Geography and Inequality

Geography and Inequality

B.E. COATES
R.J. JOHNSTON
and
P.L. KNOX

LESLIE DIENES
Department of Geography

OXFORD UNIVERSITY PRESS
1977

Oxford University Press, Walton Street, Oxford OX2 6DP
OXFORD   LONDON   GLASGOW   NEW YORK
TORONTO   MELBOURNE   WELLINGTON   CAPE TOWN
IBADAN   NAIROBI   DAR ES SALAAM   LUSAKA   ADDIS ABABA
KUALA LUMPUR   SINGAPORE   JAKARTA   HONG KONG   TOKYO
DELHI   BOMBAY   CALCUTTA   MADRAS   KARACHI

© *Oxford University Press 1977*

British Library Cataloguing in Publication Data
Coates, Bryan Ellis
    Geography and inequality.
    Bibl. — Index.
    ISBN 0-19-874069-7
    ISBN 0-19-874070-0 Pbk
    1. Title   2. Johnston, Ronald John
    3. Knox, Paul Leslie
    301.44   GF41
    Equality
    Anthropo-geography

*Set by Hope Services, Wantage, and
Printed in Great Britain by
Billing & Sons Ltd., Guildford and Worcester*

Preface

This book on geography and inequality is an introductory text, written for students and others who wish to understand some of the spatial aspects of the development, maintenance, and possible solutions to one of the world's major problems. In writing it, we have aimed at a wide audience, eschewing technical detail in favour of substantive interpretation. Much of the work to which we refer is based on statistical arguments, the validity of which can be investigated from the original source. Although we recognize that some of our discussion may be based on analyses which are rather cryptic, we feel that only by bringing these together in a general review can their relative importance be appreciated.

At least one of the words in our title is a highly emotive one. Inequality is difficult to define and measure; its converse, equality, even more so. Concepts such as economic development and under-development, civilization, and advanced industrial economies abound in the literature which we have surveyed. In portraying what we feel to be the salient features in that literature, we too have undoubtedly fallen into traps of value judgement and unwarranted synonyms. Most of our terminology is that of others, however, and we have preferred not to try and develop a standard vocabulary.

In the preparation of this book, our initial debt is to Dick Lawton, whose idea it was. Although circumstances beyond his and our control meant that he was not involved in the entire publication process, we would like to record our thanks to him for the initial stimulus. For helping us get our ideas into press and for much encouragement, we are grateful to Andrew Schuller and to the Staff of Oxford University Press. In more detail, we are indebted to Ann Barham for her efforts in correcting our English and ensuring that our bibliography is correct, to Verity Brack for her help in checking the proofs, to Joan Dunn for the wonders she has worked in producing a type-script from our three very different types of handwriting, to Stephen Frampton and Sheila Ottewell fro drawing all of the illustrations, and to Peter Morley, John Owen, and David Maddison for their photographic work.

Our major debt is undoubtedly to each other, for our mutual tolerance and the ready assistance each has given the others. This book has been produced jointly and is not a collection of essays, although each of us was responsible for the initial drafts of certain parts (we

leave the spotting of individual authorship for some geographica
party game!). And associated with this debt is that which we eac
owe to our family, for 'all that could be expected, and much els
besides'.

March 1976   B.E. Coate
                                                                  R.J. Johnsto
                                                                  P.L. Kno

Contents

Introduction

We live in an unequal world. All of us know of some people who are 'better off' than we are ourselves, and of others who are 'less well off' — however we define these emotive terms. Occasionally, the mass media bring to our attention groups who are extremely different from us, either in their degree of suffering, such as the inhabitants of drought-stricken areas in Africa, or in their extreme affluence. And most of us are concerned in some way about these inequalities. Compared to those who we know have a better 'quality of life', we feel deprived and often envious; compared to those who have a lower 'quality of life' we feel concerned and anxious that something should be done to help them. Often, we may be motivated to redress these inequalities, perhaps by supporting the activities of charitable organizations and by insisting on more inter-government aid in the case of poorer people, or by joining a militant trade union which will advance our claims relative to those who get more than us. These, we realize, are not solutions to the problems of inequalities that we perceive, but only remedies for assumed ills, and so occasionally our thoughts turn to the search for more permanent solutions to the world's inequalities.

There is awareness of inequalities among most people, but in almost every case this is very limited relative to the total extent of variations in health and wealth, happiness, and satisfaction. There are many inequalities of which we are totally ignorant, because they do not impinge directly upon our daily lives and are not brought to our notice by the mass media to which we pay attention. A lot of these may be in other countries, but many may well be in the very town or city in which we live — in parts of it which we never visit and with whose residents we have no contact. Indeed, our perceptions of inequalities may be greater at the international than at the local scale: the shanty-town dweller on the edge of a Latin American city may be more aware, through the American programmes he sees on TV, of the affluence in other countries than he is of similar affluence in other parts of his home town. Thus our perceptions of inequalities, their nature and extent, depend on the 'known world' which we live in, which is probably very small relative to the external 'terra incognita' which only occasionally impinges on our livelihood.

Although as individuals we may be unaware of many of the world's inequalities, official bodies — governments and their agencies, the United Nations, and similar organizations — ought not to be ignorant of these facts, since many of them aim explicitly at the production of a more equitable society. But in fact they are surprisingly

ill-informed. In 1974 the British government established a Royal
Commission whose standing reference began: 'To help to secure a fairer
distribution of income and wealth in the community there is a need
for a thorough and comprehensive inquiry into the existing distri
bution' (Royal Commission on the Distribution of Income and Wealth
1975, I, p. v.). Despite the great range of official statistics, the govern
ment was unable to commence a distribution of incomes policy withou
such an inquiry, and indeed its Commissioners pointed out that 'there
is much to be done to obtain satisfactory information on (various
aspects of) . . . income patterns' (p. 150). In addition to our own rela
tive ignorance, therefore, it seems that official bodies are far from
comprehensive sources of information on the kinds and amounts o
inequality in the world, and within particular countries. Thus the data
with which we can describe the patterns of inequality are far from
perfect, and we must proceed at present with 'best estimates' only.

Once we have described the patterns our next task is to try and
understand them, how they came about, how they are changing, and
what their effects are. Clearly our approach to this task can vary
enormously, since the causes are manifold and the changes complex.
Our cultural backgrounds, our moral philosophies, and our political
ideologies will all, directly or indirectly, influence how we tackle
the problem. Of major importance, too, will be the reason why we are
tackling it at all. If we are disinterested academics, our purpose may be
very different from that of a social activist with a particular ideological
axe to grind. But if our ultimate aim is to remove, or at least to reduce
very considerably, the inequalities which we perceive, then we will want
to ensure that we uncover the true causal relationships in the system
rather than the correlates: malaria may be characterized by a fever, but
treatment of the fever alone will not cure the malaria. Solution require
understanding, therefore.

The three consecutive processes of description, understanding (o
analysis), and policy present a daunting task when they relate to a
problem as massive as social and economic inequality. We make no
attempt at essaying such a task in this book. Rather, our focus is on a
single component of inequality, its spatial distribution, both because
this is our particular academic interest and because it is an aspect which
is frequently overlooked. And even within this restricted focus, ou
areal coverage is limited to capitalist countries of the 'Western' and
'Third Worlds'.

Our first task, then, is to describe the spatial pattern of inequalities
and this occupies Chapters 1, 2, and 3. The initial problem is to decide
what to measure and how to measure it, and so we begin with a

discussion of the concepts of social well-being, equity, and need. How well-off we are may, in a capitalist society, be largely dependent on our monetary income and assets, but our real income and wealth depends not only on what money we receive but what we can do with it (what we can buy, and at what price), as well as on those goods which we do not purchase directly, such as fresh air and a view, a water supply, and an educational system. In looking at spatial patterns, we almost invariably look at the conditions of populations as a whole, but must always remember that in most areas, above a minimum size, there is likely to be considerable diversity as a quick trip through any city will indicate. And so we present examples of various inequalities at different scales in Chapter 2, before turning, in Chapter 3, to attempts to find general indices of well-being which can illustrate the over-all patterns of inequality.

Given our evidence of clear spatial variations in levels of social well-being, we then try to explain why these occur, which occupies Chapters 4, 5 and 6. As indicated above, we are not presenting a full explanation of the inequalities, but only one for their spatial patterning; this does not mean a neglect of other causes, but merely indicates that our focus is on the spatial element. Three sets of reasons are suggested, and each of these is given a separate chapter. In the first, we argue that the division of labour, which has proven a vital component of the development of advanced civilizations as we know them, has a clear spatial pattern. Its original focus was in a few parts of the world and these, by and large, have remained the centres of economic power, so that, just as within a particular society one has a 'working class' and a 'ruling class', so one can recognize dominant and dominated countries in the world system, with some 'middle-class' nations, like Switzerland, who aid the system's operation. Similarly, within particular countries there are 'command centres' and 'workhouses'. Since the rewards of an economic society — wealth, status, and power — are differentially distributed, with the 'working class' generally the underprivileged, so this spatial division of labour produces a spatial pattern of inequalities.

A number of academic geographers believe that their contribution to the understanding of societies is to focus on what is termed the spatial variable. Societies occupy territories, and they must organize them, which involves the production of spatial structures. Two aspects of this spatial variable are recognized here. The first involves the time involved in moving within and between territories which, because time is a limited resource which societies wish to conserve, is a cost. Thus the costs of movement are an element in real incomes: the less travel involved in moving you to what you want and/or in moving what you

want to you, the more of your income you can spend on goods and o
services other than travel. Others will have similar aims to reduce trav€
costs, however, so spatial patterns of supply and demand are initiatec
which affect prices. Thus where one lives relative to a wide range o
other places can be an important influence on one's real income, as w
illustrate in Chapter 5.

The second way in which societies manipulate the spatial variable i
by the creation of autonomous or semi-autonomous territories. Th
most immediately relevant example of these for most of us is ou
home, a bounded area which we defend and over which we have certai
rights. But there is a wide range of such territories, both informal -
such as the 'turfs' of city gangs — and formal, such as the school an
electoral districts, the counties and boroughs, which influence so man
aspects of our livelihood. Chapter 6 focuses on these formal territorie:
discussing how our levels of social well-being can be influenced b
wh:ch we live in, and why.

Having presented our threefold explanation for spatial inequalitie:
and found evidence in support of our hypotheses concerning thes
influences, the next stage is clearly to suggest how we could manipu
late them in order to remove the inequalities. This is the theme o
Chapter 7, in which we look in turn at how the spatial division o
labour might be reorganized, how relative distances could be restruc
tured to reduce variations in accessibility, and how administrativ
territories might be revised in order to remove their contribution t
the inequalities. Evidence is presented of relevant policies in operation
and of their effects, but in virtually every example we show that th
'spatial engineering' does not remove the symptoms completely, and i
many cases never gets to the cause of the disease itself. This leads us
in our conclusions, to the view that spatial solutions to inequalities are
in themselves, insufficient. They may be ideal for reducing some in
equalities, and for bringing relatively rapid relief to suffering, bu
they do not attack the causes. Thus our purpose in this book is not t
present a panacea to the problems of inequality. But spatial plannin;
is a necessary component of any over-all policy, since we are able t
demonstrate the role of spatial variables in the development and con
tinuation of place-to-place differences in social well-being. Recognitio
of this fact should assist in the production of a more equitable world.

1 The dimensions of differentiation

Although the subject matter of this book is essentially concerned with the spatial dimensions of social inequality, it must be recognized at the outset that many of the causes, consequences, and manifestations of inequality are dominantly structural rather than spatial in nature. Nevertheless, the phenomena involved are complex, operating together as mutually reinforcing variables whose origins and effects may be seen at once in social, economic, political, and spatial terms. Although the substantive interest of geographers in social problems and social inequality will understandably be based on a perspective which places spatial variations before structural variations, this should not be regarded as the minority viewpoint of an academic discipline. Identifying the spatial component of social inequalities is crucial not only to the study of human geography but also to the improvement of social conditions within society as a whole. Indeed, it has been suggested that, in Britain at least, 'the dilemma of the "two nations" has shifted from being a class to being to an important degree a spatial problem' (Chisholm and Manners 1971, p.3). Whatever the basic causes of inequality, it is clearly a problem which affects locational, as well as occupational, social and demographic groups, and if we do not expect to discriminate against people on the bases of race, religion, colour, or social class, neither should we discriminate against people on the basis of location (Smith 1973a). In investigating inequality it is, therefore, insufficient to demonstrate that manual workers or fatherless families, for example, suffer disproportionately from poor housing conditions, dietary deficiencies, and low wages. It is also necessary to establish the extent to which these inequalities are dependent upon locational considerations and reflected in spatial patterns.

Unfortunately, geographers have traditionally ignored social problems such as these almost completely, preferring to study the production of goods and services and the distribution of resources rather than the conditions in which people live. Despite a long involvement in research into urban and regional planning, the implicit attitude in many geographical studies has been that poverty and deprivation are of little concern so long as they are spread fairly evenly and not concentrated in ghettos, distressed regions, or individual countries:

few recognized the possibility that changing spatial systems could alter over-all levels of well-being. Even in recent years there has been some resistance within the discipline to the pursuit of social relevance (see for example, Berry 1972b, Trewartha 1973), although it continues to engage the bulk of the social sciences. The result is that geographers, in comparison with sociologists and political scientists, have paid little attention to social inequalities. Nevertheless, geography should, by definition, be concerned with inequalities, since inequality represents differences and the focus of geography is surely spatial differentiation. Thus the incidence of poor people or hungry children provides as conceptually sound a topic for the geographer as the incidence of raised beaches or the distribution of place names; and a regional geography based on the quality of people's lives is potentially as informative as one based on the characteristics of the industries in which they are employed. This long neglect of social problems by geographers seems to have been rooted in academic inertia and a reluctance to become involved in issues which are both politically and morally sensitive (Smith 1972).

The inertia of academic social consciences received a substantial jolt, however, with the United States' race riots in the mid/late 1960s and it is probably no coincidence that geographical writing since then shows some welcome signs of overcoming earlier inhibitions. Studies of the geography of poverty in the United States by Morrill and Wohlenberg (1971), of the geography of health care by Shannon and Dever (1972), and of the distribution of real income within the spatial system of the western city by Harvey (1973) are examples which reflect a general awakening of interest in social well-being which is paralleled in the professional journals by a growing number of welfare-oriented articles.

In many ways, this interest in social well-being is a product of the serious public concern over social deprivation and environmental despoliation of all kinds generated throughout Western society in the late 1960s and early 1970s by the official rhetoric of planners and politicians, by the 'revelations' of the mass media, and, finally, by the evidence of people's own eyes. Underlying this concern is the realization that industrial expansion and economic growth — major goals of most nations — are, at best, mixed blessings, so that although most societies still opt for increased production and the advance of technology at the expense of some pollution and loss of amenity, economic development is now at least recognized as a process which brings qualitative changes as well as quantitative growth (Mishan 1967). It is no longer acceptable to shrug off second-order consequences of development such as the structural unemployment resulting from technological innovation and the degradation of the countryside resulting from the spread of industrialization as 'the price of progress'.

Of particular relevance to geographers and planners are the findings of research which have shown that economic growth and technological change can lead to markedly increased spatial disparities through the natural processes of national, regional, and local development. The chief exponent of such work is Myrdal, who has shown how free-market forces tend to increase inequalities between regions through 'backwash effects' resulting from a process of cumulative causation in which new increments of activity and growth are concentrated disproportionately in already-expanding regions because of their attraction to investment capital, thus depriving other regions not only of much of their locally-generated capital, but also of many of their skilled and enterprising workers and of their share of tertiary activity and welfare services (Myrdal 1957a, Hirschman 1958, Hicks 1959). Similar cyclical arguments have been applied at other spatial scales (Keeble 1967). Increasing international inequality, for example, can largely be explained by the pattern of international economic relationships: the tendency for the consumption of rich manufacturing nations to grow more rapidly than the consumption of primary producers, combined with the tendency for populations to grow faster in poor countries, produces international inequalities in average incomes which, as Seers (1973) has demonstrated, aggravate income inequalities *within* poor countries. This internal inequality hampers the development of home-based manufacturing activity and so reinforces the international trading relationships responsible for the initial international inequality.

At smaller scales, spatial inequality can often be seen as the result of second-order or 'externality' effects of the activities of producers, consumers, and public authorities. An externality effect exists if the behaviour of one individual, group or institution affects the welfare of others, and can be positive or negative. The pollution resulting from the use of rivers as dumps for industrial effluent is a negative externality effect of the industrialist's behaviour in seeking a least-cost solution to his waste-disposal problems. Similarly, the residential displacement, social disorganization, and increased costs of living which befall inner-city residents as a result of urban renewal are negative externality effects attached to corporate decisions aimed at improving the quality of urban life. The economist Mishan (1967) believes that as societies grow in material wealth the incidence of these externality effects grows rapidly. Furthermore, Harvey (1971) argues that much of the residential competition and socio-political conflict within cities can be interpreted as attempts to organize the distribution of externality effects to gain income advantages. This theme has been elaborated by Cox, who points out that even positive externalities tend to reinforce or initiate spatial disparities, simply because their intensity is a function of relative location. Thus, 'employment opportunities obviously are more available the closer one resides to such opportunities; and indirect benefits provided by a city park decline with decreasing accessibility to the park' (Cox 1973, p. 3).

The cumulative result is the localization of disadvantage in slums, shanty-towns, and ghettos. As Sherrard (1968, p. 10) says: 'the slum is the catch-all for the losers, and in the competitive struggle for the cities' goods the slum areas are also the losers in terms of schools, jobs, garbage collection, street lighting, libraries, social services, and whatever else is communally available but always in short supply'. Harvey concludes that the redistributive effects of the urban system are leading 'towards a state of greater inequality and greater injustice' (Harvey 1971, p. 229). Moreover, the problem is not exclusive to the free-market economy of the West. Konrad and Szelényi (1969), for example, attribute the failure of attempts to allocate resources in favour of less-skilled workers in Hungary to the redistributive effects of urban systems which appear to be creating even deeper patterns of inequality.

In some countries, the formal resolution of certain locational and allocational decisions within the political process has been aided by the use of highly sophisticated cost-benefit analyses which attempt to take externality effects into account. The Roskill Commission's deliberations (1969–72) over the siting of a third airport for London, for example, centred on an extensive cost-benefit approach, as did the London Traffic Survey (Greater London Council 1966). Such analyses essentially seek to specify alternatives and then attempt to evaluate their likely effects on the well-being of the community in financial terms. In practice, however, major methodological difficulties arise from our inability to measure many aspects of social well-being in terms of money. This is a recurring problem in applied economics and welfare economics, and its intractability has led to the pursuit of alternative approaches such as the social indicators movement discussed in Chapter 3. But however we attempt to quantify social well-being, it is clear that the whole is a complex product of many interrelated and sometimes conflicting parts. The following section of this chapter is therefore intended to outline the major dimensions of social well-being and to highlight some of their important interrelationships at both individual and aggregate (or territorial) levels.

SOCIAL WELL-BEING: AN ATTEMPT TO DECOMPOSE THE DEPENDENT VARIABLE

Social well-being is used here as a generic term for the family of overlapping concepts which includes level of living, the quality of life, social satisfaction, social welfare, and standard of living. As aggregate expressions of well-being, all are in common use, but few people have faced up to the problem of defining them and measuring them. Indeed, difficulties of definition have been recognized at least since the time of Aristotle, who observed that: 'both the general run of men and people of superior refinement say that [the highest of all achievable goals] is happiness [later translated as well-being], but with regard to what happiness is they differ, and the many do not give the same account as the wise' (quoted by McKean 1947, p.47). In practice, of course, all concepts are instrumental or pragmatic, being invented or adapted for some particular purpose, so that the elaboration of concepts like social welfare and social satisfaction must depend to some extent on the period, region, and context of their use. Any search for conclusive or universal definitions is therefore futile. It is pertinent, however, to make a few general observations by way of differentiation between the concepts.

To begin with, level of living is clearly established as the factual circumstances of well-being (the actual degree of satisfaction of the needs and wants of a community), whereas standard of living relates to the circumstances aspired to by that community (Knox 1975). A distinction must also be made between economic welfare and social welfare: 'the former usually refers to what people get from the consumption of goods and services purchased by money, or available as public provision, while the latter embraces all things contributing to the quality of human existence' (Smith 1973b, p.6). The notion of the quality of life is also a broad expression of well-being, but generally suggests an emphasis on the amount and distribution of impure public goods such as health care, education and welfare services, protection against crime, the regulation of pollution, and the preservation of fine landscapes and historic townscapes (Hall 1972). Similarly, although covering the whole spectrum of social well-being, the notion of social satisfaction is particularly concerned with the collective psychological response to the objective conditions of reality.

Despite these shades of emphasis, it is possible to achieve some consensus as to the main components of social well-being. Here the literature contains many suggestions. Miller *et al.* (1967), for example, propose six dimensions: money income, assets, basic services, education and social mobility, political position, and status and self respect; and Smith (1973b) has established seven 'general criteria' of social well being relevant to contemporary conditions in the United States (Table 1.1). Similar categories can be established at a more general level. There is universal agreement, for instance, as to the importance of adequate levels of nutrition, clothing, shelter, health, and other physiological requirements for survival. To these basic needs most societies would add the cultural needs of education, security, and leisure, together with certain qualitative aspects of the physical, social political, and economic environments. Beyond this, some degree of income surplus to the satisfaction of basic physical and cultural needs is generally regarded as necessary for the consumption of other goods and services available in the market place. These at least are the conclusions to be drawn from recent attempts by the United Nations Research Institute for Social Development (UNRISD) to define and measure levels of living at the international scale (UNRISD 1966a, 1966b, 1970). Using the framework provided by this research, it is possible to list nine basic components of social well-being: (1) nutrition (2) shelter, (3) health, (4) education, (5) leisure, (6) security, (7) social stability, (8) physical environment, and (9) surplus income. Since there is no social theory, even of a speculative nature, which specifies the variables of a social system and the relationships between them these components offer a convenient framework which can clarify the general scope and content of social well-being.

Nutrition. The importance of nutrition to social well-being is beyond dispute for food is an essential for survival. In addition, however, there is a mass of evidence to show that nutrition is directly related to levels of health educational achievement, and even to the economic development of whole communities. Relationships between malnutrition and disease such as avitaminosis, beriberi, anaemia, rickets, osteomalacia, and endemic goitre are long established, whilst poor nutrition clearly lowers resistance to many diseases. Children suffering from kwashiorkor (an extreme form of malnutrition), for example, are unable to form anti bodies to either typhoid vaccine or diptheria toxoid (Belli 1972). I has also been known for some time that nutrition is a key determinant of 'intelligence', brain weight, and educational achievement (Harrell Woodyard and Grates 1955); but it is only recently that malnutrition has been proven as harmful to the future economic productivity of the affected individuals. This in turn affects the distribution of real income, and so increases inequalities (Selowsky and Taylor 1974) The corollary of this, of course, is that increments of food could

Table 1.1
Smith's general criteria of social well-being

1. *Income, wealth, and employment*
   (a) income and wealth
   (b) employment status
   (c) income supplements

2. *The living environment*
   (a) housing
   (b) the neighbourhood
   (c) the physical environment

3. *Health*
   (a) physical health
   (b) mental health

4. *Education*
   (a) achievement
   (b) duration and quality

5. *Social order (or disorganization)*
   (a) personal pathologies
   (b) family breakdown
   (c) crime and delinquency
   (d) public order and safety

6. *Social belonging (alienation and participation)*
   (a) democratic participation
   (b) criminal justice
   (c) segregation

7. *Recreation and leisure*
   (a) recreation facilities
   (b) culture and the arts
   (c) leisure available

Source: Smith 1973a, p. 70.

be used as catalytic agents for development in poor communities (OECD 1973).

Shelter. If only because of man's fundamental need for shelter, housing conditions are important. But housing conditions are directly relevant to the satisfaction of many other needs, so that they must be regarded as a major parameter of social well-being. Unfortunately, the average dwelling in rural areas of most developing countries barely covers the basic need for shelter: structures of wattle and daub or of non-permanent materials without access to drinking water and with only pit latrines are the norm, while in many urban districts of the Third World these conditions are exacerbated by intense overcrowding. The effect

of such conditions on the health of poor communities is well documented (Rosser 1971) and needs no elaboration here. In more prosperou
countries, housing makes an even greater relative contribution to over
all levels of social well-being, since higher quality housing brings with i
a wide range of utilities besides shelter. These include (1) an area o
'defensible space' which helps satisfy both the occupants' need fo
privacy and their basic territorial instincts, (2) a relative location tha
has social and symbolic status, and (3) a means of storing and en-
hancing wealth.

Advanced countries are by no means lacking in poor housin;
conditions and their associated problems. At the individual level, poo
housing conditions have been shown to lead to increases in th
incidence of infant mortality rates, stress, mental ill-health, and morbi
dity from infectious diseases (Martin 1967). They also have an advers
effect on the intellectual development of children and adolescent
(Douglas 1964). At aggregate levels, they exhibit strong ecologica
correlations with deviant behaviour and social instability as well a
with demographic, racial, and occupational characteristics. In a mor
explicitly spatial context, Harvey (1973) has spelled out the inequitabl
effects of the operation of the housing market in American cities, anc
Byrne (1974) has illustrated how the public allocation mechanism o
British cities can concentrate and sometimes increase the incidence o
'problem' families.

Health. The importance of health requires little elaboration. It is fundamental to
personal happiness and the ability to enjoy and appreciate all othe
aspects of life, and has a strong influence on productivity and earnin;
capacity. The aggregate level of health in a community is therefor
vital to social well-being. Conversely, health, or the lack of it, is itsel:
a function of many aspects of well-being, and so indicators of healtl
are also indicative of these. Infant mortality rates and the averag
expectation of life, for example, reflect all of the physical, social, anc
medical influences that are brought to bear on the individual. Othe
indicators have more specific connotations. Thus the incidence o:
tuberculosis is particularly associated with poverty, malnutrition, anc
poor environmental conditions, and the incidence of bronchitis i
closely linked to atmospheric pollution, occupational hazards, and sub
standard housing. A wider interpretation of health should encompas:
the provision of health care and medical services necessary for th
prevention and cure of ill-health. Unlike morbidity and mortality
these are not subject to broad ecological determinants, but rathe
to the community's ability and willingness to pay for them. Moreover

as with all welfare services, their contribution to social well-being will depend not only on the amount and quality of facilities available, but also on their physical accessibility.

Education. Education is taken here to be the process of developing intellectual abilities, of shaping cultural attitudes, and of acquiring knowledge and useful skills. It therefore includes vocational training, adult and extra-mural education, and all forms of non-institutionalized learning opportunities as well as formal education at primary, secondary, and tertiary levels. In this broad sense, education is fundamental to the individual's enjoyment of certain recreational pursuits and to the fulfilment of democratic opportunities as well as to occupational status and social mobility. Perhaps most important of all, education is closely associated with money income. Virtually all these doors are closed to those without elementary literacy and numeracy (that is, over a third of the world's population), thus effectively limiting the extent of their well-being. Similarly, raising aggregate levels of education may be seen as an investment in human capital which pays dividends not only in economic development and material well-being but also in cultural development, social equality, and political emancipation.

Leisure. Leisure time is defined as the amount of time free from work, excluding any time spent in travel to and from work, any time spent on domestic chores, and the estimated ten hours a day spent in sleeping, eating, and dressing (Drewnowski 1974). In the context of social well-being, leisure should also be seen in terms of accessibility to cultural and recreational facilities and amenities, for without these the benefits of leisure time are limited. Moreover, since cultural and recreational pursuits are particularly sensitive to personal tastes, it is important that there should be a wide range of accessible facilities. In Western societies at least it would generally be agreed that these include provision for sport and physical exercise, entertainment, the arts, reading, and travel for pleasure. These activities clearly have implications for other components of social well-being — health and education, for example — and all are dependent on the availability of 'surplus' income, either in hard cash or in the form of public funds.

Security. This is a heterogeneous component, dependent upon prevailing political, legal, and economic systems, and related in a complex manner to many other aspects of social well-being. Without elaborating upon these relationships, the importance of security to social well-being can be indicated simply by listing the areas of life which it covers. Basically, security has two important dimensions. The first is security of the person, or public safety, which is of course at risk from the whole spectrum of violence from war, civil war, and regimes of terror to riots, gangsterism, and criminality. Second is security of the way of life — in other words, of being able to maintain a given level of well-being once it has been achieved. Such security is low when human rights are denied, when participation in politics, planning, industry, and consumer affairs is restricted, when criminal justice is partial, when property and property rights are unprotected, when unemployment, sickness, and accidents are not covered by insurance or benefits, and when the aged and the infirm are without proper care and adequate money incomes. Low security can therefore mean poverty, ill-health, ignorance and stress.

Stability. Although good relations with other members of society are felt to be a fundamental human need (Drewnowski 1974), this is the most ambiguous and culturally relative component of social well-being. Thus most would agree that economic stability (in the form of freedom from industrial strife) and social stability (in the form of freedom from high levels of prejudice, discrimination, family breakdown, crime, and delinquency) are 'good things', but we must also recognize the importance of the right to challenge dominant moral codes, to strike, to protest, and, in some circumstances, to promote social revolution. Equally important in the context of comparative studies of social well-being are the wide divergences in mores and values between societies in relation to some indicants of instability such as rates of divorce, suicide, and illegitimacy; and the ambiguous attitudes within some societies which can, for example, tolerate tobacco and alcohol whilst regarding other drugs as agents of serious personal and social instability.

Physical Environment. The strong negative relationships between environmental quality and economic growth, industrial expansion and urbanization have been well documented by widely publicized reports such as *The Limits of Growth* (Meadows 1972) and the Club of Rome's *Blueprint for Survival* (Forrester 1971). These, pointing to the numerous negative externalities of urbanization and the long-term consequences of ecological imbalance which result from industrial technology, have given rise to schools of thought apparently dedicated to restricting economic as well as demographic growth. Yet it is not growth itself which is at fault, but the tendency to see it exclusively in terms of private consumption rather than in terms of social well-being. In any case, the environmental issue is regarded in many developing countries as 'a devious excuse for the rich countries to pull the ladder up behind them' (Crosland, quoted by Cullingworth 1973, p. 80). Similarly, the conservation movement in the United States has been attacked by some black power groups as an affront to the poor and a diversion from their real problems (Hall 1972). Whatever its relative importance, however, the physical environment is clearly a distinctive component of well-being. As construed by most societies, it encompasses resource management and accessibility to certain public amenities (such as roads, parks, and street lighting), as well as the visual appearance, cleanliness, and quietness of urban neighbourhoods and rural landscapes.

Surplus income. Income which is surplus to the satisfaction of basic physical and cultural needs is the key access mechanism for the satisfaction of 'higher' needs and aspirations. In particular, it facilitates the consumption of all kinds of 'luxury' goods and services such as colour television sets, cameras, and fashionable clothes. In a more general way, surplus income determines the absolute levels of many other aspects of social well-being. It is therefore of paramount importance in the developed world, although it contributes very little in either context to the over-all social well-being of the poor or of almost the entire population of Third World countries where subsistence levels are barely achieved. For the fortunate, money income can mean quality and variety in food and shelter and the ability to indulge in sophisticated pursuits. It buys prestige and status, and even when saved it provides utility in the form of security.

Because of this, it may seem that an extended definition of income or expenditure (that is, inclusive of income spent on basic needs) could be regarded as synonymous with social well-being. Indeed, *per capita* income, consumption, and production have long been used by politicians, administrators, planners, and the mass media as surrogates for social well-being. But there are many aspects of people's well-being (health and security, for example) which these measures do not attempt to represent. Moreover, there are technical and conceptual limitations to their use which economists have long been aware of. As Drewnowski (1974, pp. 15–16) puts it, 'if all human needs were satisfied through market transactions and if the market form was perfect competition (neither of which is true), then all marginal utilities would be proportional to prices and it could be claimed that the increments in individual utility, and consequently in welfare, would correspond to the increments in the money value of products'. In addition, it should be emphasized that the ability to use money income can be as impor tant as the amount of money itself in some circumstances. A Cullingworth (1973, p.21) argues in his discussion of poverty (th negative end of the scale of social well-being), 'poverty is relative lacl of command over resources and access to opportunity. It is, therefore much more than an issue of money, important though this is. A famil may have an average income but be unable to obtain access to goo housing at a reasonable rent: their position would be disadvantaged i comparison with a family in a low-rent council house. Indeed, the may be solely "housing poor"'. The conclusion must be that althougl measures of income and expenditure probably offer the best single variable indicants of social well-being, they are by no means acceptabl surrogates. In other words, the possession of colour television set and washing machines is a poor substitute for inadequate educationa opportunities and medical care.

An alternative perspective. A rather different perspective on social well-being i evident in the psychological literature concerned with well-being. I is agreed that components such as those listed above are important but well-being is placed squarely in the eye of the beholder, with th emphasis on higher personal needs such as identity and self-fulfilment Maslow (1954), for example, argues that once the basic needs o survival and security are gratified, the need for love, affection, and sense of belonging to a community emerges as a second level in th hierarchy of human needs. This is followed by the need for self-respect self-esteem, and the esteem of others; finally, if all these needs ar satisfied, there remains the need for 'self-actualization', or the desir for self-fulfilment. From this perspective emerges the possibility o using 'life satisfaction' measures in aggregate as indicants of *socia* well-being (Stagner 1970). This is regarded as dangerous ground b Gross (1966, p.221), who asserts that 'since satisfactions and dis satisfactions are almost impossible to observe directly, we must use wide variety of "surrogates", that is indirect indicators that serve us a quantitative substitutes or representatives of the phenomena we wan to identify and measure'. But for several years now a number of re searchers (Allardt 1973, Bradburn 1969, Campbell and Convers 1972, Hall 1972) have been trying to derive subjective ('soft') indica tors of how people actually feel about the quality of their lives. Sucl work is still very tentative in nature, but some interesting results hav already emerged. In France, for example, the relatively rapid rate o national economic growth has not produced anything like a unanimou sense of satisfaction, for although 70 per cent of top managers an professionals thought that 'things had improved' since 1965, only 44 per cent of unskilled workers shared this comfortable view (INSEE 1975). In Britain, the Survey Unit of the Social Science Research Council found that satisfaction with various 'domains' of life (family life, friendships, health, housing, leisure, etc.), as well as satisfaction with life in general, varies considerably with age, sex, and socio-economic groupings (Hall and Ring 1974). More significantly, res-pondents who would score badly on conventional 'hard' data often rate themselves as highly satisfied, and vice versa (Abrams 1972). The reason is of course that satisfaction depends as much on aspira-tions and expectations as on objective reality, and it therefore seems that 'soft' indicators of social well-being should best be regarded as complementary to the more conventional indicators. As yet, however, there have been few explicitly spatial applications of the idea apart from Maclaran's pioneer study (1975) which is reported in Chapter 3. For the most part, therefore, the focus of this book will be on the 'objective' expression of spatial disparities.

THE RELATIVITY OF WELL-BEING AND THE IDEA OF NEED

However defined or measured, all components of social well-being are ultimately based on categories of need. The idea of need, however, may itself be variously defined. In theory, four different approaches can be recognized (Bradshaw 1974). The most straightforward is to take the definition that would be given by experts or administrators in any given situation, such as in the establishment of housing stan-dards or a general 'poverty line'. Need defined in this way is referred to as normative need, absolute need, or basic need. A second approach compares the actual provision in one area or community with that in others, identifying need in terms of the gap between the best-off area or community and the rest. This is known as comparative need. Thirdly, need can be defined in terms of consumer behaviour, using market demand as a measure of 'expressed need'. Fourthly, need can be equated with want, or latent demand. In this approach, needs are interpreted as feelings of relative deprivation which arise when some good, service, or amenity is wanted by a particular group or individual but is unavailable, despite being available to others (Runciman 1966).

In practice, each approach has its own limitations. The definition of basic needs, for instance, may be influenced by paternalism, as in the use of middle-class norms to assess need in a working-class context. Moreover, the theoretical distinction between the different approaches often becomes blurred. As Townsend (1970) points out, it would be very difficult to define a family's basic need for shelter, whether i terms of cubic footage or plumbing facilities, without taking accoun of social norms about the sharing of beds and rooms by people o different sex, age, and kinship. These points bring out the cruci: feature implicit in the idea of need, which is that needs are alway *relative* to prevailing environmental and cultural conditions. Clearly then, all statements about social well-being must be thus qualifiec In many cases the situation is clear enough. Nutritional levels must b seen in relation to climate, type of work, and the age and sex structur of the population; and health care needs depend to a certain extent o the range of endemic diseases.

Needs must be also seen in relation to social norms and values, an these vary much more from time to time and from place to plac* The most extreme example is surely the attitude of certain Hind* sects who see ill-health as the means of transmigration on their wa toward nirvana rather than as a bad thing; the most obvious exampl is the relativity of poverty, for what is regarded as poverty in Denmar and Sweden would clearly rank as privilege in present-day Ethiopia an Vietnam. What is most important to avoid is the 'cultural imperialism of Western intellectual thought, in which objectives appearing to b self-evidently good in Western societies are assumed to be good fo other societies too. It is only recently that this traditional perspectiv has been challenged, for, as we emphasize in Chapter 4, most of th decisions as to what is 'best' for Third World countries have been take by an élite with Westernized cultural backgrounds. In this context, car* cinemas, television sets, and universities and hospitals providin 'Western knowledge' and 'Western medicine' are seen as desirable and o high priority. Recently, however, their relevance to the well-being o the mass of people in Third World countries has been questioned b writers such as Illich (1971, 1974, 1975), who has particularly criti cized the acceptance of Western doctrines concerning the role o education, the use of energy supplies, and the utility of expensiv health care facilities. Townsend (1970) concludes that two sets o standards are required, the 'national-relational' and the 'world-rela tional'. To these we might add 'region-relational' and 'neighbourhood relational', since values, attitudes, and aspirations are dependent upo reference groups which can be traced down to the level of the indivi dual family. Pahl's study (1965) of 'Dormersdell', for example, show how the immigration of a new neighbourhood reference group (commu ting middle-classes) led to changes in both the felt needs and th* expressed needs of the indigenous population of a small community.

Finally, it is worth noting that as the spatial diffusion of informatio about other groups in society grows, so reference groups become widened and relative deprivation tends to increase, unless it is converted into expressed need via consumer behaviour. It is therefore important to recognize the influence of pressure groups, vested interests, and the media in shaping the values upon which relative deprivation is based. As Smith (1973b, p.55) comments, 'powerful forces are at work in many Western nations, inducing us to spend on automobiles, television sets, cigarettes, and so on, while there are no countervailing forces advocating the case for greater support of services such as health and education through higher taxation'. There is clearly a danger that needs generated in this way may give rise to a rather lop-sided idea of social well-being.

EQUITY AND EQUALITY IN SPATIAL DISTRIBUTIONS

The question of equity hinges to a large extent on ethical and political judgements which, as Harvey (1972) observes, geographers have traditionally avoided. Basically, those to the right of the political spectrum tend to believe in an 'economic justice' of free-market competition in which differences in ability and merit, attributable to nature, result in the more productive people and localities receiving greater rewards, so that social well-being will tend to be higher in highly productive regions than in less productive regions. Those to the left tend to believe in a 'social justice' based on the broad principle of equality of outcome. In between are those who would accept a certain amount of inequality of outcome as the price of economic efficiency. Harvey (1972), following Runciman (1966), suggests that equitable distributions need not be egalitarian, but should reflect the criteria of need, contribution to common good, and merit, whilst ensuring that the prospects of the least fortunate region are maximized. However, using these criteria to assess the equity of spatial distributions poses an enormous task: we have already seen, for example, how difficult it is to establish an adequate definition of need.

Yet in most societies, and certainly within the Western world, equity is generally identified quite simply with equality. Drewnowski (1974) asserts that this position cannot be challenged without discarding the most fundamental principles of human rights, and Donnison (1975) points out that a consensus on equality has been a recurring theme of Britain's conventional wisdom and ruling rhetoric, having been nurtured by Butskellite politics and the tradition of social thought descending from Tawney via Marshall and Titmuss. It is this overwhelming consensus which prompts the perspective on inequality which is adopted

in this book. Accepting, then, that equality approximates to equity
there is a number of well-developed techniques to which we can tur
in evaluating spatial distributions. The relative degree of inequalit
experienced in any single area can be measured against the yardstic
of some desired or ideal level, the level of the best-off area, or of th
average level in a series of areas, and can be expressed either as th
difference or the ratio between the actual level and that of the yarc
stick. For a *series* of areas, the simplest way to illustrate spatial in
equality is of course by way of a map, but in some circumstances i
is useful to have an over-all measure of inequality. Most common ar
statements which compare proportional shares, as in 'the top five pe
cent receive forty per cent of total money income.' But statements sucl
as this only tell us about one end of the distribution, so that summar
measures such as the Schutz coefficient of inequality and the Gin
coefficient of inequality are more useful (Alker 1970). The latter i
widely used, and for a series of n areas can be written as:

$$G_x = \frac{\sum_{i=1}^{n} |X_i - P_i|}{2}$$

where G_x is the Gini coefficient of inequality for 'commodity x', X_i
the proportion of item x in area i, and P_i is the proportion of the tota
population at risk resident in i. The coefficient has a potential rang
from 0 to 100, with higher values representing greater inequality. A
related measure is the Lorenz curve, which expresses inequality by wa
of a distribution curve derived from a plot of cumulative percentage
of an item against cumulative percentages of population at risk for
series of areas ranked according to the incidence of the item concerned
Perfect territorial equality results in a 45° diagonal plot, with depar
tures from this line representing some degree of inequality.

Fig. 1.1 shows a Lorenz curve of incomes for the counties of Norwa
in 1971. The area between the curve and the diagonal is representativ
of the degree of inequality in territorial (inter-county) income distribu
tion in Norway, and the Gini coefficient of 12·0 is in fact a measure o
this area as a proportion of the total area below the diagonal. The curv
itself is also useful in illustrating other features of the distribution
Tangential to the curve and parallel to the diagonal is point A. To th
left of this point on the horizontal axis the population get less tha
their fair (equal) share, and can be regarded as under-privileged. Th
élite are 'those who get most of what there is to get' (Lasswell 1958
p.13), and can be identified by locating the point B on the curv
corresponding to the median of the income distribution. Areas to th
right of this point contain the élite 30 per cent of the population

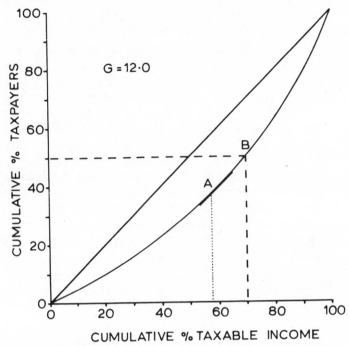

Fig. 1.1. Distribution of taxable incomes by county in Norway, 1971.

These measures are used in subsequent chapters to illustrate the extent of spatial inequality in a number of aspects of social well-being, but their sensitivity depends on the spatial frameworks employed, and, as Smith (1973b) warns, different aggregations of sub-areas can produce different results. We must therefore remember that inter-territorial equality may sometimes hide intra-territorial inequality.

CONCLUSIONS

Whatever the spatial scale, social well-being must be seen as a multi-faceted phenomenon of overlapping and sometimes conflicting parts. The most important of these constituent parts can be identified, and conveniently labelled: housing, education, health, and so on. This should not disguise the fact that each of these components is inter-dependent with others; that our knowledge of these interrelationships is rudimentary; or that we are, as yet, uncertain as to what the full list of components should be for any particular society or at any particular spatial scale.

For the purposes of describing, measuring, and analysing social

well-being, these components can be viewed in a number of differen
ways: in terms of the 'objective' environment (as reflected by co
ditions, achievements, provision, and access); in terms of the 'su
jective' environment (as reflected by feelings of satisfaction, frustratio
and deprivation); in terms of inputs to the social system (as reflecte
by the provision of hospitals and expenditure on police protectio
for example); or in terms of the outputs of the social system (as r
flected by people's health and the incidence of delinquency f
example). All are relevant to liberal humanitarian principles which see
to balance equality of opportunity with equality of outcome. This, c
course, makes the measurement and analysis of social well-bein
complex enough. The cultural, temporal, and social relativity of wel
being and the assumption that equality approximates to equity bot
impose additional qualifications on all of the statements about terr
torial variations in social well-being and its component parts whic
are made in subsequent chapters.

2 Patterns of inequality

All of the aspects of social well-being outlined in the previous chapter are of interest to the geographer concerned with social problems, since they exhibit marked variations from place to place at many levels of resolution. In this chapter, we set out to illustrate the extent of these disparities by a number of examples drawn from various cultural and socio-economic environments and to examine them at various spatial scales. The purpose is not to generalize from particular examples about the nature and causes of inequality but rather to establish the intensity of existing spatial disparities. In order to avoid the proliferation of examples that would result from an examination of the whole spectrum of social well-being, discussion is restricted to three aspects: income, health, and housing. In such an approach, the selection of the spatial scales at which to operate is a critical question. Here, attention is focused on three main levels which have been found elsewhere to provide useful frameworks for the examination of spatial patterns, spatial structures, and spatial systems (Johnston 1973): the international, the intra-national, and the intra-urban. At each level, it must be understood that data are unique aggregates of individual experience, so that observations about spatial patterns and disparities should not be imputed to other spatial frameworks or to sub-groups or individuals within them.

INTERNATIONAL PATTERNS

Income. At the international level there are a number of measures which can be used to reflect income levels, including *per capita* gross national product, *per capita* gross domestic product, *per capita* money income and *per capita* consumption. None is totally reliable, since all are based on data collected in different ways in different countries, and few countries can afford sophisticated data-collecting procedures. Direct measures of money income tend to be especially unreliable because surveys of income are hampered by persistent under-reporting in the top strata, and low income groups in many countries are often dependent upon intermittent sources of livelihood and on income in kind and so are unable to give precise information. Most data therefore relate to taxable incomes, which in developing countries are of course confined to a small fraction of the population and so tend to

overestimate *per capita* income. A more useful measure for presen
purposes is *per capita* consumption, since it reflects the sum of a
income spent on goods and services by the whole population in bot
public and private sectors. Nevertheless, as with all international dat
the figures should be treated as illustrative only.

The world distribution of *per capita* consumption is shown in Fi
2.1. At one extreme are countries such as Burundi, Ethiopia, Rwand
and Upper Volta, where the producer and consumer are usually th
same person and where annual average consumption in 1967 wa
around $50 U.S. *per capita*. At the other extreme lies the sophisticate
industrial society of the United States, in which *per capita* consumptio
was, at over $3,300, sixty times higher. These contrasts are reflecte
in the Gini coefficient of inequality of 46·2 and a distribution curv
which shows that, arranged by territories, 66 per cent of the world
population is underprivileged. A glance at the map shows that th
burden of poverty lies heavily across the developing regions of Asi
Africa, and Latin America, where almost 850 million people live i
countries in which *per capita* consumption is less than $100 a yea
Yet not all developing countries have low levels of consumptio
Countries like Chile, Uruguay, Venezuela, Libya, and Namibia, wit
favourable resource endowment, vigorous export industries, and
degree of economic diversification, enjoy ten times the *per capit*
consumption of their neighbours; whilst in some small countries suc
as Israel, Kuwait, and the Netherlands Antilles, human and physic;
capital have been combined to give consumption levels of the sam
order as those in some developed market economies.

There was not, however, any marked tendency for the lov
consumption countries to catch up during the 1960s. According t
U.N. figures, the average annual rate of increase for consumption i
'developing' countries between 1960 and 1968 was 4·4 per cent, bu
most of the countries with the lowest absolute levels of consumptio
had growth rates which were well below this. Nigeria, for example
had a rate of 0·1 per cent, whilst Haiti, Tanzania, and Sri Lanka ha
rates of 0·8 per cent, 1·8 per cent, and 2·2 per cent respectively. Mos
disconcerting of all are those cases in which growth in consumptio
lagged behind the growth of population. These include Burund
Dahomey, Haiti, Indonesia, Madagascar (the Malagasy Republic), Nepa
Nigeria, Tanzania, and Upper Volta. At the other end of the scale, th
high-consumption 'developed market' economies achieved an averag
annual growth in consumption of 5·0 per cent whilst almost all ha
population growth rates of only about 1·0 per cent. Thus, France, wit
a *per capita* consumption of $1702 and a growth rate of 5·3 per cen

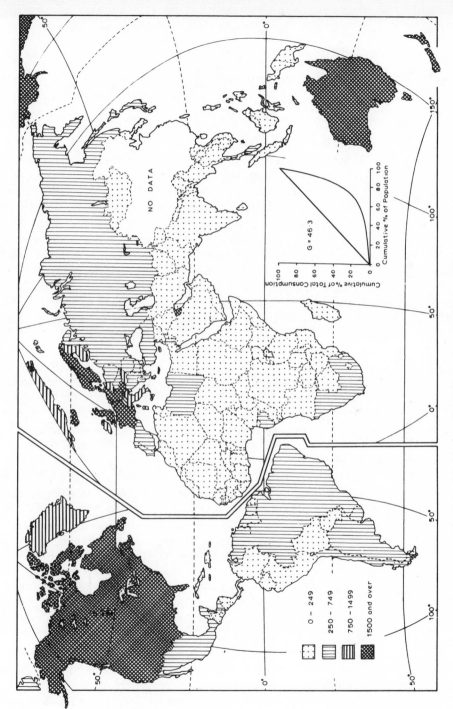

Fig. 2.1. World annual consumption *per capita*, 1967, in U.S. dollars.

had a rise in population of 0·6 per cent a year; and Canada, with
consumption level of $2138 and a growth rate of 4·8 per cent, had
population growth rate of 1·0 per cent. In short, people in the ric
countries are getting richer, and those in the poor countries are gettin
poorer.

Health. As indicated in Chapter 1, the physical well-being of a population ca
be indirectly gauged from the incidence of certain diseases and ag
specific mortality rates. Among these parameters, the infant mortalit
rate is probably the most sensitive measure of community healt
although many countries still have inadequate recording systems ar
so may tend to underestimate the incidence of mortality of all kind
The distribution of known infant mortality rates in 1970 is shown
Fig. 2.2. Without attaching too much importance to the precise figure
the disparities depicted on the map are clearly daunting: Australi
New Zealand, South Africa, and the Soviet Union, together with mo
of Europe and North America, experience rates of less than 40 deatl
per 1000 live births, but the populations of countries in central ar
western Africa, the Indian sub-continent and South-East Asia suff
rates at least three times as high. Indeed, the contrast between nort
European countries, where the rate starts at around 14, and countri
like Haiti, Lesotho, and Mauritania, where the rate approaches 20
is even greater. Fortunately, the 1960s saw an almost universal r
duction in infant mortality rates, with the most dramatic improvemen
occurring in some of the worst-off countries. This continues the patte
of the last fifty years (Fig. 2.3). In Chile, for example, the rate declin
from 125 in 1960 to 92 in 1968; in the People's Democratic Republ
of Yemen it fell from 120 to 80; and in Liberia from 188 to 160. B
even in countries with more moderate infant mortality, substanti
reductions were achieved, as in Thailand (51 to 28), Panama (54 to 41
and Spain (44 to 30), with comparable reductions being recorded
the more advanced countries. Despite the general trend towards i
proved conditions, therefore, it is likely that international dispariti
will be slow to diminish.

In the long term, improvements in physical well-being may be r
flected in a decline in the use of medical facilities, but it is still realist
to regard an increase in the availability of such facilities as an increa
in social well-being. Most important in this context are those faciliti
to which the ordinary citizen can resort in case of need: the traine
physician, the trained nurse, and hospital accommodation. An approx
mate measure in this field is the average incidence of these facilitie
although several qualifications need to be kept in mind in using suc

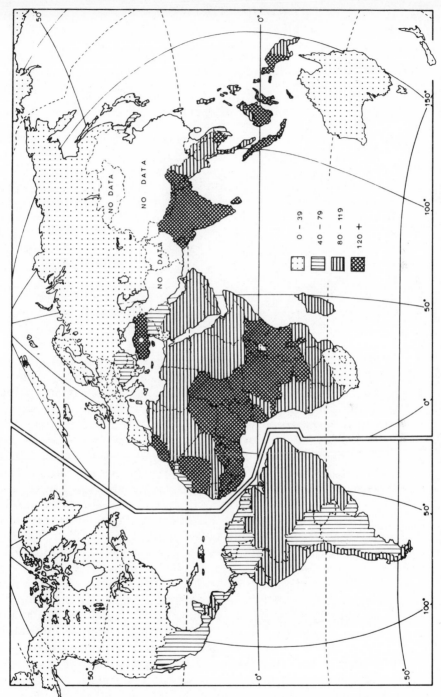

Fig. 2.2. World infant mortality rates: deaths under one year of age per 1000 live births, 1970.

0 — 39
40 — 79
80 — 119
120 +

NO DATA
NO DATA
NO DATA

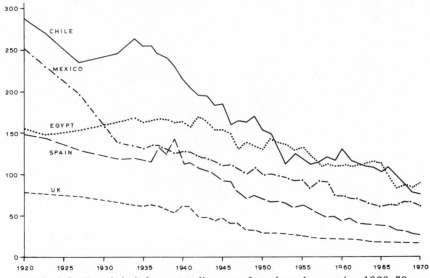

Fig. 2.3. Trends in infant mortality rates for selected countries, 1920–70:
deaths under one year of age per 1000 live births.

indicators. The quality and experience of medical personnel may vary,
and what constitutes an adequately equipped hospital bed is open to
wide interpretation. In addition there is the important qualification of
accessibility: this depends to a large extent on geographical dispersion
and available transport facilities, but it is also dependent upon more
subtle barriers, such as language and culture. In the case of physicians.
a familiar pattern emerges (Fig. 2.4). The worst-off are those in the
developing countries of Africa and Asia, where there are six times
more potential patients per physician than in North America, Eurasia
Australia, and New Zealand. Overall, 66 per cent of the world's popu
lation by national units is underprivileged in terms of the provision o
physicians, whilst an élite 18 per cent live in countries able to call upon
50 per cent of all the world's physicians. As Fig. 2.5 shows all too
clearly, the situation has hardly improved at all in the last twenty years
In Ethiopia, Rwanda, Chad, Niger, and Upper Volta there were mor
than 50,000 inhabitants for every qualified physician in 1971, com
pared to figures of less than 500 in Israel, Czechoslovakia, and Hungary
Put in another way, Indonesia, with 6 per cent of the world's popu
lation, has 0·25 per cent of the world's physicians, compared to th
United States' 10 per cent of the population and 20 per cent of th
physicians. However the figures are viewed, the disparities ar
enormous. Moreover, despite encouraging trends in many countrie

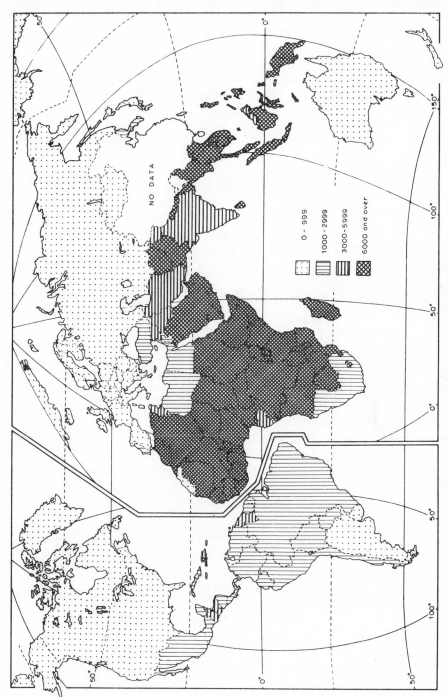

NO DATA

0 - 999
1000 - 2999
3000 - 5999
6000 and over

Fig. 2.4. World distribution of physicians: inhabitants per physician, 1970.

the biggest improvements typically occur in those countries with
relative abundance of health personnel, a tendency which is cor
pounded by the growing phenomenon of international migration b
physicians (UN 1975b). Should the reader need still more evidence
inequality, UN data show that the provision of physicians actual
deteriorated in almost a third of the developing countries in the 196(
including Algeria, Angola, Chile, Cuba, Gambia, Haiti, Kenya, Malaw
Mexico, Morocco, Paraguay, Thailand, and Zambia.

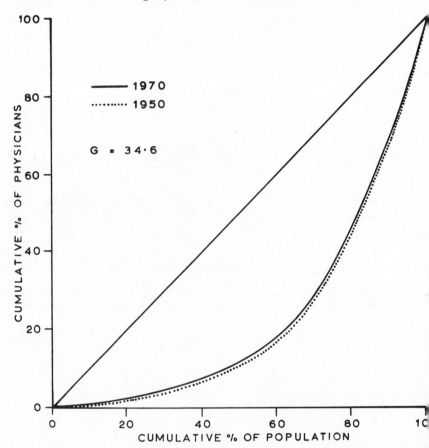

Fig. 2.5. Lorenz curves of the world distribution of physicians, by country,
1950 and 1970.

Housing. Because of the great diversity in climate and construction materi
and in household size, customs, and practices, it is extremely diffic
to measure and compare the housing situation on an internatior

basis. Most difficult to assess are conditions in the rural areas of developing countries, where dwellings are rarely surveyed for census purposes. It is evident, however, that conditions are, in general, abysmally bad, with a predominance of structurally unsound, insanitary, crowded, and poorly ventilated dwellings being only occasionally relieved by the more comfortable accommodation of small towns, slowly growing provincial cities, and government-sponsored housing schemes associated with construction projects, resettlement schemes, and agrarian reform programmes. Greater attention is generally paid to the more dramatic deficiencies of the larger and more rapidly growing urban centres of the same countries, where the inability to cope with rates of immigration of up to 10 per cent a year has led to the development of squatter settlements holding between 30 and 50 per cent of the population (Dwyer 1975). Together, the combination of these urban and rural housing problems means that the developing countries of the Third World fare very badly on all the conventional indicators of housing conditions (Table 2.1). Although definitions in this field are often vague, coverage often incomplete and comparability doubtful, the broad contrasts are all too clear, and the magnitude of the disparities is alarming. Almost 50 per cent of Zambian and Sri Lankan housing is severely overcrowded (at an average level of more than three persons per room), compared to a figure of 0·2 per cent in Canada and West Germany. In Korea, less than one in 50 dwellings has a flush toilet, compared to almost 19 out of 20 in Canada; and whereas almost all French homes have mains electricity, only one-third of those in Réunion are thus privileged.

There are many more examples, and the figures quoted are by no means extremes: they simply represent a cross-section of available data. What is plain is that, as with *per capita* consumption, infant mortality rates, and the provision of physicians, there is an enormous rift between the rich and prosperous countries of Europe, North America, and the 'Old' British Commonwealth on the one hand and the poor countries of Asia, Africa, and, to a lesser extent, Latin America on the other. As we shall see in Chapter 4, the mechanics of the international spatial system seem designed to keep it that way.

INTRA-NATIONAL PATTERNS

Income. It has been suggested that, as individual countries progress through various stages of development, regional income disparities change from being moderate in the subsistence phase to acute in transitional stages of rapid urban and industrial growth, finally narrowing in the mature stage of a diversified industrial economy. Williamson (1965), for example, has shown that the extent of regional inequality is low in many countries with low *per capita* national income, high in rapidly developing countries of the middle-income group, and relatively low in high-income nations with sophisticated free-market economies. Such a progression accords quite well with Myrdal's ideas (1957b) of cumulative causation with 'backwash' effects being moderated by 'spread' effects in later stages of economic development. It has also been suggested that inter-regional income differences may be largely attributable to the increasing inter-personal income differences associated with a more complex division of labour. But we are unable to draw on many detailed analyses of inter-regional income differentials for confirmation of the model, as, notwithstanding the inevitable data problems, geographers have been remarkably slow to investigate regional variations in income levels, even at a fundamental descriptive level. Important exceptions to this are studies of the geography of income distribution by Brunn and Wheeler (1971), Burghardt (1972), and Morrill and Wohlenberg (1971) in the United States, Coates and Rawstron (1971) in Britain, and Klaassen, Kroft, and Viskvil (1973) in Holland.

These studies reveal that, whatever the disparities may have been like in the past, there certainly remain substantial and unacceptable variations between national sub-regions. In the United States in 1969 the median annual family income ranged from around $6000 in Mississippi, Arkansas, and Alabama to over $11,500 in Hawaii, Connecticut, and Alaska; in Britain, Coates and Rawstron (1971, p.15) found the pattern of total net incomes to reflect 'an island of prosperity stretching from Essex to Worcestershire and from Sussex to Leicestershire'. Around this island, incomes everywhere were below the national average, falling to less than 80 per cent of this statistic in Armagh, County Down, Londonderry, and Tyrone. In Fig.2.6 we have plotted the distribution of the average amount of income tax paid per resident population of each département in France in 1970. These data contain even greater variations, although it must be recognized that the range of the disparities reflected by this sort of indirect measure of income is to a certain extent a function of the progressiveness of the tax system. It is clear at any rate that in France there also an 'island' of prosperity, centred on Paris and surrounded by what Gravier (1947) has called the 'French Desert', in which live the underprivileged 70 per cent of the population, whose average taxes amounted to less than 250 francs per head in départements like Cantal, Haute Loire, Lot, and Lozère. By contrast, the 2·5 million inhabitants

Table 2.1

Housing conditions in selected countries, c. 1970

	% Dwellings with only 1 Room	% Dwellings with over 3 persons per room	% Dwellings with piped water	% Dwellings with flush toilet	% Dwellings with electricity
Canada (1971)	1·5	0·2	96·1	94·5	N.D.
Federal German Republic (1968)	2·1	0·2	99·7	87·4	99·9
France (1968)	12·0	2·8	90·8	51·8	98·8
Yugoslavia (1971)	6·7	9·2	34·0	26·5	87·9
Greece (1971)	12·4	3·0	65·0	45·0	88·3
Brazil (1970)	2·8	4·8	27·4	13·2	47·6
Panama (1970)	37·4	38·6	26·1	41·3	52·4
El Salvador (1970)	60·8	63·1	26·0	22·5	34·1
St. Helena (1966)	1·2	4·7	43·9	38·4	45·1
Mauritius (1962)	27·5	28·6	14·9	22·4	46·9
Réunion (1967)	18·0	17·8	27·3	N.D.	29·3
Republic of Korea (1970)	7·3	N.D.	19·6	1·8	49·7
Zambia (1969)	51·3	47·4	12·4	15·1	N.D.
Sri Lanka (1971)	35·3	47·7	4·4	6·7	9·0

Source: United Nations 1975b, pp. 724–58.

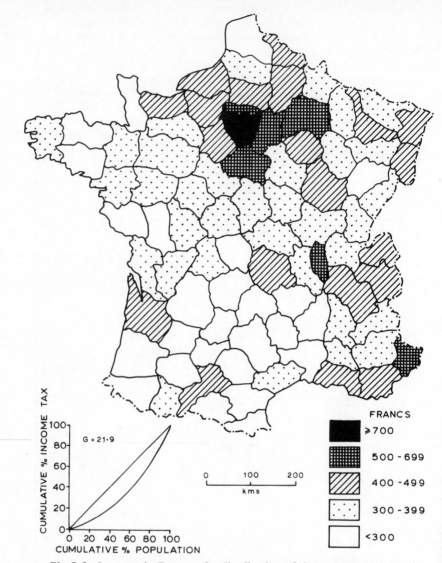

Fig. 2.6. Incomes in France: the distribution of the average amount of income tax paid per inhabitant in 1970

Paris were prosperous enough to generate a figure of 1676 francs pe head, four times the national average (just under 400 francs). Outsid the Paris region and adjacent parts of Picardy and Upper Normandy this average figure was exceeded only by a few départements i Lorraine, Alsace, Franche-Comté, Provence, and the Cote d'Azu together with the outliers of Gironde and Haute-Garonne.

In less-developed countries, the pattern is often more explicitly one of urban-rural contrasts, though if there is any marked degree of primacy in the urban hierarchy the spatial expression of income disparities will clearly be more akin to the British and French experience of a centre–periphery dichotomy. The reasons for an urban–rural dichotomy are several. In the first place, incomes from agricultural employment are, on average, much lower than in the non-agricultural sector: available data suggest that incomes derived from non-agricultural pursuits are usually between two and four times higher than agricultural incomes, and in some cases the ratio is as high as 10 to 1 (ILO 1972). In addition, average incomes in rural areas are depressed by large-scale underemployment and unemployment resulting from the inability to support the burden of productivity and income generation for expanding populations. Conversely, the marked concentration of industrial activity and overhead capital in urban centres of developing countries has caused a localization of what prosperity there is to go round. Regional income gradients are therefore steep, despite the fact that absolute levels of income are low everywhere. Thus in Malaysia the gross domestic product *per capita* in some states is estimated to be five times that of others, and in Indonesia in the mid 1960s, regional monthly *per capita* expenditures varied from 70 to 200 per cent of the national average (UN 1975b). More detailed breakdowns are difficult to find, for in all these countries the difficulties of measuring income are exacerbated by the very problem of mass poverty. Karan and Bladen (1975) have been able to estimate the average *per capita* income of local districts in India, however, using survey data derived from the National Council of Applied Economic Research (Fig. 2.7). Broadly speaking, the distribution of high *per capita* incomes corresponds closely to the spatial pattern of urban and industrial development, and the lowest incomes are found in the rural areas of northern Bihar and eastern Uttar Pradesh in the Middle Ganges Valley.

Health. At the regional level, major variations in health and health care delivery persist in most countries, regardless of levels of economic development and the structure of the health services. Studies of the geography of disease mortality show that even in the most advanced countries of the world with universal national health service coverage, regional differentials are significant (Howe 1970). Within England and Wales, for example, male Standardized Mortality Ratios (that is, standardized for areal variations in age structure) for tuberculosis for the period 1959–63 range from less than 4·5 in Oxfordshire, Dorset, Huntingdonshire, Norfolk, and Canterbury, to over 200 in Bootle, Salford, Dudley,

Liverpool, West Bromwich, and Stoke-on-Trent. Differentials are of course much greater in developing countries with small and weakly developed public health sectors, although reliable data are scarce. In Orissa, Ahmad (1973) found mortality from the major endemic diseases — fever, cholera, smallpox, dysentery, and respiratory diseases — varied by factors of between four and thirty between the thirteen sub-regions of the State.

Similar disparities exist in the regional provision of health care facilities in many countries. Access to these facilities clearly depends to a great extent on distance and travel time, so that much of the literature on the spatial organization of health care delivery systems emphasizes cheapness and proximity, relying heavily on fairly sophisticated applications of gravity models and linear programming (see, for

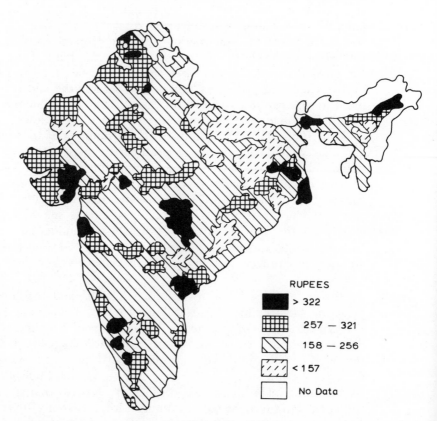

RUPEES

> 322

257 — 321

158 — 256

< 157

No Data

Fig. 2.7. Incomes in India: the distribution of estimated *per capita* incomes in 1955/6. (Source: Karan and Bladen 1975, p.5.)

example, Gould and Leinbach 1966, Godlund 1961). But an approximate measure of provision, as at the international scale, is provided by
the density of physicians and hospital beds. Here again, regional
variations within Britain, despite a long-established National Health
Service, have been shown to be extensive. Coates and Rawstron (1971)
found that the *per capita* provision of hospital beds in the North East
Metropolitan hospital board area in 1963 was 20 per cent above the
average for England and Wales, in contrast to the level of provision in
the Sheffield area, which was almost 20 per cent below the average.
Similarly, the number of principal general medical practitioners per
100,000 patients in 1966–7 ranged from 32 in Barnsley, Burton-upon-
Trent, and West Hartlepool to over 100 in Sutherland (Coates and
Rawstron 1971). In the United States, where medical personnel are
able to move more freely in pursuit of higher incomes and better
working conditions, Shannon and Dever (1972) have demonstrated a
marked imbalance in health care facilities, exemplified by the distribution of general practitioners (Fig. 2.8). In general, the Mid-West and the
Black South have been losing ground to the Atlantic and Pacific Coasts,

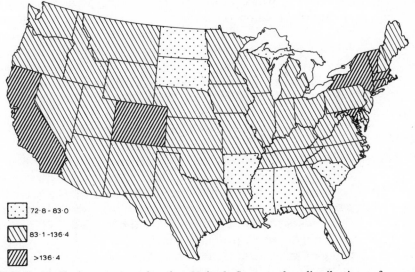

72·8 - 83·0

83·1 -136·4

>136·4

Fig. 2.8. Medical resources in the United States: the distribution of general
practitioners per 100,000 inhabitants in 1970. (Source: Shannon and Dever 1972,
p. 39.)

and in particular to California and the North-East. Such disparities
were the reason for the Emergency Health Personnel Act of 1970,
which created the National Health Service Corporation, whereby

physicians and other health personnel can be assigned to communities where there is a critical shortage of manpower. By 1972 about 200 communities with a total population of some 900,000 were benefiting from this initiative. Nevertheless, in the United States the uneven application of the national systems of medical insurance, Medicare and Medicaid, is still a major source of regional variation in health care. As Rivlin (1973, p.91) says, 'some states have generous Medicaid programs covering the near-poor, and others do not. As a result half the Federal expenditures go to three generous states — New York, California, and Massachusetts — and equally needy people in other states go without help' (see also Boulding and Pfaff 1972).

In less developed countries, the spatial distribution of qualified physicians and 'Western' medical services is highly centralized, so that spatial variations are often dramatic. In Thailand in 1968, more than 50 per cent of the physicians served the 10 per cent of the population in the Bangkok area. In India, although 80 per cent of the population is rural, only 11 per cent of the physicians practise in rural areas. And in the Lebanon the ratio of physicians to patients ranges from one to 490 in Beirut Province to one to 5277 in the predominantly rural province of South Lebanon (UN 1975b). A similar situation obtains in relation to hospital beds. Thus 60 per cent of the hospital beds in Iraq are located within the three urban areas of Baghdad, Basrah, and Nineveh, with the average number of beds per 100,000 persons ranging from 29 in Baghdad to six in Thi-Qar province. In Sierra Leone, well over one-third of the hospital beds are located in the Western Area (encompassing Freetown), where there is only one-eleventh of the population. The contrast between this area and the provinces, where some parts are almost totally devoid of medical centres, is well illustrated by Fig.2.9, which shows the population per hospital bed by provincial districts. Arranged by these units, 62 per cent of the population can be regarded as underprivileged. As Riddell (1970) points out, this pattern is attributable to the attitude of the old colonial administrations, whose attention focused on the provision of medical services for government personnel and administrative centres. Subsequently, independent governments have had to contend with shortages of capital, materials, and trained staff which have delayed the construction of facilities which might otherwise have allowed a more equitable distribution of resources.

Housing. The inevitable problems of data availability and reliability which beset the measurement of housing conditions mean that there are relatively few data sources and even fewer case studies from which to

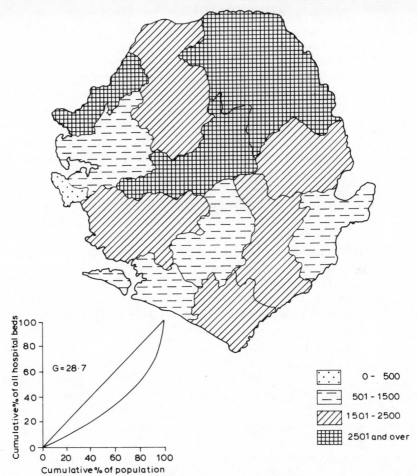

Fig. 2.9. Medical resources in Sierra Leone: the distribution of population per hospital bed, by province, 1964. (Compiled from data in Clarke 1966, p. 66.)

draw examples with which to illustrate the extent of regional disparities. Britain is one of the few countries in which housing conditions at the regional level have attracted the attention of geographers (see, for example, Burnett and Scott 1962, Hillyard *et al.* 1972, Humphrys 1968), and only a few other countries publish reliable data at regular intervals. For the most part then, we are limited to very sweeping generalizations based on scanty evidence which suggests that whereas rural areas experience the most extensive problems, the most acute problems are found within the larger urban areas of the world (UN 1973b). Comment is therefore restricted to one country for which reliable data are readily available for a fairly fine mesh of data units —

the United States. Ironically, there have been few geographical analyses of these data, so that our knowledge of the spatial disposition of the housing problem in the United States is far from complete.

Until recently, housing conditions in the United States were commonly measured in terms of 'substandardness', defined by census variables relating to structural conditions and the provision of basic plumbing amenities; but questions on structural condition were dropped from the 1970 census because of the difficulties of enumeration, so that we are left with no universally accepted yardstick of housing conditions. Feasible alternatives are provided by several combinations of other census variables, but the most efficient is probably the dual measure of dwellings which are both overcrowded (that is, have an occupational density of more than one person per room) and lack one or more of the basic plumbing facilities (hot running water, a flush toilet, and a fixed bath or shower). In order to avoid confusion with definitions of substandardness, dwellings which fulfil these criteria will be referred to as *inadequate*. By this test there were some 700,000 occupied inadequate dwellings in the United States in 1970, or 1·1 per cent of the total. These figures clearly represent only the hard core of the housing problem, yet there is considerable variation between the 3108 counties of the conterminous United States (Fig. 2.10).

What in fact emerges is an oppressive picture of spatial inequality, with the incidence of inadequate housing in the worst areas thirty times the national average, and three hundred times the proportion found in the best-off areas. Such disparities are a poor advertisement indeed for the world's richest nation, however small the absolute numbers of inadequate dwellings may be in some counties. Some of the worst conditions of all are associated with the rural poverty of the Black South. Major concentrations of inadequate rural housing exist in coastal South Carolina, central Georgia, central Louisiana, and the Delta Country of northern Mississippi, reflecting the meagre level of living of the black population which is the legacy of share cropping, tenant farming, severe underemployment, and systematic racial discrimination. In Marshall County, Mississippi, over 12 per cent of all occupied dwellings were inadequate in 1970. This figure is by no means exceptional, and certainly gives some indication of the miserable state of housing conditions in the Black South. But an even more disturbing impression is given by supplementary sources. A recent survey of ninety-six families in the Louise-Midnight district of the Mississippi Delta Country found that over three-quarters of the families live in rat-infested dwellings, whilst children were forced to sleep, on average 2·2 to a bed. Other aspects of life for these families were equally

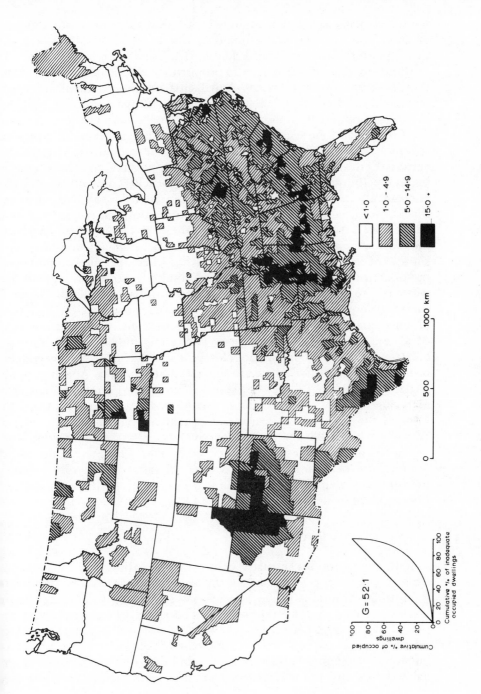

Fig. 2.10. Housing conditions in the United States: the distribution of 'inadequate' housing in 1970. Categories indicate the percentage of housing classified as 'inadequate'.

wretched. Only two-fifths could afford to eat meat on more than on
or two days a week, whilst one-fifth had never seen a physician and
three-quarters had never seen a dentist (Dunbar 1969).

Rural poverty of less dramatic proportions extends northwards from
the Black South to encompass Appalachia and the southeastern coastal
plain. Within these areas, the incidence of inadequate housing is highest
in the groundnut and tobacco areas of North Carolina and Virginia
the Cumberland Plateau and Cumberland Mountain areas of Tennessee
together with the Black Mountain areas of southwestern Virginia and
eastern Kentucky, where problems of rural poverty have been exacer
bated by the decline of the Kentucky coalfields. Beyond these areas
concentrations of inadequate housing are chiefly associated, as in th
Black South, with the rural poverty of ethnic or racial minority groups
Numerically, the most important of these is the Mexican-American
population of southeastern Texas which was originally imported as
source of cheap agricultural labour. For these people, employmen
opportunities outside agriculture are limited, and since agricultural
workers are paid extremely low wages poverty is widespread. It i
therefore not surprising to find that in several counties the incidenc
of inadequate dwellings is over 20 per cent. Finally, the highest rate
of all are to be found in counties containing Indian reservations, th
location of which correspond closely with the most barren and un
productive agricultural areas of the United States. Thus Apache Count
(Arizona), Navajo County (Arizona), San Juan County (Utah), and
McKinley County (New Mexico), which encompass the Indian reserva
tions of the Colorado plateaus, had inadequate housing of the order o
38, 23, 27 and 28 per cent respectively in 1970. Similar condition
prevailed around Wounded Knee and the Cheyenne and Sioux
reservations of South Dakota, where 38 per cent of the occupie
dwellings in Shannon County and 29 per cent of those in Ziebacl
County were inadequate.

INTRA-URBAN PATTERNS

With the enormous diversity of the world's cities, it is impossible t
make comprehensive statements about either the extent or pattern o
intra-urban variations in income, health, or housing conditions. Never
theless, we can at least base some general assumptions on the regulari
ties of Western and Westernized cities which have been catalogued b
urban geographers, and we can supplement these with the evidence o
individual examples which serve to indicate the magnitude of im
balance. As with the international and intra-national patterns described

above, a more detailed consideration of the processes involved is reserved for later chapters.

Income. Not surprisingly, we are unable to make more than the most general of assumptions about income distributions in non-Western cities because of a simple lack of information. The most that can be said with any confidence is that income distributions are likely to follow the broad trend of severe deprivation in the interstitial squatter areas and peripheral shanty zones, relative affluence in central areas and some suburbs, and spectacular affluence in a few enclaves. The extent of income disparities between these areas is at present a matter for speculation, but if living conditions in general (see below under 'housing') are at all a function of incomes, then the gap must be enormous. Conversely, for Western cities there is plenty of evidence, both direct and indirect, pointing to a general pattern of inner city deprivation and suburban affluence, with secondary sectoral variations. As we shall see, income distribution is closely related to similar patterns of health and housing. In addition, income variables are common constituents of studies of the residential patterns of cities, and have been found to be closely associated with the dominant 'socio-economic status' dimension of residential differentation which characterizes the ecological structure of most cities (a full summary of such studies is given in Timms 1971, Herbert 1972, and Johnston 1976h). Mapping of these income variables reveals that neighbourhood gradients, as with social class, housing quality and ethnicity, are fairly steep. Mogridge (1968), for example, estimates that average incomes in the southwestern sector of London increase by 40 per cent from the innermost to the outermost districts. It is possible to be more explicit about variations within North American cities, since detailed census data are available. The typical pattern is well illustrated by the distribution of median family incomes within the Atlanta and St. Louis metropolitan areas (Fig. 2.11 A and B). Both exhibit regions of luxury adjacent to regions of brutal poverty, as in the pattern identified by Bunge (1975) in Detroit. The median annual income of families living in inner city areas encompassing the downtown commercial districts barely exceeds the official poverty level for individual families ($4000 p.a. in 1970), whereas the most prosperous suburban neighbourhoods contain families whose median annual income is at least five times as great. As Bederman and Adams (1974) show, the poor are typically unskilled and black, from large families with a high proportion of female heads of household for whom job opportunities are extremely limited. In contrast, the rich élite is comprised of the small, white families whose economic position is threatened only by the envy of the poor.

A

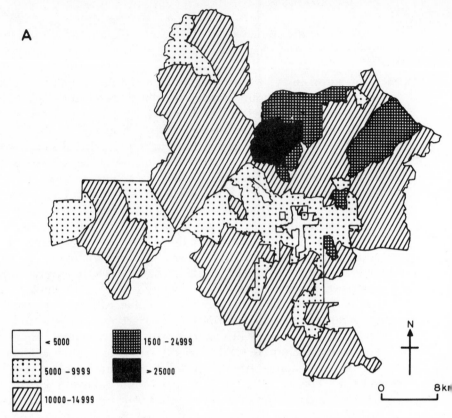

☐ < 5000	▦ 1500 – 24999		
⋮ 5000 – 9999	■ > 25000		
╱ 10000–14999			

N

0   8km

Fig.2.11A. Intra-urban variations in income: median family incomes by census
tract in Atlanta, Geogia, in 1970.

Health. Strong relationships exist between health and urban structure, since
the incidence of many diseases is dependent upon population density,
sanitation, and environmental quality. Thus, just as the 1854 outbreak
of cholera in London was linked with contaminated water supplies in
the densely populated area around Broad Street (Stamp 1964), many
contemporary outbreaks of disease can be traced to the poorest and
most overcrowded districts of cities in the Third World. This sort of
relationship is not exclusive to Third World cities, however. A simple
map of infant mortality rates within the London boroughs between
1968 and 1972 (Fig.2.12) reflects the contrast between the poorer
central boroughs of Camden, Hackney, and Tower Hamlets and the
affluent and spacious suburbs which surround them. At one extreme
of this distribution is Harrow, with a rate of 13 infant deaths per
1000 live births; at the other extreme the residents of Hackney

B

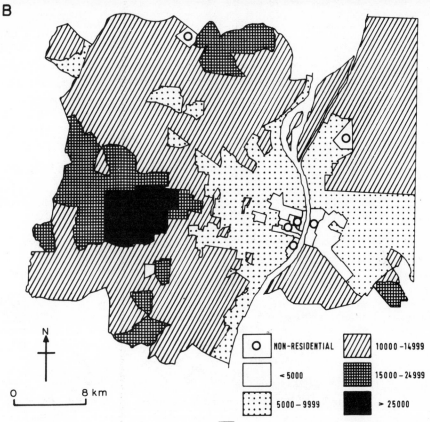

Fig. 2.11B. Intra-urban variations in income: median family incomes by census tract in St. Louis, Missouri, in 1970.

experience a rate almost twice as high. A more comprehensive approach to patterns of urban health has been taken by Pyle (1968) who identified 'poverty areas' and 'health syndromes' in Chicago. Three of the first five factors delimited exhibited distinctive spatial patterns, and the most important of these, which Pyle calls a 'poverty syndrome', revealed a close correspondence between the incidence of tuberculosis, syphilis, and infant mortality and the poorest neighbourhoods of the densely populated central city. A second factor, labelled a 'density syndrome', was also linked with poor, overcrowded neighbourhoods, and had associations with three diseases — mumps, whooping cough, and chicken-pox — which thrive on close personal contact. His third and fourth factors showed no clear spatial pattern, but the fifth, a 'water syndrome', highlighted the relationship between stretches of open water in the city and the incidence of infectious hepatitis.

Chicago is also the city for which we have the most detailed knowledge about spatial variations in health care facilities, thanks to the work of geographers like Earickson, Morrill, Pyle, and Rees in the lavish Chicago Regional Hospital Study (CRHS) (see de Visé 1973).

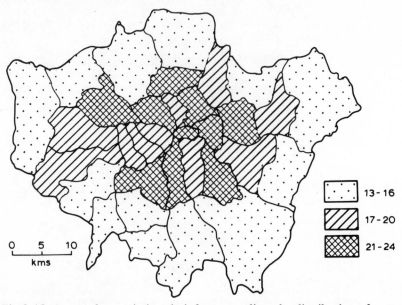

	13-16
	17-20
	21-24

Fig. 2.12. Intra-urban variations in infant mortality: the distribution of average infant mortality rates per 1000 live births in London, 1968–72.

These workers and others have established the extent of imbalance in Chicago's provision of physicians and hospitals. Working papers published by the CRHS have described the health system as 'apartheid', discriminating on the basis of race, residence, age, and sex, not only in terms of the location of physicians and hospitals, but also in terms of waiting time, quality of care, and cost. Hospitals, for example, have always had an excess central city capacity and a shortfall in the suburbs, especially the less prosperous suburbs (Morrill 1966). Physicians are equally badly distributed, their location being determined more by the socio-economic status of communities than by need. Fig. 2.13 shows the present distribution of physicians in Chicago which is the product of locational shifts which have meant heavy losses of physicians in the Loop, a small net gain in the inner city, a slight loss in the outer city, and heavy gains in the suburbs (Rees 1967). Physicians in private practice vacating the poor black neighbourhoods of the southeast for the more affluent inner suburbs o north, northwest, and west Chicago leave welfare physicians to serve an average of 7000 people rather than 700, to see 80 patients a day rather than 80 a week, and to care for the sick without making home visits (de Visé 1968). The same movements have led to the improvement of the ratio of physicians to population in Chicago's ten most affluent communities from 1·78 per 1000 in 1950 to 2·10 per 1000 in 1970; at the other end of the spectrum, the ratio in the ten poorest communities deteriorated from 0·99 to 0·26 per 1000 (de Visé and Dewey 1972). If Chicago is as much the 'model' for intra-urban variations in health care delivery as it seems to be for the other urban patterns, there must be a high probability that inequalities of similar dimensions exist in other cities.

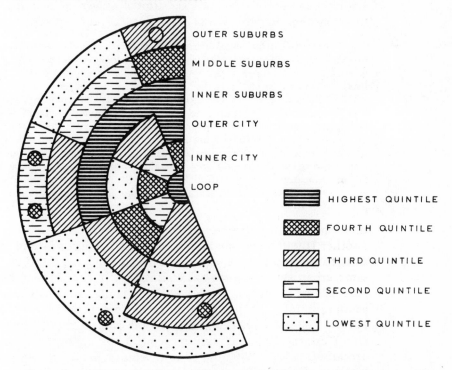

OUTER SUBURBS

MIDDLE SUBURBS

INNER SUBURBS

OUTER CITY

INNER CITY

LOOP

HIGHEST QUINTILE

FOURTH QUINTILE

THIRD QUINTILE

SECOND QUINTILE

LOWEST QUINTILE

Fig. 2.13. Medical resources in Chicago: the distribution of physicians per 1000 inhabitants in 1970, ranked by quintiles. (Source: Dewey 1973, p.14.)

Housing. All cities have their share of slum dwellings, but some are less fortunate than others and, as the reader will have come to expect by now, the cities of the Third World suffer most of all. The UN estimates that slums and squatter settlements presently constitute the living environment for at least one-third of the urban population in all developing countries, and that they are growing at a rate of 15 per cent per annum, which will cause them to double in six years (UN 1975b). Although these cities, like Western cities, have slum environments in decaying inner areas, the bulk of the slum conditions are the result of rapid urbanization which has forced the poor into transitional squatter settlements on unoccupied land between more prosperous suburbs, and on peripheral sites.

As such, these shanty settlements afford essential shelter which cannot be provided by conventional private or public housing markets; and in many cases there is evidence of the spontaneous development of active participation and social organization which provides a relatively stable community for the transitional stages of assimilation to the urban system. But the actual housing conditions are appalling:

The degree of environmental deprivation is severe. Families establishing themselves in these areas will commonly begin their existence at the meanest of subsistence levels. Access to water will be difficult, irregular and expensive, and the water itself will in all probability be contaminated. Inadequate or more likely non-existent sewage and garbage disposal services will provide fertile conditions for breeding of vermin and pestilence. The living accommodation will be overcrowded, lack privacy and will be very hot in summer and cold and wet in winter. The surrounding area will suffer from a high density of population, without open space or ready access to transportation to other parts of the city. Fire will be a constant hazard, threatening devastation. Access to normal community facilities such as health, education and recreation facilities will be difficult or impossible. Sickness and infant mortality rates will be high and life expectancy short (UN 1971, paragraph 44).

In Bombay alone there were 500,000 shanty dwellings in 1971, and another 100,000 lived in the streets. Such conditions stand in sharp contrast to the prosperous suburbs and élite enclaves that exist within the same urban systems, such as Petaling Jaya in Kuala Lumpur, Chanakyapuri in New Delhi, and Forbes Park in Manila. In Hong Kong (Fig. 2.14) housing conditions for the European and Chinese élites in the Mid Levels, Repulse Bay, Peak, and Jardine Hill areas are as luxurious as in any Western city, but, despite a massive building programme (which produced nearly 250,000 new dwellings between 1965 and 1970), housing shortages were so acute that nearly 2 million people are officially recognized as being inadequately housed: 400,000 of them live in squatter huts and other makeshift accommodation. The density of population in parts of New Kowloon approaches 1,000 persons per acre, a figure which finds few parallels in other Asian cities (Pryor 1973).

By comparison, the problems of slum dwellings in Western cities

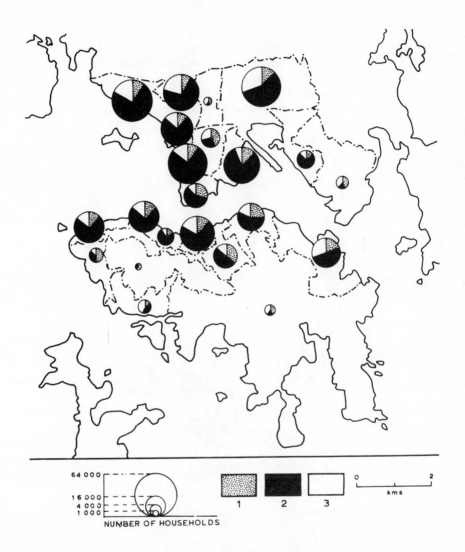

NUMBER OF HOUSEHOLDS

Fig. 2.14. Housing conditions in Hong Kong: households in different types of accommodation, by census tract, 1961. Key to numbers: (1) Permanent housing (self-contained): whole concrete, brick, or stone house, or self-contained flat in a concrete, brick, or stone building; (2) Permanent housing (not self-contained): rooms, cubicles, bedspaces, basements, and verandahs or cocklofts not being part of a self-contained flat in a concrete, brick, or stone building; (3) Non-permanent housing: whole wooden house, shack or part thereof, or non-domestic living space in a whole concrete, brick, or stone building; or a space not in a building. (Source: Pryor 1973, p. 30.)

are much less dramatic, although they are no less significant for those who live in them. Generally speaking, slums in Western cities are localized in inner city areas: this is certainly the case in our two examples of Philadelphia and Paris (Figs. 2.15 and 2.16). These inner city areas are becoming increasingly unattractive to the middle classes, who are moving to the suburbs; and as the working classes also look forward to newer homes further out, the inner cities are left more and

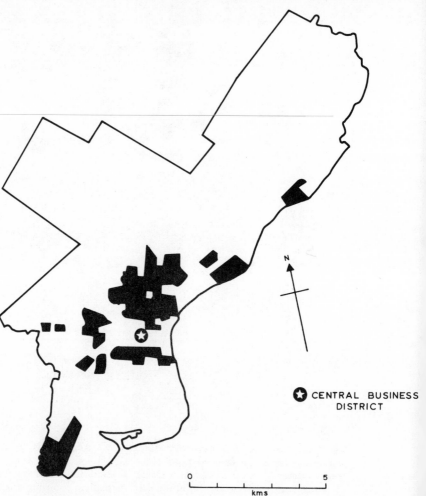

CENTRAL BUSINESS
DISTRICT

0   5
kms

Fig. 2.15. Housing conditions in Philadelphia: the distribution of census tract⸱ with at least 3 per cent of dwelling units having no plumbing facilities *and* at leas⸱ 7·5 per cent of dwelling units classed as overcrowded (that is, at an occupationa⸱ density of more than 1 person per room), 1970.

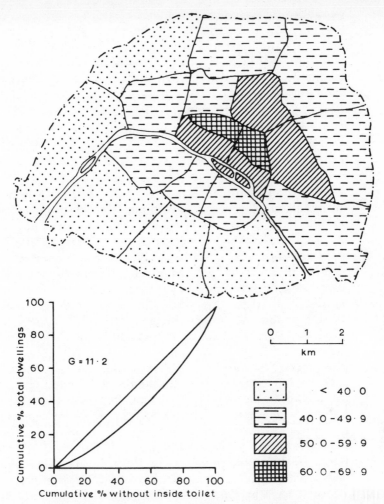

Fig. 2.16. Housing conditions in Paris: the distribution of the percentage of dwellings without an inside flush toilet, by *arrondissement*, 1968.

more to the poor, the old, and the racial minority groups. In Britain and other countries with large public housing markets, those with the lowest incomes are not necessarily those with the worst housing, since these markets are far from being governed by commercial considerations alone. But on the whole it is still the inner city environments which contain the worst housing conditions, regardless of the status of the occupants.

An examination of census data on overcrowding (persons per room) and the provision of basic amenities (hot water supply, fixed bath or shower, and an inside flush toilet) for the 3093 rural districts, urban districts, municipal boroughs and wards that in 1971 formed a nested hierarchy within the major local authority areas of England and Wales shows that all except eight of the 310 worst areas (that is, the lowest tenth) ranked on an index combining the two criteria* are inner city wards, and that 177 of these are located within inner London. From an examination of those wards falling within the worst decile, it appears that the most common denominator is privately rented nineteenth century by-law terraced housing. Among many possible examples of wards whose housing stock is dominated by dwellings of this type are Hudsons and Ordnance in Newham, Deritend and Duddleston in Birmingham, Everton in Liverpool, Beswick in Manchester, Attercliffe in Sheffield, Byker in Newcastle, and the well-documented case of St. Ann's in Nottingham (Coates and Silburn 1970). The problems of such areas are clearly rooted in the familiar process of inner city decay. In a number of wards, however, these problems are intensified by gross overcrowding resulting from the concentration of low-income minority groups, and where this occurs, the worst housing conditions of all are to be found. Examples include Golborne ward (Kensington and Chelsea), Harrow Road ward (Westminster), Northcote ward (Ealing), Kilburn and Roundwood wards (Brent), and Holloway ward (Islington); these six wards are at the bottom of the list, and all contain large clusters of Irish and New Commonwealth immigrants. Students also form substantial minority groups in some wards, concentrated by economic necessity into converted low-rent apartments in older dwellings. Examples here include Abercromby ward in Liverpool and Westgate ward in Newcastle upon Tyne. Finally, in wards such as Thorntree (Teesside), Dockyard (Southwark), and Moorfields (Hackney), where the housing stock consists of a mixture of nineteenth century terracing and older local authority housing, the combination of the under-provision of basic amenities associated with the former and the high average densities of occupation associated with the latter produces equally poor over-all index scores.

CONCLUSIONS

The cartographic and statistical evidence presented here shows unequivocally that, from a spatial perspective, inequality is always present and often extreme. Beyond such fundamental statements,

---

*Standardized, normalized scores for the two variables (the average number of persons per room in occupied dwellings and the proportion of households without exclusive use of one or more of the basic amenities) were summed to give an index of housing conditions.

however, any conclusions drawn from this brief investigation must be very tentative. Existing sources of information are too fragmented, and our approach too selective, to allow us to make any conclusive statements about the spatial expression of social inequality. Some broad patterns do recur, such as the basic disparity between the Third World and the 'white north' and its settler colonies, the urban–rural contrasts within developing areas, the centre–periphery dichotomy of many advanced space-economies, and the various inner-city/suburban gradients of cities everywhere. These generalizations must be treated with caution, however, for another recurring theme of this chapter has been the individual complexity of socio-spatial patterns. The territorial manifestations of inequality are never neat or simple, and inductive 'explanations' based on associated characteristics can only be first approximations of the truth. What we have been able to demonstrate with the available (and often crude) statistics is the existence of disparities which are unacceptable in intensity, complex in pattern, and persistent in occurrence. An awareness of these inequalities and their magnitude must be the first step towards their removal.

3 Integrated approaches to social well-being

Because academics, planners, administrators, and politicians mus often ask questions of a specific nature, the measurement of socia well-being must often be fractional, through the examination anc analysis of single components such as health or housing. But thes components are ultimately interrelated, overlapping and sometime conflicting in a complex way, so that in many circumstances it i necessary to take a more general view of the situation. The human mind, no matter how specialized or sophisticated, persists in wanting to know whether things in general are getting better or worse; and th policy-maker must know the effects of particular decisions on socia well-being in general. Moreover, if we accept the need for social policie of any sort, then we must also have some means of evaluating anc monitoring their success in terms of maintaining or increasing socia well-being. Traditionally, the yardsticks used to measure progress in national and regional well-being have been the economist's indices o production and consumption, supplemented by income levels anc rates of unemployment and industrial growth. As we have seen, how ever, these are by no means satisfactory surrogates for social well being. Similarly, the conventional economic criterion of Pareto efficiency (by which no person can become better-off without other becoming worse-off) becomes a precarious concept in the social sphere New developments and changed social conditions will be judged a Pareto-optimal if some people are made better off without reducing the well-being of anyone else, with money or real income being th measure of well-being. But, as Drewe (1973) points out, Pareto optimality takes no account of externality effects or of the impact o change on different social groups.

These deficiencies have led to the search for more appropriate yardsticks of progress and well-being. Several attempts have been made to modify such traditional national accounting indicators as Gros National Product (GNP) to take account of negative externalities anc disamenities such as environmental pollution, traffic congestion, anc crime. In the United States, a measure of 'Net Economic Welfare exhibits annual growth rates significantly below those of GNP anc Samuelson (1973) suggests that we have to think in terms of a trade-of relationship between them. A similar measure has been developed in Japan, and is now used officially in parallel with GNP and Ne

Domestic Product (NDP) as an indicator of prosperity. Termed 'Net National Welfare' (NNW), it includes measures of current government social expenditure, services derived from government social capital, services derived from consumer durables, the value of increased leisure and the contribution of female housework (at female wage rates). On the debit side, it seeks to account for any deterioration in environmental conditions (by way of the estimated costs of offsetting the deterioration), and for the negative externalities associated with urbanization (for example, commuting time and the cost of injury and death from traffic accidents). As Table 3.1 indicates, NNW in 1970 was lower than the estimate of NDP. Indeed, the increased costs of pollution have meant that the rate of growth of NNW for the period 1960–70 averaged more than 1·5 per cent a year less than the growth measured conventionally by NDP.

SOCIAL INDICATORS

Interesting as these new departures may be they must still rely, ultimately, on the measuring rod of money and therefore overlook the many aspects of social well-being which are impossible to gauge in

Table 3.1

Japan: Composition and growth of net national welfare 1960–70

	Distribution (percentage)		Growth rate (annual average)
	1960	*1970*	*1960–70*
Government consumption	6·8	6·9	8·3
Private consumption	72·8	74·1	8·4
Services from capital:			
Government	1·0	2·0	15·4
Consumer durables	1·0	5·8	29·4
Leisure	14·3	14·2	8·1
Non-market activities	12·5	14·4	9·8
Less			
Environmental maintenance	−0·2	−0·8	25·8
Environmental pollution	−4·6	−13·8	20·9
Urbanization losses	−3·6	−2·7	5·1
NET NATIONAL WELFARE	100·0	100·0	8·2
compared to:			
NET DOMESTIC PRODUCT	93·8	108·6	9·8

Source: Economic Council, Government of Japan 1973, pp. 124–5.

financial terms alone. As a result, most of the initiative in developing
new yardsticks of social conditions has sprung from the so-called
'social indicators movement'. Beginning in the United States in 1966
with the North American Space Administration's desire for quantitative measures of the 'social spin-off' of its activities (Bauer 1966)
the idea of measuring social well-being and its various components by
aggregate bundles of social variables — social indicators — has now
gathered momentum. The objective is to develop integrated systems of
social reporting using indicators that could be related to policies in
much the same way as the cost of living index and rates of inflation
are related to economic policies. A major obstacle to this task is the
lack of basic data on social conditions that was so apparent in our
examination of single components of social well-being in Chapter 2.
Nevertheless, several countries have managed to make a start at the
national level, if not the regional. In Britain, the Central Statistical
Office has since 1970 produced *Social Trends*, a package of statistical
series relating to social conditions which attempts to present a 'rounded
picture of British Society' (Moser 1970). In the United States, the
seminal document *Towards a Social Report* which appeared in 1969
(U.S. Department of Health, Education, and Welfare 1969), has been
followed by the Management and Budget Office's *Social Indicators
1973* (1974); and in France the equivalent statistical package is the
annual *Données Sociales* (INSEE 1975). The Organization for Economic
and Cultural Development (OECD), which had for a long time been
wholly growth-orientated, determined in 1971 'to devote more attention to how the extra wealth which the growth process creates may be
better directed to improvements of the quality of life and the meeting
of social aspirations' (OECD 1971, p.1), and has now instituted its
own programme of social indicators.

Similarly, as an awareness of the limitations of traditional economic
yardsticks has spread, other institutions have also turned to social
indicators in order to help formulate and evaluate policies. For
example, local government agencies in Liverpool (1970) and Newcastle
upon Tyne (1974) have produced social reports based on social indicators, and in the *Strategic Plan for the North West* (North West Joint
Planning Team 1974) a series of social indicators was used to establish
sub-regional variations in social well-being. With the practical application of social indicators there has developed a substantial literature on
the aims, scope, and limitations of their use (Agoc 1970, McVeigh
1971, Plessas and Fein 1972, Zapf 1975). The bulk of this literature
is concerned with social indicators in an aspatial context, but there is
an increasing interest amongst geographers in territorial social

indicators which is reflected in works by Smith (1973a) and Knox (1975). Of particular interest to us here are those indicators which aim at some comprehensive measure of well-being: the sort which Elaine Carlisle (1972) calls 'informative' indicators, as opposed to 'problem-oriented' or 'predictive' indicators. These are usually operational versions of one or other of the concepts outlined in Chapter 1: level of living, quality of life, social welfare, and so on. The technical and conceptual problems associated with the construction of these informative indicators are discussed in a number of papers (Knox 1974a, Kamrany and Christakis 1970, Perle 1970, Terlekyj 1970). As Smith (1973b, p.46) concludes: 'we are apparently faced with the problem of trying to measure something which is not directly observable, for which there is no generally accepted *numéraire*, and which theory tells us is some function of things which ultimately rest on societal values'.

It is this problem of values which is the most difficult to resolve. What is needed is some system of allocating weights to the variables representing different aspects of the various components of well-being. These weights should ideally reflect the relative importance attached to the components by the population whose well-being is under consideration, but there is no easy way of discovering these priorities. One way of setting about the problem is to regard the market-place as a mechanism for ordering priorities through supply and demand, so that the weights can be derived from the 'revealed' preferences of consumer behaviour. But this approach only accounts for *effective* demand and is subject to the dubious influence of advertising. Moreover, it is in practice very difficult to incorporate the revealed preferences for public goods, especially impure public goods (items which are supplied both privately and by central and local governments, such as housing and education), which are available in more than one 'market' at the same time.

A common solution to the problem of value judgements is to fall back on the priorities of professional 'experts' or politicians, although this approach is seen by many to contain an undesirable élitist or paternalistic element. Whatever the principles of democracy, it is probably unrealistic to assume that the preferences and priorities of politicians approximate to those of people in general; and it is clear from the experience of public inquiries that 'expert' opinion can be found to support most reasonable points of view. A more reliable strategy is to deduce priorities from the explicit aims of national or local governments in the form of plans or targets. One potential source in the United States, for example, is the report of the U.S. President's Commission on National Goals (1960). A related approach would be to gauge priorities from a content analysis of newspapers, politic: manifestos, textbooks, and articles in learned journals. But probabl the best solution of all is to evaluate priorities through some surve of attitudes. There are clearly many dangers in such surveys, for th questions asked of people must be extremely carefully worded. Mor over, it is quite probable that attitudinal surveys will reveal division of opinion which are difficult to build into quantitative indicator Environmental quality, for example, is highly income-elastic becaus: as Engels saw, the poor have more urgent needs to satisfy. A mo practical difficulty lies in the sheer size of the task of surveying att tudes. Nevertheless, it should be possible to make some use of th results of sample surveys in determining weights for social indicator Koelle (1974), for example, reports that the degree of consensus amon a sample of 200 people in Berlin as to the priorities for the improv ment of the quality of life was almost twice as great on items such : the preservation of the natural environment and the improvement c educational facilities as on the reduction of violence and the improv ment of cultural facilities. In Britain, a national survey by Know (1976 using a stratified sample of 1450 persons, revealed substanti: differences in the importance attached by respondents to ten maj dimensions of well-being (see Table 3.2). Moreover, an analysis c these aggregate priority preferences suggested that they were generall more related to place of residence than to class, occupation, incom or stage in the life-cycle. Finally, a pragmatic and commonly-use 'solution' to the weighting problem is to give each variable equ: weighting in the absence of any relevant evidence. This, of cours only transfers the weighting procedure to the selection of variable so that achieving the right 'balance' of variables becomes imperativ and this is a matter of choice potentially as subjective and élitist as th 'expert' allocation of weights. Nevertheless, it is often the only pract cable option, and must be regarded as legitimate as long as th derivation of the resultant indicator is clear to everybody concerne As Smith (1973a, p.47) says: 'the imperative of empirical analysis i welfare geography means that we must be prepared to move in whe the angels fear to tread'.

TERRITORIAL INDICATORS OF SOCIAL WELL-BEING

Given the nature of these problems, and the infancy of the soci indicators movement, it is not surprising to find that there is no estal lished paradigm for the analysis of spatial variations in social well-bein It follows, therefore, that it is difficult to compare the results c

Table 3.2

Weights assigned to ten life-domains by 1450 survey respondents in Britain using an eleven-point scale (0 = completely unimportant, 10 = overwhelmingly important)

DOMAIN	*Mean Score*
The housing conditions you live in (number of rooms, state of repair, provision of running water, sanitary facilities, garage, garden)	8·5
Your neighbourhood and its environment (friendliness, cleanliness, appearance)	7·9
Your state of health (freedom from illnesses and the availability of medical services if you do feel ill)	9·1
Opportunities and facilities for education (being able to go to well-equipped schools, colleges, and so on)	7·6
Job satisfaction (how happy you are with the sort of work you do; how interesting it is)	8·1
Family life (being close to your family and relatives)	8·8
Your social status (what other people think of you; their respect for you in general; your standing in the local community)	6·1
Opportunities and facilities for leisure and recreation (things like parks, theatres, cinemas, sports centres, and so on; and having the time to make use of these things)	6·6
A stable and secure society (a society without a lot of crime, vandalism, and industrial strife, and one where you are taken care of if you are thrown out of work, or become ill, and when you retire)	8·5
Your financial situation (the sort of money you earn and the amount you are able to save if you want to)	7·9

Source: Knox 1976, p. 16.

different studies and impossible to generalize about the spatial expression and common dimensions (if any) of social well-being in the way that it is possible to generalize about regional economic geography or urban residential structure. What we seek to do here, therefore, is simply to review the development of territorial indicators of social well-being whilst extending our perspective on the extent of spatial inequalities from the single-component approach of Chapter 2.

Table 3.3

Level of living indexes, per capita consumption, and gross national product for 20 countries, c. 1960

	Level of living index	Consumption per capita ($US)	G.N.P. per capita ($US)
USA	171·3	2290	2790
Denmark	119·8	1020	1300
Belgium	119·4	1020	1250
Israel	115·2	620	680
Japan	81·9	270	440
Greece	80·2	340	390
Argentina	79·6	450	570
Yugoslavia	76·7	200	300
Spain	72·0	270	340
Chile	67·6	530	570
Mauritius	59·0	220	260
Venezuela	54·7	720	960
Jamaica	49·3	340	400
UAR	46·4	130	160
Ecuador	44·2	150	180
India	41·4	70	80
Morocco	39·1	140	160
Thailand	38·2	80	100
Ghana	37·2	160	200
Uganda	37·1	50	70*

*G.D.P.

Source: Drewnowski and Scott 1968, p. 268. From *Ekistics*, vol. 25, 1968, published by the Athens Center of Ekistics, Athens, Greece.

International indicators. At the national and international levels, the UN has long been the main initiator of attempts to develop over-all measure of social well-being, largely because of its fundamental commitment to increase the level of living of member nations. Without such measures there is clearly no way of telling whether this particular aim is being achieved. Preliminary investigations into possible ways of measuring international variations of levels of living began in the early 1950s and since then considerable progress has been made towards establishing the framework of an index of levels of living (Drewnowski 1974) The chief problems involved here have been those of data availability and of the wide range of social, physical, and cultural environment which makes the interpretation of many variables very difficult. As result, the efforts of the UN have yet to come to fruition in the form of an official series of measurements. Nevertheless, the results of the application of a prototype index to 20 nations by Drewnowski and

Scott (1968) give a clear indication of the extent of international disparities (Table 3.3). This index was constructed using a system of sliding weights for variables representing seven components of level of living: nutrition, shelter, health, education, leisure, security, and surplus income. A value of zero represents conditions under which human beings are just able to survive; a value of 100 represents 'full satisfaction' of basic physical and cultural needs, and a *per capita* surplus income of $50 per annum. The actual figures for the over-all index range from 37 for Uganda to 171 for the United States.

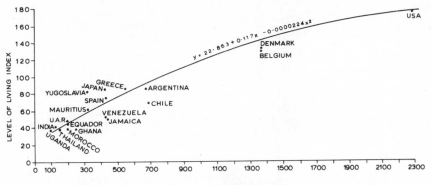

PER CAPITA CONSUMPTION, EXPENDITURE IN U.S. DOLLARS (PURCHASING POWER PARITIES)

Fig.3.1. The relationship between level of living and *per capita* consumption for 20 countries, *c*.1960. (Source: Drewnowski and Scott 1968, p.269. From *Ekistics*, vol.25, 1968, published by the Athens Center of Ekistics, Athens, Greece.

Fig. 3.1 emphasizes the dangers of using income data as surrogates for over-all measures of social well-being such as these, for whereas the level of living index exhibits a positive relationship with *per capita* consumption, it is only a loose curvilinear relationship. Thus Jamaica, Venezuela, Spain, and Japan, all with consumption levels of around $400, had index values of 49, 55, 72, and 82 respectively. Drewnowski and Scott (1968) found that in the advanced industrial nations, high levels of living are the result of a high degree of satisfaction of all needs, with the marked exception of security. In the slightly less developed countries, levels of living are somewhat lower, with relatively high levels of satisfaction of physical needs (nutrition, health, shelter) tending to be offset by a moderate satisfaction of cultural needs (education, leisure, security) and an even lower degree of satisfaction of higher needs (surplus income). At the foot of the ladder, countries such as India, Morocco, Ghana, and Thailand are characterized by extremely low levels of living, with particularly low scores on health and security, and an almost negligible degree of satisfaction of higher needs.

Regional Indicators. Within these developing countries, it is difficult to establish the extent of regional variations in social well-being, and there have been few attempts to do so, although a number of writers have

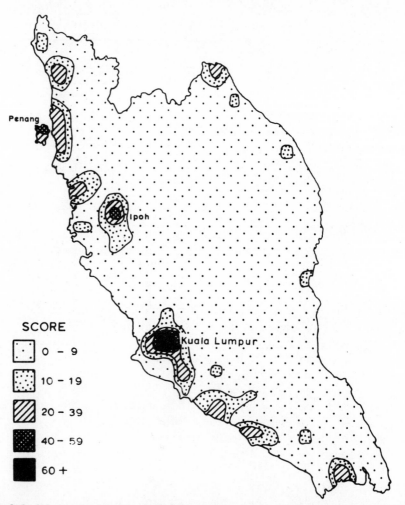

SCORE

- 0 – 9
- 10 – 19
- 20 – 39
- 40 – 59
- 60 +

Fig. 3. 2. 'Modernization' in Malaya in 1969. (Source: Leinbach 1972, p. 275. This sort of map may reflect Western ideas of social well-being, but does no necessarily represent an adequate reflection of the welfare of the indigenou population. High scores are indicative of a high degree of 'modernization'.

proposed systems or sets of territorial social indicators for developing areas (Andrews 1973, Cant 1975, Gostkowski 1974, Wilson 1973). Some evidence of over-all spatial patterns is afforded, however, by the results of multivariate analyses of 'modernization', which use input variables of a socio-economic nature. Leinbach (1972), for example, in an analysis of the spread of modernization in Malaya, used over 40 variables relating to health facilities, educational characteristics, public services, communications, and commercial activity. The 'modernization surface', an isoline map of component scores synthesized from these data, shows a marked urban–rural contrast (see Fig. 3.2). If we can assume that 'modern' Western facilities such as cinemas, newspapers, family-planning centres, hospitals, schools, and banks are indicative of well-being, then it is clearly the dominant urban centres of Kuala Lumpur, Ipoh, and Penang which are the healthiest parts of the country, contrasting sharply with the inaccessible core areas of Pahang and Kelantan. A similar metropolitan–rural contrast is discerned in an analysis of local socio-economic structure in India (Horton, McConnell, and Tirtha 1970) (see Fig. 3.3). High positive values here are the result of high levels of manufacturing activity, high *per capita* incomes, trade, urbanization and literacy, and are found in the Bombay metropolitan area, the Calcutta–Hooghly–Howrah conurbation, the Simla area, and the industrial districts of Ahmadabad, Indore, Kanpur, Bangalore, and Hyderabad. Conversely, high negative values are associated with the desert areas of southwest Rajasthan and the less productive rural areas of southwest Orissa, Uttar Pradesh, and Assam. Comparable analyses of other developing countries also reveal urban–rural contrasts: for example Riddell (1970) describes a dominant urban–rural dimension of modernization in Sierra Leone. On the other hand, the 'welfare' surface derived by Board, Davies, and Fair (1970) for South Africa shows high levels of welfare (high incomes, high gross domestic product *per capita*, high levels of education, and favourable age and employment characteristics) to be associated primarily with white-dominated poles of intensive economic activity, and markedly lower levels, outside the prosperous Witwatersrand, occur in the black areas of Ciskei, Transkei, and Zululand. The weight of available evidence, then, suggests that patterns of social well-being in developing and pluralist countries are closely related to patterns of urbanization and industrialization. It should be added, however, that equating 'modernization' with social well-being in developing countries, even in a tentative way, reflects a degree of cultural bias for which there is no substantive justification (Brookfield 1973).

Our knowledge of the extent and patterns of regional variations in

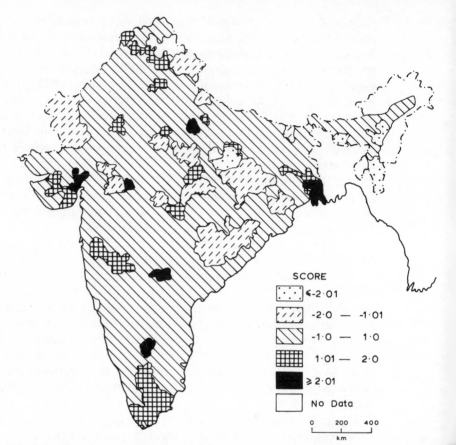

SCORE

.∴. < -2·01

/// -2·0 — -1·01

\\\ -1·0 — 1·0

▦ 1·01 — 2·0

■ ≥ 2·01

☐ No Data

0   200   400
⊢———⊢———⊣
km

Fig. 3.3. Socio-economic sub-regions in India. Negative scores reflect low levels of literacy, low incomes, low urbanization and low industrialization; conversely, areas with high positive scores are associated with high levels of literacy and income, and a high degree of urbanization and industrialization. (Source: Horton, McConnell, and Tirtha 1970, p.105.)

social well-being within a number of advanced industrial countries is much more precise. In the United States there has long been an interest in such matters, stemming from the work of Margaret Hagood and the United States Department of Agriculture (USDA), in developing the Farm Operator Level of Living Index (Hagood 1943). Published at regular intervals on a county basis (see Fig. 3.4), this index was a simple aggregate of unweighted scores on four variables: the percentage of farms with a telephone, the percentage of farms with a car, the average value of farm produce sold or traded each year, and the average value of land and buildings per farm. Sociologists found the index to be useful in analyses of social structure, and produced a large volume of literature in the 1940s and 1950s dealing not only with levels of living at the county scale but also with the investigation and measurement of levels of living among families and neighbourhoods. This conception of level of living was clearly based on the rather narrow idea of consumption and wealth, however, and it was not until the late 1960s that more comprehensive measures of social well-being were developed to measure territorial variations within the United States.

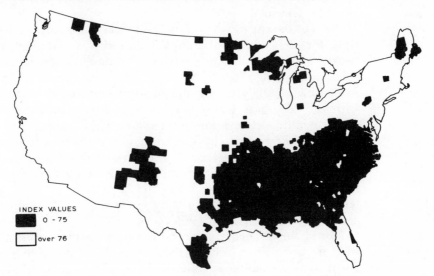

INDEX VALUES

■ 0 - 75

□ over 76

Fig.3.4. The Farm operator level of living index: the bottom 40 per cent of U.S. Counties, 1959. Actual index values ranged from 12 (the worst) to 243 (the best).

In 1968, Lewis analysed the concept of level of living with a broader set of variables designed to reflect twelve socio-economic characteristics in an attempt to analyse the population geography of the northeastern United States. These characteristics were:

(1) The extent of recent in-migration (a measure of socio-economic attraction)

(2) The extent to which the adult population had received an inadequate formal education

(3) The extent to which the adult population had received an advanced formal education

(4) The extent to which the labour force was employed in relatively complex occupations

(5) The extent of unemployment

(6) The extent to which the population was adequately housed

(7) The extent to which the population was inadequately housed

(8) The extent of access to a widely used means of communication (telephone)

(9) The extent of political awareness (size of poll)

(10) The extent to which the population was served by and had adequate access to medical services

(11) The extent to which adequate standards of hygiene and sanitation prevailed

(12) The extent to which family life was reasonably stable.

Data for each of the variables (by county) were ranked from 'best' to 'worst' and combined into a relatively simple index, with each variable given equal weighting. In terms of extremes, the 'best' area to emerge from Lewis's analysis was the highly urbanized core of 'Megalopolis', with the very best scores being achieved by counties with rapidly expanding middle-class commuter suburbs and booming service industries. At the other end of the spectrum was the area extending eastwards from the Allegheny plateau of southern West Virginia to the Delmarva peninsula on the Atlantic coast. This is a relatively backward agricultural region, where the very lowest levels of living are associated with the tenant-operated peanut and tobacco farms of the Inner Coastal Plain and the Piedmont (Lewis 1968).

More comprehensive surveys have been conducted by Wilson (1969) who measures inter-state variations in the 'quality of life' basing his selection of variables on nine of the 'domestic goal areas' set out in the report of the U.S. President's Commission on National Goals (1960), and by Smith (1973a) who employs a set of 47 variables to represent the seven general criteria outlined in Table 1.1. Both portray virtually the same picture of a solid block of 'poor' states in the South, with the 'best' states in the West, the upper Midwest, and the Northeast (Fig. 3.5), but Smith, using more elaborate statistical techniques, is able to disaggregate this basic pattern and demonstrate the existence of two major independent dimensions of inter-state variation in social well-being:

there is a predominant dimension within which relatively high incomes are associated with good housing, high occupational status, good education, and good access to health care. This is the dimension in which the South shows up so poorly and which picks out the relatively wealthy industrial states at the other end of the scale. The level of social well-being on this dimension represents poverty and affluence in the broadest sense and must largely be attributed to income. The other dimension has to do with social disorganisation and the incidence of social pathologies. This identifies the states with large cities, especially those with substantial deprived minority populations, and also some of the most rapidly growing states where some aspects of social disorganisation are related to population in-stability rather than to poverty (Smith 1973a, p. 102).

Regional variations are at least a great in other countries for which information is available. In France, an extensive survey of regional variations in social well-being undertaken shortly before President Giscard d'Estaing's appointment of the first French Minister for the Quality of Life in 1974 has shown that existing disparities between the 95 départements of Metropolitan France are acute (*Le Point* 1974). Altogether, 48 variables were examined, each relating to one of six basic components of the quality of life: health, environment, social stability, material well-being, economic growth, and culture and recre-ation. Thus health was assessed by five variables relating to infant mortality, life expectancy, and the provision of doctors, hospital beds, and pharmacies; environment was assessed by nine variables relating to water pollution, land use, climatic conditions, the availability and use of outdoor sports facilities, the presence of tourist sites, and, this being France, of good restaurants; social stability was assessed by seven variables relating to crime, delinquency, divorce, suicide, and the inci-dence of social pathologies such as alcoholism; material well-being was assessed by eight variables relating to housing conditions, car and

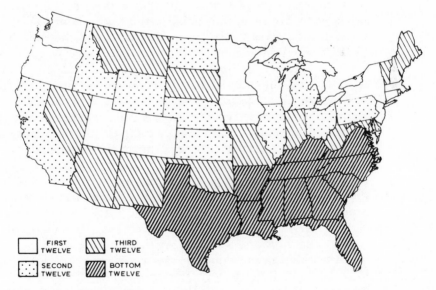

FIRST TWELVE   THIRD TWELVE

SECOND TWELVE   BOTTOM TWELVE

Fig. 3.5. Social well-being in the United States in the 1960s: the conterminous states ranked on an index derived from indicators of six criteria of social well-being: Income, Wealth and Employment; Housing; Health; Education; Social Disorganiza-tion; and Alienation and Participation. (Source: Smith 1973, p. 89.)

telephone ownership, and social welfare benefits; economic growth was assessed by seven variables relating to income, productivity, unemployment and migration; and culture and recreation were assessed by 12 variables relating to educational opportunity and achievement, television ownership, newspaper readership, and the provision of cinemas, theatres, libraries, and museums. An over-all index was devised by combining the scores for the 48 variables, with each being weighted according to its relative importance as agreed by a panel of 'expert' economists, sociologists, and psychologists. In relation to Smith's findings, it is worth noting that subsequent investigations have shown that the resultant index values correspond closely to those derived from an index based on equal weightings.

The pattern of regional inequality in France described by these index values is illustrated in Fig.3.6, which shows the départements mapped by quintile divisions. There is clearly no direct relationship with patterns of economic activity or material wealth (see Fig.2.6), or with the traditional distinctions which geographers make between Le Nord and Le Sud and between a relatively poor western half and a richer eastern half of the country. The regional variations in the quality of life may be seen in terms of three main zones which run broadly from west to east across the country. The poorest zone stretches from Brittany to Lorraine and includes the lower Loire valley, Normandy, the industrial areas to the north, Lorraine, and the suburbs to the east of Paris. The richest zone skirts the Pyrenees and the Alps and stretches from the Landes of Aquitaine, through the Mediterranean coastlands to Lyon and the Alps of Savoy. Paris and its outer eastern suburb of Yvelines together form a favoured outpost in the north. Between these contrasting zones is a wide intermediate band embracing the Massif Central, Burgundy, and the eastern part of the Paris Basin. Conveniently, the départements with the most extreme scores offer good examples of representative types of area. Thus Seine-Saint-Denis (ranked 90th) represents the worst of the Parisian suburbs; Nord (92nd), Aisne (93rd), and Pas-de-Calais (94th) represent the worst product of a mixture of industrial and rural depression; and Cotes du Nord (91st) and Morbihan (95th) represent the worst of the purely rural communities of Brittany. At the other extreme the départements of Alpes-Maritimes, Alpes-de-Haute Provence, Hautes Alpes, Var, Hérault, and Isère reflect the favourable climate and recreational amenities of the Alps, the Riviera, and the Languedoc coast, as well as the long cultural tradition of the Midi and the economic prosperity based on the exploitation of new hydro-electric power sources.

In Britain, Knox (1974b) has analysed variations between the

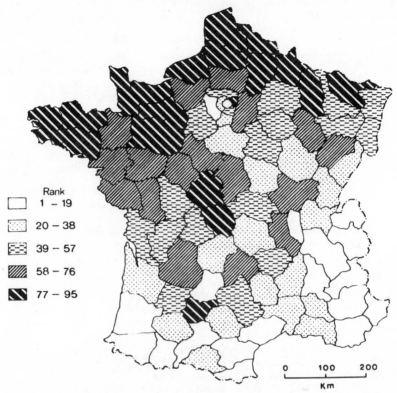

Fig. 3.6. Social well-being in France in 1970: a map of the 'quality of life' based on an index derived from forty-eight variables. High ranking areas, shaded lightest, have the best 'quality of life'. (Source: *Le Point* 1974, p. 46.)

counties and county boroughs of England and Wales in 1961 on the basis of 53 unweighted variables selected to represent a 'balanced' definition of level of living. Here we present in summary the results of an updated analysis using 1971 data for the equivalent administrative units — counties, county boroughs, and London boroughs. Because of changes in the availability of data, the operational definition of level of living has changed somewhat from the 1961 analysis, but the character and balance of the set of 29 variables used here is essentially the same. The full list of variables is given in Table 3.4. Following the methodology of the earlier study, a multi-variate statistical analysis was used to identify the major independent dimensions of regional variation in levels of living. In this case, seven significant dimensions accounted for 72 per cent of the total variation in the data. As in the earlier analysis, variables measuring overcrowding, unemployment, a lack of household amenities, and the proportion of pensioners were

Table 3.4

Variables used in the analysis of levels of living
in England and Wales, 1971

1   % households overcrowded (more than 1·0 persons per room)
2   % households without exclusive use of all three census amenities
    (hot water supply, fixed bath/shower, inside flush toilet)
3   % households sharing a dwelling
4   % dwellings with only 1 or 2 rooms
5   % dwellings owner-occupied
6   % dwellings privately rented
7   New dwellings completed per 1,000 households
8   Infant mortality rate
9   Local health services: expenditure per 1,000 resident population
10 Average list size of principal general medical practitioners
11 % students in age group 15–19
12 Ratio of pupils to teachers in primary schools
13 % professional workers
14 % unemployed
15 Female activity rate
16 % persons aged 0–14
17 % persons of pensionable age
18 % households of only 1 or 2 persons
19 % population change per annum 1961–71 due to migration
20 % poll in local elections
21 % households without a car
22 Index of rateable property values ($\frac{\text{product of 1d. rate}}{\text{total population}}$)
23 Public libraries: expenditure per
       1,000 resident population
24 Cinemas per 1,000 resident population
25 Population per social worker
26 Police services: expenditure per 1,000 resident population
27 Divorce rate
28 Illegitimacy rate
29 Child care referrals per 1,000 population aged 0–17

found to be highly 'diagnostic' of the spatial patterns exhibited by the
aggregate data set, although two more variables — measuring rates of
divorce and illegitimacy — had to be added to these four in order to
arrive at a properly representative set of diagnostic variables. Finally,
an index of level of living was computed from scores on the six
diagnostic variables.

The spatial expression of this index is illustrated by Fig.3.7.
Theoretically, the index has a potential range from −18·0 to +18·0;
in practice, the values range from −12·3 in Southwark (the worst)
to 11·1 in Solihull (the best). Broadly speaking, the regional pattern is
similar to that which existed in 1961: high levels of living are found in
the Home Counties and the Midlands, with lower levels of living in the

peripheral counties of northern, eastern, and southwestern England
and northwestern and central Wales. Within this regional framework,
county boroughs tend to have lower levels of living than the encompassing administrative counties, and among the county boroughs the
worst-off are those in the industrial conurbations of the northwest
and northeast of England. Worst of all, however, are conditions within
inner London: of the 174 areas examined, 11 out of the bottom 20
were London boroughs, with Southwark, Hammersmith, Kensington

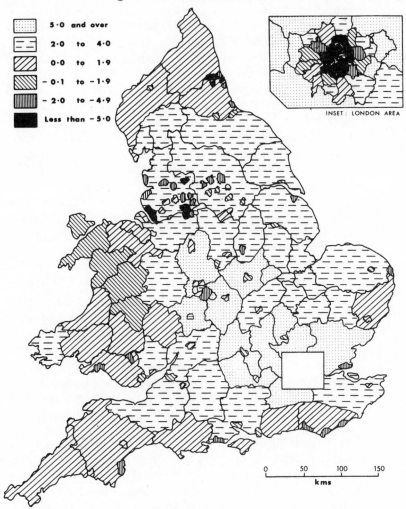

Fig. 3.7. Social well-being in England and Wales in 1971: an index of level of living
based on twenty-nine variables. Negative scores are indicative of low levels of living.

and Chelsea, Hackney, and Islington occupying the bottom five places
Some idea of the prevailing conditions in these areas is given by the raw
data on the diagnostic variables. In Kensington and Chelsea, for
example, the proportion of overcrowded households was 21·7 per cent
(compared to an average of 12·7 for the 174 areas studied), the pro
portion of households without exclusive use of all three basic amenitie
was 36·6 per cent (compared to 19·9), the level of unemployment was
6·9 per cent (compared to 5·52), the female divorce rate was 3·4 pe
cent (compared to 1·2), and the rate of illegitimate births was 19·!
per cent (compared to 9·2). Only in terms of population structure dic
the borough have a favourable score, with 14·6 per cent of its popu
lation of pensionable age, compared to the average of 17·1. At the
other extreme, the prosperous Midlands dormitory town of Solihul
had only 5·1 per cent of its households living in overcrowded con
ditions, only 2·7 per cent having to manage without the basic ameni
ties, only 2·2 per cent unemployed, a divorce rate of only 0·8 per cent
a rate of illegitimacy of only 3·1 per cent, and a retired population o
only 12·3 per cent. Similar conditions, and correspondingly high index
values, are found in the affluent London suburbs of Havering and
Hillingdon and the prosperous agricultural and metropolitan dormitory
counties of Hertford, Bedford, and Buckingham. Between the two
extremes, the index values exhibit a complex and interesting pattern
although it is not within the scope of this chapter to pursue a detailec
regional social geography of England and Wales. Moreover, many o
the features on Fig. 3.7 parallel those of Knox's 1961 map, which i
given detailed consideration elsewhere (Knox, 1974b).

Inter-urban indicators. Turning to inter-urban variations in social well-being, we
find that the earliest evidence of interest is the study reported by
Buckatzsch (1946), who constructed an 'index of social conditions
for the county boroughs of England and Wales based on scores derivec
from a multi-variate statistical analysis of data relating to income
unemployment, housing conditions, and social class composition. There
followed a long period during which the analysis and classification of
cities by geographers and others was dominated by economic and
functional considerations, but the interest in territorial social indicators
which developed in the 1960s has produced several analyses of inter
city variations in social well-being. These are exemplified by the work
of Coughlin (1970) and of Jones and Flax (1970) who have examined
'goal attainment levels' and 'quality of life indicators' respectively for
metropolitan areas in the United States. In Britain, the pioneer study
by Moser and Scott (1961) on the socio-economic characteristics of

British towns illustrated the extent of inequality in relation to many aspects of social well-being in the 1950s.

An examination by Sally Holtermann (1975) has revealed dramatic differentials in the extent of urban deprivation that exist between smaller parts of the urban areas of Britain. Taking the 87 578 Enumeration Districts (EDs) which made up the urban administrative districts of Britain in 1971, a measure of 'multiple deprivation' was derived by identifying those EDs which fell in the worst 15 per cent of all EDs on each of three criteria:

(1) the percentage of households classed as overcrowded
(2) the percentage of households without exclusive use of all three basic amenities — hot water, a fixed bath or shower, and an inside toilet
(3) the level of male unemployment.

The deprivation reflected by this measure is therefore only 'multiple' in the sense that an *area* is disadvantaged in terms of three different criteria, and not in the sense that the area necessarily contains large proportions of *individuals* who suffer multiple deprivation. This is a qualification which of course applies to all aggregations of variables based on spatial data, but which needs to be made especially explicit when terms such as 'multiple deprivation' are used. It is nevertheless likely that EDs which are 'multiply deprived' *will* contain large numbers of individuals who are themselves similarly deprived. Table 3.5 lists those cities having ten or more of their constituent EDs classed as 'multiply deprived', together with an indication of the number of people living in the deprived areas. Since the three criteria employed in this study were also used as 'diagnostic variables' in our earlier examination of levels of living in England and Wales, it is not surprising that the cities and boroughs listed in Table 3.5 mirror the distribution of cities and boroughs with the worst scores on the level of living index (Fig. 3.7). The inclusion of the Scottish data, however, shows that deprivation is most serious in Clydeside. Glasgow alone, with 578 'deprived' EDs containing over 165,000 people, suffers more than all of the London boroughs together. Indeed, the proportional share of multiple deprivation in Clydeside is far greater than for any other conurbation. Location quotients (which have values of 1·0 if the percentage in the area is the same as the national percentage, greater than 1·0 if above the national average, and less than 1·0 if below) reflecting the degree of localization of EDs in the worst 15 per cent on all three criteria range from 0·13 for the 'outer' London boroughs through 1·07 for the Merseyside conurbation and 2·10 for the 'inner'

Table 3.5

*Cities and boroughs with 10 or more enumeration districts (EDs)
in the worst 15 per cent on all three criteria of multiple deprivation*

	Number of EDs	Population in private households in these EDs	% of city's total population
Northwest			
Blackburn	11	4891	4·9
Bolton	12	6021	4·0
Liverpool	60	27 444	4·6
Manchester	93	36 794	7·0
Salford	32	13 565	10·6
North			
Gateshead	14	4966	5·3
South Shields	20	7425	7·5
Sunderland	22	9134	4·3
Newcastle upon Tyne	29	11 944	5·6
Teesside	27	12 290	3·1
Yorks and Humberside			
Kingston-upon-Hull	12	6048	2·2
Bradford	84	31 684	11·0
Leeds	35	13 897	2·9
West Midlands			
Wolverhampton	25	12 832	4·8
Birmingham	170	70 831	7·2
Coventry	22	9793	3·0
Southeast			
Brent	23	7637	2·8
Camden	42	11 268	6·1
Hackney	35	13 456	6·2
Hammersmith	40	13 592	7·5
Haringey	11	3532	1·5
Islington	69	22 131	11·3
Kensington and Chelsea	57	16 719	10·1
Lambeth	46	15 942	5·3
Newham	13	6051	2·6
Southwark	23	8354	3·3
Tower Hamlets	30	7271	4·6
Wandsworth	16	5673	2·0
Westminster	51	12 744	6·5
Bournemouth	14	3446	2·5
Southampton	14	4023	1·9
Brighton	12	3968	2·6
Hove	10	2631	3·7
East Midlands			
Leicester	36	17 715	6·4
Nottingham	52	24 864	8·5

Table 3.5 (continued)

	Number of EDs	Population in private households in these EDs	% of city's total population
Southwest			
Bristol	16	6794	1·6
Wales			
Cardiff	10	4387	1·6
Scotland			
Dundee	70	12 904	7·3
Edinburgh	101	24 810	5·8
Glasgow	578	165 422	18·9
Clydebank	10	2967	6·2
Rutherglen	10	2493	10·1
Paisley	35	9319	10·0

Source: Holtermann 1975a, Table VII, p.42.

London boroughs to 6·19 for the Clydeside conurbation (Table 3.6). Moreover, whilst Scotland as a whole has a location quotient of 3·21, the only other regions with more than their 'share' of multiple deprivation are the Northern (location quotient= 1·11) and the West Midlands (location quotient= 1·10).

Intra-urban indicators. Despite a widespread interest in territorial indicators of specific problems within urban areas (Krendel 1971), there have been few attempts to evaluate intra-urban variations in over-all social well-being. The best known example is the analysis of Tampa, Florida, by Smith and associates (see Smith 1973a). In this study, territorial indicators were constructed from forty-seven variables. The aggregate pattern of social well-being revealed a sectoral division of the city, with the poorest areas extending from around the central business district to the city limits in a northeasterly direction, and the best areas occupying the opposite sector. The factor analysis showed that this general pattern is a product of several overlapping and partially conflicting independent dimensions of social well-being: a 'social problems' dimension identifying the neighbourhoods around the inner city Model Cities area (Model Cities are designated areas of urban renewal set up under a Federal aid scheme: see p. 235); a 'socio-economic status' dimension identifying the affluent, well-housed, and well-educated people of the southwestern sector of the city; a 'racial segregation' dimension identifying the poor, black, northeastern sector of the city; and a 'social deprivation' dimension identifying the 'hard core' social problems concentrated in and around the Model

Table 3.6

Localization of 'multiple deprivation' within the regions and conurbations of Britain

Regions	Location quotient
North	1·11
Yorks and Humberside	0·74
North West	0·81
East Midlands	0·84
West Midlands	1·10
East Anglia	0·20
South East	0·66
South West	0·25
Wales	0·28

Conurbations	
Tyneside	1·60
West Yorkshire	1·37
Merseyside	1·07
S.E. Lancs	1·15
West Midlands	1·76
'Outer' London Boroughs	0·13
'Inner' London Boroughs	2·10
Clydeside	6·19

Neighbourhood Area and Model Cities area to the north and east of the central business district. These findings prompt Smith to suggest that, when the largely demographic and economic data which form the conventional input for studies of urban residential patterns are augmented or replaced by information on the broad range of conditions contributing to social well-being, the spatial structure of cities appears to take on a somewhat different form: 'the limited evidence available suggests that the population of the sub-areas of the city may be primarily differentiated according to the incidence of social problems rather than according to their socio-economic status, stage in life cycle, or ethnic background' (Smith 1973a, p. 133).

In Britain there have been no comparable sutdies using multi-variate techniques in this way, but an interesting departure from previous approaches to the measurement of territorial variations in well-being is represented by Maclaran's investigation of intra-urban patterns of social well-being in Dundee (Maclaran 1975). Using questionnaire data relating to the various components of social well-being, Maclaran has not only established the pattern of social well-being in terms of aggregate unweighted scores on conventional 'hard' data (Fig. 3.8A), he has also established the corresponding variations in people's feelings o satisfaction (Fig. 3.8C) and has been able to weight both of these according to the preferences expressed by the respondents (Figs. 3.8B and 3.8D). At present only the preliminary results of the study are available, and it would therefore be unwise to place much emphasis on the general features common to the four maps or on the points of difference between them. More important is the evidence in Maclaran's approach of a step in the direction of a well-structured set of psychologically-based and need-oriented indicators which do not have

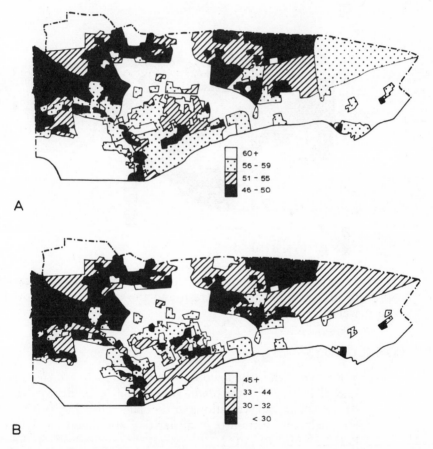

Fig. 3.8. Social well-being in Dundee in 1974: (A) an index of level of living based on 'objective' data; (B) an index based on 'objective' data and weighted by individuals' priority preferences; (C) an index based on levels of satisfaction; (D) an index based on levels of satisfaction weighted by individuals' priority preferences. Darker shadings represent areas with low levels of living. (Source: Maclaran 1975, p. 10.)

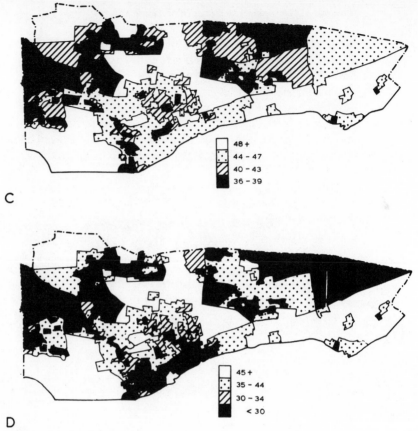

	48 +
	44 – 47
	40 – 43
	36 – 39

C

	45 +
	35 – 44
	30 – 34
	< 30

D

Fig. 3.8. (C) and (D).

to rely on the availability of published data and which can be aggregate
to illustrate both the pattern and the extent of territorial variations i
well-being.

CONCLUSIONS

As with the single-component approach to the measurement c
spatial inequality, the main conclusion to be drawn from existing ev
dence of spatial variations in social well-being is that internationa
regional, and intra-urban disparities are daunting. Whilst patterns o
health, employment, housing, education, and all of the other compo
nents of social well-being sometimes play conflicting roles in shapin
the socio-economic landscape, they do not, by and large, cancel eac
other out. Rather, the tendency is for inequalities to be reinforce
producing familiar patterns of territorial differentiation. The availab

means of measuring and portraying these patterns (despite the use of sophisticated statistical techniques) must be regarded as crude and approximate yardsticks which, because of their relative insensitivity, probably underestimate the true intensity of spatial inequalities. Nevertheless, they are able to provide the sort of information that must form part of the educational diet of administrators, politicians, and the general public if the task of reducing inequality is ever to be seriously entertained. In the first instance at least, the availability of these crude 'facts' of the geography of social well-being is more important than the need for methodological perfection. Once public interest and academic conscience have been awakened, attention can be given to better ways of monitoring social well-being.

In addition to the problems of the availability of data, of weighting, and of accounting for the interrelationships between variables, the examples of territorial indicators of social well-being outlined above all suffer from the disadvantage of lacking an established theoretical framework within which to accommodate explanation and promote systematic investigation. This has been recognized by David Smith, who has suggested that much of the existing theoretical framework of welfare economics could be borrowed by geographers for use in a spatial context (Smith 1973b, 1974). Thus the conventional analysis of consumer choice and welfare through indifference curves, budget constraints, utility functions, and production frontiers would be transposed from the spaceless or single-point world of the economist to the multi-point world of the geographer. Territorial indicators, for example, could be written in algebraic form in the same way that the welfare economist models the welfare of the individual as a function of the utility (and disutility) derived from various quantities of a number of goods and services: the result would be a *social welfare function* for the territory in question. Further possibilities are elaborated by Smith, and such an approach may well provide the foundation for a 'welfare geography' capable of integrating our fragmentary knowledge of spatial variations in social well-being. For the present, however, we are limited to more modest approaches. Having established the magnitude of spatial inequalities at several levels of resolution, we now turn to a closer examination of the various factors and processes involved in shaping these patterns.

4   Inequality, location, and the economic system

We have seen how social well-being varies from place to place, noting especially variations between and within countries, regions, and urban areas. This chapter focuses on some of the economic reasons for these spatial differences. We observe how spatial inequalities are produced, fortified, and changed. The argument concentrates upon the influence of the market economy of the Western advanced industrial countries, for it is the working of this economy, and the way in which it has developed over the last two hundred years, that accounts for many of the important spatial differences observed in chapters 1, 2, and 3.

Economic activity is not equally distributed in space. On the contrary, there is often a high degree of geographic specialization in the space economy, with some areas producing the food and raw materials, others the 'nuts and bolts', and yet others the 'high technology' of the economic system. Though the industrial districts of this Western capitalist system are relatively small in area and concentrated in a few parts of the world, the system itself is the dominant influence over much of the earth's surface, albeit to a more muted degree in China and the more industrially advanced countries of Eastern Europe and the Soviet Union than in the underdeveloped countries of Asia, Africa, and Latin America.

Spatial economic specialization is most apparent at the international, intra-national (regional) and inter- and intra-urban scales. These different geographic scales are often chosen for convenience of analysis, for obviously the market system itself, being a complex whole, does not operate at or within these distinct levels. Few nation states (and no regions or cities) are powerful enough and sufficiently well endowed in human and natural resources to contemplate an isolationist existence, although every country today attempts to guard itself against the chill winds of foreign competition by erecting tariff barriers, quotas, and many other forms of restriction on the free international movement of selected factors of production and goods.

In this chapter we pay particular attention to the operation of the dominant economic system at the international and regional scales. We contend that the social livelihood of the individual (or any group of people) is in the first instance related to the economic function of the place in which he lives. For the time being, therefore, we are taking for granted that the role assigned to, or occupied by, the individual will also depend upon personal circumstances such as age, family size and composition, education, ambition, and ability to exploit the opportunities available to him, and, unfortunately, perhaps race or some other genetic characteristic. Here we emphasize that the perceived needs of the individual and his ability to satisfy them are in effect broadly governed by the role played in the economic system by his town, region, and country. If one lives in one of the great metropolitan centres of the advanced industrial world, one's wants and livelihood will reflect the opportunities available in a community commanding economic wealth, power, and influence, able to buy technical knowledge and utilize the fruits of innovation for the few or the many, and serviced by its infrastructure of trade, finance, marketing, public investment, housing, and so on. The metropolis offers a relatively high wage economy, a great variety of jobs, and a high level of job security, as well as a social infrastructure geared to meet not only the basic needs of health, education, and social security benefits, but also to satisfy the sophisticated demands of the few — the investment decision-takers in government, industry, and the professions. In contrast, if one lives in Niger or the Deccan or northeast Brazil, one will experience life in an area playing a very different role in the world economic division of labour. Rewards will be very different to those of one's countrymen who have emigrated to the great metropolises of London, Paris, or New York. For by comparison with the metropolitan centres such regions and countries are powerless and poorly paid and thus the average quality of life is poorer.

In general terms, therefore, the geography of social well-being is primarily a reflection of the role played by (some would say allocated to) countries, regions, and towns in the economic system. Our argument is then that the spatial distribution of social inequalities is a consequence of the spatially segregated functions within the dominant economic system. Some areas are more important than others; one might say that some areas, like the animals in George Orwell's *Animal Farm*, are more equal than others. As a result, the economic rewards accruing to areas are unequal and this leads to a spatially segregated quality of life. At the global scale, the extent of the gap between the spatial distribution of population and of economic rewards is dramatically illustrated in Figs. 4.1 and 4.2 showing Warntz's mapping (1975) of 'the socio-economic terrain' of world population and world income potential about 1960. ('Potential' is defined as 'a measure of influence at a distance or of macroscopic aggregate accessibility to a population/income', expressed as a density distribution in the plane: Warntz 1975, p.77.) *Per capita* income is used by Warntz as an

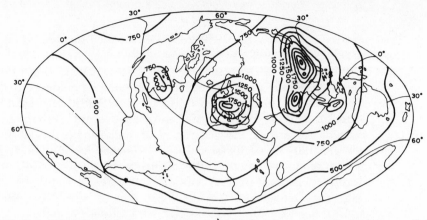

Fig.4.1. World population potential, c. 1960 (in thousands of people per mile showing the huge concentration of humanity in southern Asia, especially Chir and India. Comparing this distribution with that shown on Fig.4.2 one discern the overwhelming 'gap' between the spatial distribution of mankind and the spati distribution of income produced by the dominant economic system. (Source Warntz 1975, p. 81.)

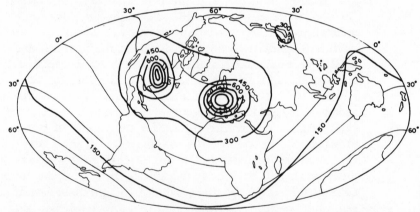

Fig.4.2. World income potential, c. 1960 (in millions of U.S. dollars per mile Some people, some regions, and some nations count for more than others. Whe weighted by income, by far the 'heaviest' areas are eastern North America an Western Europe. (Source: Warntz 1975, p. 82.)

'acceptable substitute' for 'social mass *per capita*', that is, the good consumed to support and sustain the level of living in a given place a a given time. Thus Americans have a heavier 'social mass' (here ex pressed by weighting of incomes) because their homes, railways, road automobiles, bridges, washing machines, food etc. (and *per capit* income) greatly exceed the social mass of Asians, Africans, and Lati Americans, as well as Europeans in general. Figs.4.1 and 4.2 thu display the gross maldistribution of economic rewards at the world scale.

Inequalities are present at all scales. There are rich (so-called developed) and poor (so-called developing or undeveloped or under-developed) nations, there are 'North' and 'South' regions; and there are 'East' and 'West Ends' within towns and cities. Perhaps the most important feature of the geography of social inequality is that the rich are generally spatially segregated from the poor. The segregation is seen nationally (compare the affluence of the United States with the deprivations and poverty of Mali), regionally (compare Megalopolis with the Deep South or the Paris Region with the Massif Central) and locally (compare Westchester with Harlem in New York or Tower Hamlets with Kingston in London). We now turn to some of the economic reasons behind these patterns.

ECONOMICS AND INTERNATIONAL INEQUALITIES

Thoman and Conkling (1967), Freeman (1973), and Johnston (1975b) demonstrate that basic social and economic inequalities between countries are sensitive reflections of the roles played by individual countries in international trade. As a result of the findings of Berry (1961a) and others, Johnston is able to take it as 'axiomatic' that social and economic inequalities are associated with various parameters of a country's trade patterns. He examines the feasibility of raising living standards in the underdeveloped world by means of a reordering of the trade system or of the trading patterns of countries. After discussing the problems associated with the size of a country, its export specialization (in both commodities and countries traded with), terms of trade, economies of scale, regional trade groupings, and 'growth pole' development, Johnston reaches conclusions which 'must be pessimistic: that it is in the nature of such a spatial system, as it has evolved and currently exists, to produce inequalities. Perhaps this is a product of the division of labour, especially the spatial division of labour, itself . . . The problem is the economic system. The spatial system is a part of it, but not independent of it; manipulation of the spatial system alone cannot solve the problems of the economic system' (Johnston 1975b, pp. 149–51).

Far more important than the nature of the present international trading system are the underlying reasons producing it. This is well summarized by Johnston as follows:

> The international trade system is the product of international capitalism. Each country's roles are a function of comparative advantages but these advantages

do not exist in the vacuum of economic models but in the matrix of the history
international capitalism, in which the major comparative advantage is initial adva
tage. Economic growth was initiated in a few places according to an econom
system which was developing contemporaneously. Slowly at first, and then rapidl
this system spread its growth processes across the earth. Some of the areas we
allowed to "grow" through the system and join the upper echelons of its hierarcl
of control; most were prescribed a role and the system was so structured that th
have been unable to escape from the imposed strait jacket (Johnston 1975
pp. 149–50).

We examine each of the pillars of this spatial concentration of pow
within the capitalist economic system in turn. The pillars are tl
international division of labour, the comparative advantage of initi
advantage, and the structures which perpetuate the major inequaliti
in the spatial pattern which now exists, for instance internation
trade and international investment.

International division of labour. A not unexpected conclusion of many analys
of the international pattern of economic well-being is that unde
developed countries have subsistence economies and developed cou
tries have specialized commercial economies. Some writers take tl
measure of economic health or development to be the degree to whi
the money economy and modern technology have been effectively a
sorbed into the national economy (Rostow 1971). These chang
involve, and derive from, a progressive change in the division of labo
within a nation state embarked upon economic development. /
specialization increases the proportion of the workforce engaged
agriculture falls, and there is a corresponding increase in the proportic
employed in manufacturing and services. This relationship is exemp
fied in the work of Chenery and his associates (1971). Taking a samp
of 100 countries over the period 1950–65 they compiled from multip
regression analyses the normal variations one would expect in tl
values of selected variables at different levels of economic developmei
measured in terms of gross national product *per capita*. Table 4
indicates, for a country of 10 million people in 1960, that the valu
of most of the variables chosen, ranging from literacy to industri
employment, and from urban population to overseas trade, rise as tl
level of economic development increases. The link between econon
and society is dramatically brought out in the rapid escalation of tl
school enrolment and adult literacy ratios as gross national produ
per capita is increased. In stark contrast, the primary share of gro
domestic product and the percentage of the labour force engaged
primary employment both fall from very high to relatively low level
These two variables are commonly taken to be useful measures

Table 4.1

Normal variations in economic structure with level of development

	Level of GNP *per capita* (in 1964 US dollars)								
	50	100	200	300	400	600	800	1000	2000
ACCUMULATION									
1 Gross national savings, as % of GNP	9·4	12·0	14·8	16·4	17·6	19·3	20·5	21·5	24·6
2 Gross domestic investment, as % of GDP	11·7	15·1	18·2	19·7	20·8	22·2	23·0	23·7	25·4
3 Tax revenue, as % of national income	9·8	12·7	16·7	19·5	21·8	25·3	28·0	30·3	28·0
4 School enrolment ratio	17·5	36·2	52·6	61·2	66·9	74·2	78·9	82·3	91·4
5 Adult literacy rate	15·3	36·5	55·2	65·0	71·5	80·0	85·4	89·4	93·0
OUTPUT COMPOSITION									
6 Primary share of GDP	58·1	46·4	36·0	30·4	26·7	21·8	18·6	16·3	9·8
7 Industry share of GDP	7·3	13·5	19·6	23·1	25·5	29·0	31·4	33·2	38·9
8 Services share of GDP	29·9	34·6	37·9	39·2	39·9	40·5	40·5	40·4	39·3
9 Utilities share of GDP	4·6	5·7	7·0	7·7	8·3	9·1	9·7	10·2	11·7
LABOUR FORCE									
10 Primary labour, as % of total labour force	75·3	68·1	58·7	49·9	43·6	34·8	28·6	23·7	8·3
11 Industrial labour, as % of total labour force	4·1	6·9	16·6	20·5	23·4	27·6	30·7	33·2	40·1
12 Services labour, as % of total labour force	20·6	22·3	26·7	29·3	31·7	35·8	39·2	42·2	51·6
13 Urban population, as % of total population	4·1	20·0	33·8	40·9	45·5	51·5	55·3	58·0	65·1
TRADE									
14 Exports of goods and services, as % of GDP	9·9	13·2	16·3	18·0	19·1	20·7	21·8	22·5	24·8
15 Imports of goods and services, as % of GDP	16·6	18·7	20·6	21·6	22·3	23·2	23·8	24·3	25·5
16 Primary exports, as % of exports	89	78	68	61	56	50	46	42	33
17 Primary imports, as % of imports	10	18	25	27	28	29	30	30	30

Source: Chenery 1971, pp. 30–1.

economic development. Ginsburg (1961, p.32), for instance, deeme
the proportion of the labour force in agriculture to be 'particularl
sensitive for identifying situations where some economic diversificatio
exists, as in Malaya [Malaysia] , Ceylon [Sri Lanka] , and the Philippine
in Asia, Nigeria and Rhodesia in Sub-Saharan Africa, and in severa
countries in Latin America'.

Although these variables serve as useful general indicators of strengt
and prosperity within the international economic system, we mus
recognize that economic diversification resulting from participation i
the world economy has negative as well as positive effects. The rich i
poor countries are often those engaged in the international economy a
producers, traders, bankers, and administrators. Their economi
rewards are far in excess of those of their countrymen who continue t
participate in the local economy. Thus two main systems co-exist i
the same geographical space. The imported system creates point-centre
enclaves of export development and its 'backwash' effects are expo
bias in the infrastructure of the national economy and social an
economic stratification. The enclaves contain the more well-to-do an
form the basis of a hierarchy of places and often generate a tendenc
towards polarization around privileged points across the country. It
factors such as these which prompt Williamson (1965) to argue tha
further economic growth in the developing countries only serves t
widen regional inequalities in growth which are already more accentu
ated than in the developed countries (Berry 1969, Friedmann 196
Hay 1974).

There are, in addition, several other important qualifications to th
simplistic assertion that less agriculture and more secondary an
tertiary activity equals 'development', 'growth', and 'prosperity'. It
true that, with only a few exceptions, countries which have undergon
a sustained increase in income *per capita* over the long run have e
perienced a continuous decline in the percentage of their economicall
active population engaged in agriculture. In the United Kingdom an
the United States the proportion is now as low as 3 per cent, and i
only a few developed countries does it exceed 20 per cent. By contras
in much of the underdeveloped world the proportion is still well abov
51 per cent, the proportion of the world's economically active popu
lation engaged in agriculture in 1970 (Grigg 1974, 1975). The propo
tion engaged in agriculture is falling in both advanced and developin
countries but the fall in the latter is occurring from very high leve
and there is no guarantee that the experience of the developin
countries will be similar to that of the advanced countries over rece
decades. Indeed, as a result of population growth the numbers engage

in agriculture are increasing. As Grigg has shown, despite more than a century's decline in the relative importance of agriculture in the world economy and a fall in the proportion engaged in agriculture from 72 per cent in 1900 to 51 per cent in 1970, the absolute numbers of people working on the land have risen from 541 million to 761 million over the same period. Of crucial importance is the marked spatial contrast in the trends in the numbers in the agricultural labour force. There has been an uninterrupted increase in the underdeveloped countries and they now have twice as many workers in agriculture as in 1900, whereas there are now only half as many engaged in agriculture in the developed world.

These facts are indicative of deep-seated factors affecting agricultural productivity, farm incomes, and hence social well-being. Agricultural employment has fallen in developed countries in response, on the one hand, to 'push' factors such as increasing productivity resulting from mechanization, rationalization of holdings, and other inputs such as artificial fertilizers, new strains, and government support programmes, and, on the other hand, 'pull' factors such as the demand for labour in industry and services, high wages in urban areas, and the supposed attractions of city life. For the most part, therefore, the rural exodus has been gainfully employed. Even so, many millions of European farmers and peasants left their ancestral holdings for the 'new life' overseas when Europe was undergoing its industrial revolution in the nineteenth century. No less than 35 million Europeans crossed the Atlantic to the United States in the hundred years after the Battle of Waterloo, and 16 million settled the 'empty lands' of Australasia, South Africa, and Canada (Hansen 1941). 'The Great Frontier' was still open (Webb 1953) and many Europeans opted to try their luck overseas rather than remain on the land or migrate to the booming industrial towns of Europe.

By 1920 most of the 'empty lands' had been settled (Turner 1920, Williams 1974) and migration overseas has not been a realistic possibility for displaced or dissatisfied farmers in the underdeveloped world. Instead, the doubling of the agricultural labour force since 1900 has been accommodated by extending the cultivated acreage, intensifying the utilization of existing farmland and, where possible, cultivating commercial crops for the overseas market. Incomes are kept low through the competition of an increasing number of small-scale producers, and the malnutrition and hunger endemic in many underdeveloped countries is in no small measure the result of this under-capitalized, dominantly subsistence type of agricultural base (Fig. 4.3). Thus the proportion of the workforce engaged in agriculture

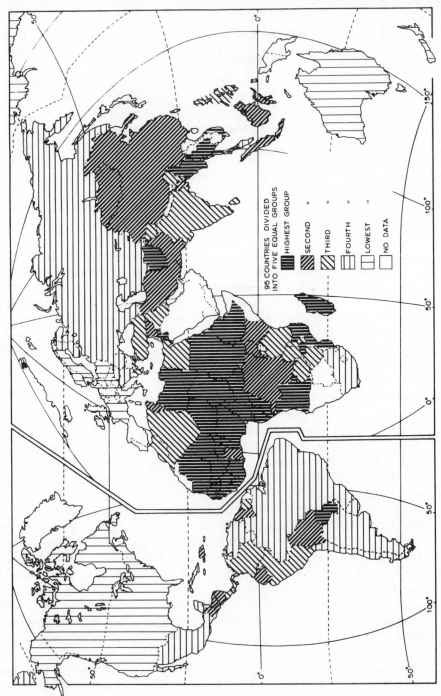

Fig.4.3. The Technological World: countries are grouped according to level of development as measured by indices of accessibility, transportation, trade, external relations, technology, industrialization, urbanization, national product, and the [?]mination of population. The scale has been inverted to emphasise the large areas of Asia, Africa and Latin America with low

95 COUNTRIES DIVIDED INTO FIVE EQUAL GROUPS

- HIGHEST GROUP
- SECOND "
- THIRD "
- FOURTH "
- LOWEST "
- NO DATA

is not merely an index of a changing economic system. It is a matter of great significance in the developing world that such large, and increasing, numbers are engaged in agriculture. It is indicative of the failure of diversification into the industrial sector to reduce the dependence of the whole economy on agriculture, and it reflects the fact that population growth in the developing world is operating almost independently of changes taking place in the economic system; more and more people are pushed onto the land or into the ranks of the under- and un-employed (Thorbecke 1971). Mabogunje (1972, p.837) writes, 'the problem of urban unemployment in African cities has assumed during the last decade gigantic proportions. Paradoxically, it is in the metropolitan areas where new employment opportunities are constantly being provided that unemployment is also most striking. There is, of course, no real paradox here since people flock mostly to those centres where the prospects of rather than necessarily the actuality of employment is high'. Many of these job seekers are school leavers of twelve to fifteen years of age!

A fall in the proportion of a country's labour force employed in agriculture may then be the cause for either optimism or pessimism. In so far as workers are leaving the land for gainful employment in industry and service trades, the post-war changes give a measure of hope. By 1970 the agricultural sector was below 70 per cent in all Latin American countries and in much of Asia and Africa. Only in tropical Africa and southeast Asia are there many countries with proportions above 70 per cent (Grigg 1975). If, however, the fall in the proportion is accompanied by, as seems to be the case in most developing countries, an increase in the absolute numbers working on the land, and the proportional fall is in large part the consequence of rural–urban migration transferring some of the unemployed and underemployed from the rural areas to a similar economic state in the urban areas, then it is a cause for pessimism. Moreover, this proportional fall in the underdeveloped countries has not resulted in a narrowing of the gap between them and the developed countries. In the same post-war period the developed countries have not stood still — the proportion of the population engaged in the agricultural sector has fallen below 10 per cent in Britain, Canada, the United States, Belgium, the Netherlands, Switzerland, and Australia, and to below 20 per cent everywhere else in Western Europe and also in New Zealand. All these countries have the might of advanced chemical industries, high-powered research institutes, and strongly entrenched political lobbies as the handmaidens of their agricultural industries. Though the sector is itself small in terms of employment, its high productivity is the result of inputs of technology and organizational skills. Such inputs are for the most part at much lower levels in the underdeveloped countries. As Maizels (1963) points out, there are few areas where output per man (and *per capita* income) can be raised as high in agriculture as in industry, because of the limited extent of returns of scale and the weak bargaining position of the many primary producer countries against the few manufacturing centres.

It is the misfortune of underdeveloped countries to be dependent on primary produce in the world trade system and to be relatively unimportant in the total pattern of trade in most of the primary products upon which they depend for their foreign earnings (Johnston 1975b). As a result, the terms of international trade are loaded against them and in favour of an increasingly prosperous élite: a relationship which has been exacerbated by recent economic events. An analysis of how underdeveloped countries which are heavily reliant on the export of basic commodities have been affected by the massive oil price rise since 1973 and of the persistence of inflation in the developed countries is given in a report on international trade, 1974–5, published in August 1975. The General Agreement on Tariffs and Trade (GATT) constructed an index for the price of twenty-four commodities, and compared it with world prices of manufactured goods, steel, fertiliser, fuels, and grains, taking 1967–71 as a base period. It found that the terms of exchange of five of the commodities – tea, jute, iron ore. tobacco, and bananas – declined even during the general commodity price boom in 1972–3. For eleven developing countries at least one of these commodities accounts for between a fifth and a half of all export earnings. The terms of exchange of another ten commodities – including copper, cotton, rubber, and coffee – had in the first quarter of 1975 fallen below the 1967–71 base, thus losing some of the ground gained in the commodity price boom. For twenty-six developing countries at least one of this group of ten commodities accounts for between a fifth and a half of all export earnings. These figures are doubtless being paid for in terms of increasing human misery.

For the underdeveloped countries the harsh fact of life is that 'it is only in the later stages of the industrialization and demographic process that a high rate of migration to the cities and a falling rate of natural increase in the countryside leads to an absolute decline in the numbers employed in agriculture' (Grigg 1975, p.195). Few nations have accomplished this long and difficult process. Those that have together constitute the developed world and exercise a spatial control through their pre-eminence in the products and services of their accumulated technology, capital, and skills (Figs.4.3 and 4.4) (Berry 1961a

This spatial control is so far confined to the manufacturing regions of Europe, east-central North America, the Soviet Union, and Japan. Two of these areas — Western Europe and North America — form 'the upper echelons of the hierarchy of control', and these 'metropolitan centres' have for a century or so been the dominant partners in the international capitalist system. We now turn to examine the statement that their major comparative advantage in the world economic system exists 'in the matrix of the history of international capitalism, in which the major comparative advantage is initial advantage' (Johnston 1975b, pp. 149–50).

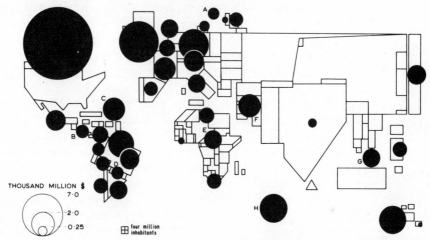

Fig. 4.4. Total book value of direct United States foreign investments in 1969: two-thirds of the total investment is in the developed nations of the White North. Key to letters: (A) unallocated Western Europe; (B) other Central America; (C) other Western hemisphere; (D) other Latin American republics; (E) other Africa; (F) Middle East; (G) other Asian/Pacific; (H) International, unallocated. On Figs. 4.4, 4.5, and 4.6, countries are depicted in relation to the size of their population rather than the extent of their geographical area. (Source: Buchanan 1972, p. 42.)

Initial Advantage. The current pattern of the international division of labour is clearly rooted in the past, particularly in the nineteenth century, when, contemporaneously, a new economic system was being fashioned in northwestern Europe and eastern North America (Kuznets 1966). Predöhl's model of worldwide spatial economic organization shows the modern world economy as having evolved in the industrial core area of Britain and the continent of Europe to give, initially, a unicentric world economy (this discussion is based on Grötewold 1971). In the last three decades of the nineteenth century the development of a second industrial core area in the eastern United States introduced a bicentric world economy. Both of these core areas expanded most vigorously in the half-century before 1914, and, by means of the railway and the steamship, overland and overseas expansion gave rise, according to Grötewold, to the development of the Louisiana Territory and the Argentine Pampas, the modernization and reorganization of the sugar industry in Cuba, the rapid increase of coffee cultivation in Brazil, the nitrate boom and the beginnings of the modern copper industry in Chile, the development of iron mining in the arctic lands of northern Sweden, the growth of cotton cultivation in Egypt, the beginnings of cocoa production in West Africa, the growth of the jute industry in Bengal, the first tea exports from Ceylon (Sri Lanka), and the development of rubber plantations and tin mines in southeast Asia. This list is by no means complete, it misses out the 'development' accruing from capital transfers from the metropolitan core areas of the North Atlantic to ensure cheap supplies of food and raw materials from Australia, New Zealand, South Africa, the Cotton Belt of the Deep South, and so on. Predöhl's world is now a multicentric world economy with the relatively recent development of industrial core areas in the Soviet Union and Japan.

There can be little disagreement with Predöhl's broad generalizations regarding the emergence of the spatial pattern of metropolitan core areas and the chronological sequence of the major developments. There is, however, very considerable controversy as to how it was done. Why, for instance, did the pivotal historical experience which we call the Industrial Revolution take place where and when it did? Economic historians differ in the emphasis they place upon the importance of various factors in Britain's transformation from a handicraft-handicapped medieval world to a modern industrial state reliant upon machines inanimate power, and great productivity. One may conclude from their findings that the interplay of various aspects of Britain's social and economic structure enabled it to take the lead in economic development and establish a long-held initial advantage (Parsons 1971) Structural changes were associated with a relative decline in agriculture the development of large-scale units of production, the introduction o machines driven by inanimate energy, the beginnings of modern urbanization and transport systems, and the increased tempo of exploitation of the relatively widely available coal and iron ore resources (Perkin 1969). Concentration within factories, on a limited range of product with specially trained and increasingly specialized workforces, increase productivity and lowered costs (Coates 1973). Goods were produce more quickly, more cheaply, more reliably, and above all in far greate quantities. Concentration, within towns and regions, produce geographic specialization, leading to economies of scale, accelerating the diffusion of innovations, creating a pool of skills, and calling forth new methods of organizing finance, marketing, and trade (Mathias 1969). These changes occurred in an environment (political as well as social and economic) in which innovation was widely diffused, expansion — of personal wealth, overseas territory, and production — was widely accepted and acclaimed, technical innovation was widely adopted by many producers in many industries, the supply of labour (and perhaps the number of innovators) was increasing as a consequence of population growth, and local market areas were being replaced by regional and national markets. Whatever the causes of Britain's industrialization, it rapidly spread across western Europe and across the Atlantic to North America. How did these metropolitan areas extend their influence and create 'the periphery'?

Neo-classical economists see the world division of labour as the natural consequence of the beneficial principle of specialization. Each country is seen as pursuing its own interest by exploiting its comparative advantage, so ensuring the best use of given resources (Barratt-Brown 1974). Orthodox economists thus attribute the unequal outcome to relative market strengths between the industrial countries and their trading partners, coupled with a degree of political as well as economic colonial coercion (Helleiner 1972). On the other hand many economists (and not only Marxists) judge the unequal outcome as a logical consequence of the exploitive capitalist system (Galbraith 1975), which brought with it further large surpluses that played an important part in the historical development of the metropolitan countries themselves. To Marxists the international division of labour is not a 'natural consequence' but an 'artificial' system deliberately imposed on the rest of the world by the capitalists of the metropolitan areas. The underdeveloped lands are seen to be in a special condition of underdevelopment rather than just undeveloped. Vents were closed for export of finished products and opened for the primary products of the periphery, and the structure of colonial production changed from independent village agriculture and handicrafts to plantations of slave and indentured labour in India, Africa, Latin America, and the Cotton States of the Deep South. 'The very success of capitalist industry in Britain, and the enormous power it developed [is] attributable to the accumulation of treasure and the use of slave labour, to an artificial world division of labour (established by the British Empire and retained down to our own times), and to the extension of the area of capitalism, which imperial expansion made possible . . . This was the way it [industrialization] was accomplished in Britain . . . the first nation state to succeed in the long and difficult process' (Barratt-Brown 1974, p. 145).

Both sides agree that the spatial arrangement of economic and social inequalities we have inherited is undoubtedly the result of the key decision-makers — those who called the tune in industry, commerce, and empire — being spatially concentrated in the metropolitan cores. The metropolitan areas gained most and the periphery least from this arrangement. In biblical terms the periphery may be judged to have picked up the crumbs from the rich man's table. In Marx's words the division of labour was 'suited to the chief centres of modern history'. Four major consequences of the division of the world into metropolitan cores and peripheral areas are selected here for brief comment.

First, there is the unequal distribution of economic rewards and thus the possibility of social well-being to which we have already referred. Mill recognized more than a century ago the advantage of initial advantage in stating that 'the superiority of one country over another in a branch of production often arises only from having begun it sooner'. The 'first-comers' benefited from the processes of cumulative causation, and their specialization became more and more marked, so strengthening their bargaining power in the rest of the world. 'The power of the European metropole to coerce and to control, the concentration of economic power and market strength within many of the European industries engaging in overseas investment and trade, and the relatively weak market strength of the inhabitants of the host (undeveloped) economies, combined to turn the terms of whatever bargains were struck to the advantage of the metropolitan interests (Helleiner 1972, p. 17). Widespread concern about the terms of trade of the underdeveloped countries suggests that this unequal trial of strength is still a feature of the spatial economy (Theberge 1968).

Secondly, the economic development of the periphery itself was designed to serve the interests of the metropolitan areas, particularly in the European Empires. This resulted in distorted economic and social development and all-round vassal status. European settlement overseas was associated with, and geared to, enormous and unprecedented expansion of world trade. Large parts of the world were brought within the capitalist system, basically to supply food and raw materials and take in return its manufactured products. Intra-metropolitan trade has long been far more important than metropolitan/periphery trade and one should not therefore exaggerate the importance of peripheral markets. India undoubtedly did become an important market for the products of the Lancashire cotton textile industry, taking in 1913 no less than 43 per cent of the cotton piece goods exported from Britain

(Smith 1953), and the rapid development of the Indian market was reflected in the enormous increase in cotton manufacturing in Lancashire before World War I. But there were (and are) few trading relationships between the core and the periphery as important and as influential as that between the Indian market and the Lancashire cotton textile industry. This qualification does not, however, invalidate the main point of the argument — that comparative advantage in peripheral areas was decided by metropolitans (as plantation owners, mine developers, traders, and colonial government officers) in terms of what they judged to be the needs of the metropolitan areas. They provided the know-how, the capital, and the transport systems as well as the markets. The overseas trade engendered by these developments ensured export-led growth in the period of rapid industrialization of the capitalist countries. Rostow (1971) considers that the 'take-off phase' began in England in the 1780s, in New England in the 1820s, in France in the 1830s, in Germany in the 1850s, in Japan in the 1880s, and in Russia in the 1890s. Kindleberger (1958) also recognizes export-led growth in Sweden and Denmark after 1880, and in Switzerland, the Netherlands, and Canada between 1900 and 1913. In part, take-off was achieved by 'incorporating' the rest of the world into the capitalist system. Overseas markets were, in effect, pre-empted by those with the initial advantage. Knapp (1973) aptly summarizes the condition of the underdeveloped countries since the fifteenth century to be one of stagnation because of peripheral location in relation to actual capitalist development. The spatial distribution of political and economic power meant that 'advances of prosperity that would (may) have occurred in the now underdeveloped world were aborted by the impact of the now developed world upon them' (Barratt-Brown 1974, p.118).

Thirdly, as a result of the process of cumulative causation, once the gap between the developed and undeveloped world has been established it is difficult for countries to break out by changing their role in the international division of labour. The dilemma facing the weak countries is well summarized by Barratt-Brown (1974, pp.99–100), as follows:

The problem for countries (one could also consider regions and towns) which had historically a narrow range of possible goods to offer on the world market has been that of their being able to change a division of labour once established. Free trade in manufactures made it especially difficult for a country, once committed to primary production for export, to develop a manufacturing capacity able to compete with established industrial centres. Yet the advantages of industrialization for any country were, and are, not only the possibility of diversification, so as not to be dependent on the vagaries of world prices for one or two crops or minerals, and on the monopolistic positions established by manufacturers in the world market,

but also the general increase in productivity to be obtained from industr
mechanization.

As these advantages accured in particular parts of the world — tl
metropolitan areas — their power multiplied. The twin processes
urbanization and industrialization gathered pace and specialization i
creased in the industrial countries (Rostow 1975). Each major techn
logical breakthrough called for new resources and products, bett
methods of organization, new transportation systems, and addition
sources of energy, more capital investment, more sophisticated financi
services, and more extensive trading links. As 'know-how' multiplie
it became difficult for a new industrial area to develop without he
from an older one. Spatial inequality accelerated as the strong countri
became richer and the weak became poorer.

Fourthly, the capital and technology of the industrialized capitali
countries were employed for their own benefit. (The trials and trib
lations of foreign development of 'the riches of the tropics' a
explored in Jackson (1968).) Countries which 'pushed through' tl
market system to join the 'élite' were, with the major exception
Japan, both occupied *and* settled by Europeans — countries such
the United States, Canada, Australia, New Zealand, and South Afric
These permanently settled European lands were developed, the rest
Asia, Africa, and Latin America was only temporarily settled, and l
comparison left underdeveloped. Areas of permanent settlement wer
for the most part, in temperate latitudes and it was to these are
climatically suited to Europeans that most attention was directe
These countries, as a result of their development by settlers from tl
'core', became a part of the metropolitan system.

Capital flows, especially from Britain, aided the upward transitic
of these white settler countries and helped them to join the ranks
the metropolitan countries. In 1914, 90 per cent of all internation
capital movements took the form of portfolio investment; that is, tl
acquisition by individuals or institutions of securities issued by forei
institutions, without the purchasers taking any control over or parti
pation in their management (Dunning 1972a). The establishment
branch plants overseas by metropolitan-based companies was tl
exception rather than the rule and most of the plants were in any ca
generally set up in other advanced countries, for example, those
Singer, General Electric, and Nestlés. Richardson (1972) argues that
the period 1870–1914 labour and capital moved from Britain
response to increased economic opportunity in regions of recent settl
ment overseas. He suggests a demand-determined model in which risi

investment creates an increasing demand for labour and expanding natural increase induces an increase in investment demand. Thus imported capital and immigrant labour were particularly important in periods of rapidly expanding economic opportunity. In other words, inward flows rose when domestic factor supplies of labour and capital were inadequate to meet demand in boom periods.

Most of British capital exports went to the overseas descendants of Western Europe — the United States, Canada, Australia, and New Zealand — which are now in the world's top income bracket as a result of undergoing their own industrialization and urbanization process. 'Much of their infrastructure was built up on the savings of the British private investor' (Thomas 1972, p. 39). Feis (1930) and Thomas (1972) estimate that in 1913 of the estimated £3763 million invested overseas by the British in publicly issued securities 47 per cent was invested in the British Empire (mainly in the 'white settler colonies'), 20 per cent in the United States, 20 per cent in Latin America (especially in railways and public utilities), and 6 per cent in Europe. By 1913, however, *NB* Britain's capital exports were at the rate of 9 per cent of her national income and Thomas asks whether Britain, by investing so much abroad, was paying too high a price in terms of domestic productivity and employment. He concludes, 'the pursuit of private investment profits overseas had become inconsistent with the long-run social productivity of the British economy in a changed environment. The technical performance of British industry and the welfare of the wage-earners would have been improved if foreign lending had been on a smaller scale, with the domestic rate of interest reduced to the level consistent with full employment of home resources' (Thomas 1972, pp. 55-6). The fruits of this fall from grace, especially after two world wars, were picked by industrial competitors such as the United States, Germany, Sweden, and Japan rather than by the underdeveloped countries within the capitalist system. Indeed, for several decades intra-metropolitan competition has been a far greater economic concern for individual metropolitan countries than their relations with the periphery; intra-metropolitan trade far surpasses in value metropolitan–periphery trade.

International Trade. We have seen how capitalist economies in the metropolitan areas expanded their influence over the rest of the world by means of exporting labour, capital, and manufactured goods. Trading partners were, and are, not equally endowed and equally competitive and did not equitably share the benefits of trade. Many underdeveloped countries still have a rigid production structure, often the consequence of their limited resource base and specific soils, climate, and disadvantageous economic and locational position in the world space economy. In consequence they respond relatively inflexibly to altering market conditions. Moreover, they are not operating in free trade conditions, having to surmount a variety of trade barriers and having to accept, in some instances, that their export volume is determined by foreign firms with global, rather than national, interests. Yet international trade has played a strategic role in Asia, Africa, and Latin America: it has been relied upon to stimulate economic development (Myint 1969). Production for export now accounts for 10–25 per cent of total gross domestic product in these areas and for an equally large share of aggregate national expenditure spent on imports (Helleiner 1972).

Thoman and Conkling (1967), after an exhaustive analysis of the *Yearbook of International Trade*, conclude that regardless of the political and economic system to which it subscribes, a country appears to derive benefits from international trade roughly in proportion to its position on the scale of economic development. The world trading pattern is therefore dominated by non-communist developed economies, accounting for over two-thirds of all exports and imports (Table 4.2). Indeed, Western Europe and the United States together send and receive over one-half of the value of all international trade. The spatial spread of the power and influence (socially and politically expressed as well as economically) of the individual metropolitan core areas required that the system be linked together by trade and now ensures that it continues to be so.

Predöhl distinguishes three types of trade flows: intra-core trade, inter-core trade, and core area–periphery trade. International trade statistics do not permit a separation of these three flows, but Freeman (1973) and Johnston (1975b) have shown that the greatest amount of trade is between neighbours at similar economic levels and Grötewold (1971) suggests that perhaps one-half of the total foreign trade of industrial core countries in Western Europe is accounted for by intra-core trade: the impressive trade volume of Western Europe is thereby largely a consequence of the political fragmentation of an industrial core area. By contrast only one national boundary cuts the industrial core area of eastern North America. Much of the remainder of Western Europe's 'foreign' trade is inter-core trade, leaving core area–periphery trade relatively small in volume, value, and importance. This reinforces the point made above that it is 'metropolitan' trade that is so important to the developed countries, though they do require the raw materials of the underdeveloped world to maintain their industrial output.

Inter-core and intra-core trade are now so complex and sophisticated

Table 4.2

International trade, 1971

f.o.b. value in million US dollars

EXPORTS FROM \ EXPORTS TO	World	Developed market economies	Centrally planned economies	Developing market economies	Western Europe	USA
World	348 230	246 560	34 060	65 480	161 160	45 080
Developed market economies	250 390	191 890	9020	47 910	128 400	33 660
Centrally planned economies	35 920	8760	21 860	5230	7500	240
Developing market economies	61 910	45 910	3170	12 340	25 260	11 180
Western Europe	156 760	126 560	6930	21 840	105 330	12 990
USA	43 490	29 820	380	13 280	13 970	–
Japan	24 020	13 160	1150	9700	3420	7610
USSR	13 810	3160	8020	2630	2660	60

Source: United Nations 1973a, pp. 406–11.

LESLIE DIENES
Department of Geography

that it is difficult for the peripheral areas to break into the system
particularly with respect to trade in manufactured goods. Exports of
industrial and semi-processed goods accounted for 7 per cent in 1955
and more than 20 per cent in 1969 of exports of underdeveloped coun
tries. But their share of world trade in manufactured goods (about 7
per cent) scarcely altered and remained small. Moreover, this increase
in manufactured exports was geographically concentrated, with 48 per
cent of total manufactured exports of 'underdeveloped countries' in
1969 coming from Hong Kong, Taiwan, India, and Yugoslavia, and no
less than 75 per cent derived from thirteen countries. The least
developed countries have the least developed industrial infrastructure
and such countries are at a serious disadvantage relative to such semi
industrial countries as Argentina, Mexico, and Brazil (Helleiner 1972).
Meanwhile the great trading nuclei are exporting increasing amounts of
manufactured products and are continuing to dominate the trade of
non-communist, underdeveloped countries.

In recent decades the old-established nuclei around the North Atlan
tic have been challenged by Japan and the centrally planned Commu
nist countries. Countries at the other end of the scale of economic
development have experienced only indifferent success in maintaining
their export income: between 1953 and 1963 more than two-thirds of
the underdeveloped countries failed to keep up with the rise in the
world average of exports measured on a *per capita* basis (Thoman and
Conkling 1967). The gap between the 'haves' and 'have nots' ha
widened.

It is easy to forget the extent to which the United States dominate
the world market economy. For example, in 1972 the gross domestic
product (GDP) of the United States exceeded the combined totals of
the European 'Six', the United Kingdom, the Caribbean and Latin
America, and Africa. The *increase* in GDP in the United States from
1970 to 1972 was greater than the *total* GDP of the Caribbean and
Latin America in 1970 and more than twice as great as the total GDP
of Africa. The total GDP of the whole of Africa in 1970 was barely
more than half that of France, whilst the total GDP of the Caribbean
and Latin America fell below that of West Germany (UN 1975a). It is
indeed a disheartening fact that between 1960 and 1967, the mere
increase in the annual *per capita* income of the major developed coun
tries exceeded the *total* average annual *per capita* income of lesser
developed countries (Meier 1970). Even if the poor countries were to
proceed at a much higher rate of growth than in the last two decades
their problem would still be to produce a surplus for expending on
projects designed to raise the quality of life for the majority.

There are several reasons why the gap between the 'haves' and 'have nots' is increasing. First, countries at the 'periphery' of the trade system pay locational penalties whereas most of the advanced industrial countries have neighbours at a similar stage of economic development and benefit from short-distance exchange of manufactured goods (Johnston 1975b). Secondly, because this type of intra-metropolitan exchange dominates international trade, countries outside the metropolitan areas are often peripheral in both location and importance in the system, giving them weak bargaining power. Thirdly, analysis of changes in the 1960s leads to the conclusion that while the underdeveloped countries are broadening their search for new markets and new commodities in which to trade, the developed countries are becoming more introverted, concentrating on the goods which they are already successfully marketing among themselves. The nucleus of the world trading system is becoming more intense; the periphery is struggling to hang on. Fourthly, amongst the 'haves' the technically advanced countries which emerged from World War II with basically undamaged and active manufacturing plant have expanded their already formidable trade but at lower rates than Japan, the Soviet Union, and occupied Europe, areas which have thrust forward at unprecedented rates of absolute growth (Thoman and Conkling 1967). Finally, the underdeveloped countries have faced a series of severe problems in international trade since 1945. Few of them, in the words of Thoman and Conkling,

possess sufficient reserves of natural resources, educated and trained human resources, and capital to keep pace with world growth in development and trade. Serious problems in deteriorating terms of trade, over-specialization in the export of a few primary products, lack of adequate investment capital and of the means of raising such capital, and low levels of technology all mitigate against the chances of these economies moving forward toward what might be taken as their logical places in the world scheme of things. Moreover, the very high rates of population growth in many of the less developed countries further weakens their positions in world trade as they are forced to substitute food crops for commercial crops in agriculture, to sell their limited mineral resources from weak bargaining positions, to invest heavily in consumer goods industries when producer goods industries are so vitally needed for long-term development, and to concentrate on labour intensive types of production when capital intensive output was demonstrated a superiority except where wages of labour are low and efficiency high. The aggregate results of these and associated problems are that most of the less developed countries are trapped in economic conditions, sensitively reflected in world trade, over which they have little control and from which they cannot hope to rise without generous assistance from the outside.*

*Richard S. Thoman and Edgar C. Conkling, *Geography of International Trade*, ©1967, p.171. Reprinted by permission of Prentice-Hall, Inc., Englewood Cliffs, New Jersey, U.S.A.

In arguing the current need to modify the economic theory of comparative advantage, Helleiner (1972) cites the following characteristics of the world economy — the demand by the poor countries for a rapid augmentation of stocks of skill and capital, the substantial blockages to free trade in the international market system, the presence in world markets of monopolistic and oligopolistic elements, the instability of demand (and price) in world markets, the limited price and income elasticities of demand for many goods exported by underdeveloped countries, the substantial foreign ownership of domestic factors of production, and the distorted infrastructure in poor countries because of export activities. Johnson (1968), however, argues that only a small fraction of the big differences in *per capita* incomes of different countries is assignable to differences in the gains derived from international trade. He asserts that the traditional causes of international (and regional) inequalities are differences in technological levels, accumulated capital, educational levels, economies of scale, specialization, and division of labour. The differences in these levels are not, however, unrelated to the nature and pattern of international trade as developed over the last two centuries between the metropolitan cores and the periphery. Indeed, Galbraith (1975) argues that we need to recognize two capitalist economic systems — the market and the 'corporation planned'. In the former prices are a function of supply/demand factors and primary producers are at the mercy of the market in the developed world. In the latter corporations and producer cartels fix prices irrespective of the market (within broad constraints). Hence industrial goods from the United States and now oil from the Middle East do not vary in price with general fluctuations in supply and demand.

Space does not permit elaboration of all these and many other factors affecting global inequalities, and this section on international inequalities is concluded by drawing attention to the part played by international investment in the capitalist economy and to some of the problems faced by the primary producers in exporting their agricultural products and minerals.

International Investment. International investment takes many forms. Here we are concerned with investment consequent upon multi-national corporations engaging in manufacturing, agriculture, and mining in countries outside the ones in which they have their headquarters. All the great multinational corporations are based in the metropolitan cores and are owned, managed, and directed by metropolitans. Their growth since 1950 has been very rapid. In 1969–70 the gross sales of General

Motors (then the biggest multinational corporation) exceeded the gross national product of Switzerland, of South Africa, and of Denmark, and by the same measure Ford Motors, Royal Dutch Shell, General Electric, IBM, Mobil Oil, Chrysler, and Unilever each ranked above Colombia, Egypt, New Zealand, and Portugal (Brown 1973). (As a result of the oil crisis since October 1973 the oil companies have emerged as the richest of all corporations. Eight of the ten biggest world companies are oil companies, led by EXXON (formerly Esso), with Shell not far behind.) Brown found fifty-nine nation states and forty-one multi-national corporations in the top 100 in a merged list ranking companies according to gross sales and countries by gross national product.

Many decisions once considered the province of the nation state are now being made by externally based multi-national corporations, particularly in such matters as the nature, timing, and location of investment. These decisions may affect the employment level, the rate of economic growth, the balance of payments or whether a given natural resource is developed. A planning commission sitting in Accra, the capital of Ghana (a country not in the Top 100 list), may make certain decisions concerning the creation of additional employment, but critical decisions influencing the number of new jobs to be created in Ghana may be made in the executive offices of multi-national corporations' headquarters in New York or Osaka (Brown 1975, p. 9).

Not only the smaller nation states are concerned about the operations of these economic collossi; see, for instance, Dickenson's (1974) summary of the importance of foreign investment in Brazil's industrialization.

The division of the world into nation states is being overlaid by a network of giant corporations with their annual sales expanding more rapidly than the gross world product. The volume of goods produced abroad by American companies alone — with management, technology, and often capital from the United States — is four times that of U.S. exports. Production, finance, and ownership are being internationalized and economic relations between countries, traditionally dominated by international trade, are today increasingly dominated by international production (Dickenson 1974). Thus, although spatial specialization of production may explain some forms of trade (for instance, between raw material rich countries and manufacturing oriented nations) it is often quite inapplicable in the case of other forms of commodity exchange (for example, flows between highly industrialized nations), where phenomena such as risk-spreading, cultural or traditional preferences, and competitive behaviour among international companies have some relevance (Freeman 1973).

The concentration of control over direct foreign investment is in the developed world, especially the United States. Countries receiving foreign investment may benefit from the transplantation of superior technical and managerial knowledge, the taxed profits, and the ability to acquire knowledge more quickly and more cheaply than by developing home-based industries. Disadvantages are, however, numerous — the fact that untaxed profits may be exported back to the parent company, the sense of being exploited, the loss of long-term gains from home-based knowledge accumulation, the employment of foreign nationals in key positions, and the utilization of technology developed elsewhere for different markets (Johnson 1972b). Liberia is the classic example of a country which 'has become a state of foreign concessions for the production of rubber, iron ore and timber, for the provision of public utilities and for the development of industry' (Church 1969, p.431). The Firestone rubber plantations there exhibit, in large measure, the characteristics of plantation agriculture (Courtenay 1965) — large-scale production by a uniform system of cultivation; location in sparsely populated tropical areas; recruitment of labour from outside the environs; employment of considerable financial resources; scientific research and management by a large overseas-based company; advanced production techniques, including factory-type organization; and export to an external and usually large market. Rubber is still Liberia's only significant cash crop. In acreage and production it has, however, been overtaken within West Africa by Nigeria, where development has followed a very different course. British distaste for the social and economic ill-effects of plantation agriculture led the colonial rulers to restrict the development of plantations in Nigeria. This action, however, may have been counter-productive by restraining the economic development of the largest state in West Africa (Udo 1965).

Many developed countries as well as all underdeveloped countries are in a 'second-best' position. American corporations lead in most technologically advanced sectors of industry. The large rich market, high wage levels, and relative abundance of capital in the United States tend to give American firms a comparative advantage in the production of new technology. Despite having a smaller population, the United States spends about four times as much on research and development as Western Europe and about twice as much in proportion to gross national product (OECD 1968). Most other countries are unable to invest with profit in the development of rival advanced technologies because of inadequate market size, income levels, availability of scientifically trained personnel (Johnson 1972b), and the fact that American firms were the first in the field.

Fig. 4.4 shows the pattern of the 'total book value' of direct United

States foreign investments in 1969. These investments are not distributed equally among nation states, nor are they related to basic
distributions such as population potential (Fig.4.1). (On Figs. 4.4 and
4.5, after Buchanan (1972), countries are depicted according to population size rather than geographical area actually occupied.) On the

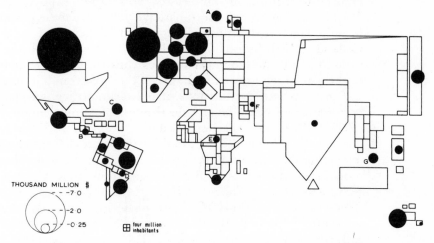

Fig.4.5. United States investments in overseas manufacturing industry in 1969:
over four-fifths of the total is in the developed nations of the White North. For key
to letters see Fig.4.4., p.91. (Source: Buchanan 1972, p.46.)

contrary, the investment is heavily concentrated in the developed
nations of the northern hemisphere and in Latin America (Fig.4.4).
Over four-fifths of American investment in manufacturing industry
is located in the 'developed nations of the White North' (Fig.4.5).
Even within the developed countries of Western Europe, American
investment has been directed to those countries with the most rapid
growth and to two main sectors of industry: (1) science-based or
research-intensive industries supplying both producer and consumer
goods, and (2) industries subject to economies of scale and producing
products with a high income elasticity of demand (Dunning 1972b).
'Knowledge industries', such as the manufacture of computers, instru-
ments, electronics, and chemicals, provide an infrastructure of knowledge, create substantial spill-over effects, and act as a catalyst for
growth.

A rather different and more recent phenomenon of rapidly increasing
importance is the 'putting out' to developing countries, by multi-
national companies, of unskilled labour-intensive processes. Thus 'data
are sent by air from New York to the West Indies to be punched on

computer tape by relatively cheap labour, following which they are sent back again by air. Components of complex electronic equipment are manufactured in Taiwan, Hong Kong, South Korea, and on the Mexican border with the United States. It may well be that in such "processes" rather than in "industries", as conventionally thought of, lies the immediate future of the Third World; but export enclaves could develop, within which multi-national firms purchase cheap labour and outside which little impact is registered (Helleiner 1972, p.76; see also Holland 1975, Barratt-Brown 1974). This vision of the 'immediate future' of the developing countries constitutes a pertinent illustration of the gap which now exists between the 'haves' and 'have nots'.

The long-term implications of the technological and managerial gap between the United States and the rest of the world are by no means clear. Switzerland and New Zealand (Franklin 1967) fare well by importing the products of technology, Japan and Germany fare well by importing the technical know-how and producing technology-embodied products, and the United States reigns supreme as the producer of the technological know-how itself (Fig.4.3) (Dunning 1972b). Political fragmentation in Europe, Latin America, and elsewhere hampers attempts to pool technical resources, rationalize industrial structure and create a large, free-trade market able to meet the challenge of American and Japanese companies. Layton (1969, p.50) quotes a European research director as saying, 'if America wishes to close the technological gap with Europe, all she needs to do is erect 51 different sets of customs barriers, tax systems, space and defence programmes, science policies and public buying arrangements'. Meanwhile, the comparative advantages of initial advantage widen the technological gap between the United States and the rest of the world.

Problems of Primary Producers. Inequality is a basic feature of our world. Each member state of the United Nations has one vote irrespective of its economic power or the number of its battle-ready air squadrons, missiles, and atomic bombs. This sense of equality is illusory, for the world is split up into a collection of unequal member states. Some are huge in terms of population and resources, such as the Soviet Union, China, and the United States, and others are very small, for example Gambia, Guatemala, and Sri Lanka. Size should also be seen in relation to spatial extent, population, access to technological know-how, share of world trade, and diversification of trade. In 1968 about 60 member states of the United Nations had populations of less than ten million each. Such a base gives little scope for economies of scale and is unlikely to provide sufficient human expertise to tackle the social economic, and technological issues involved in economic development (Odell 1971). There is, for instance, a significant relationship between country size and the share of finished as opposed to semi-finished goods in total manufactured exports (Balassa 1969).

In this unequal world underdeveloped nations are faced with the task of trying to catch up at a time of very rapid, and accelerating, advance in science and technology. They are competing overseas with the mighty, well-established, multi-national corporations and in a few well-organized markets; and at home they face a population explosion, low educational levels, shortage of skilled entrepreneurs, managers, and engineers, slow build-up of capital formation (Nurkse 1953), small domestic market for industries needing economies of scale, high price of imported goods, high interest rates, high oil prices, debt repayments, and high royalty payments (Myrdal 1971, 1974, Buchanan 1971). To these obstacles to expanding their international trade Johnson (1968) adds the problems created in the underdeveloped countries themselves by their nationalistic orientation to economic policy, preference for centralized economic planning, exploitive attitude toward traditional agriculture, commitment to import substitution, and policies of inflation and currency overvaluation. Thus, though international trade and private overseas investment are fundamentally economic phenomena, reflecting vested interest decisions, the political element is never absent. By way of trade, countries pursue their political self-interested ends with varying degrees of success (Thoman and Conkling 1967, Itagaka 1973). Buchanan (1971) argues that economic development is not indeed primarily an economic process in the Third World but a social and political process.

The fundamental problem facing underdeveloped countries is, indeed, their dependent relationships with the developed countries (Santos 1970). For instance, Gilbert (1974) argues that Latin America, like the rest of the Third World, *depends* on the United States, Western Europe, and Japan for trade, capital, and technology. The continent's major markets and suppliers are few in number: the United States supplies 40 per cent or more of Latin America's imports and Europe much of the rest. But the mutual dependence of this international trade is limited and one-sided, for Latin America imports mainly machinery and manufactured goods and exports agricultural and mineral products. It is therefore in a fundamentally weaker trading position than its partners. The export specialization of many Latin American countries places them in a difficult supply and demand situation: 63 per cent of Colombia's export revenue comes from coffee (and Colombia is not in a monolopy situation), 72 per cent of

Chile's derives from copper (and there are other major world producers) and 91 per cent of Venezuela's accrues from petroleum (the great rise in the price of oil since late 1973 has produced a bonanza but made the country even more dependent on this one commodity). These exports are, of course, susceptible to the vagaries of external demand, unless producers can dominate a relatively inelastic market, for example petroleum-exporting countries.* Foreign exchange is needed to pay for the imports on which much of Latin America's development relies. This dependence upon imports arises from Latin America's need for overseas technology. This in turn leads to the perpetuation of a third form of dependence, the need for injections of foreign capital. The mechanism of capital transfer, by loans from foreign governments, international banks, private investors etc., increases the measure of dependence upon 'outsiders' with their own vested interests (see Figs. 4.4 and 4.5). Finally, Gilbert argues that a further manifestation of Latin America's foreign dependence is reflected in its cultural relationships. Many Latin Americans are culturally biased towards Paris, London, Rome, and New York. Their external orientation means that many of the forms of dependence are accentuated: imported products are valued more highly than local goods, foreign degrees more than local degrees, foreign consultants more than local experts. One of the most dramatic examples of cultural transfer is highlighted by Buchanan who illustrates the power of advertising, capital, and market control residing in American corporations by mapping the Coca-cola empire (Fig. 4.6). The map shows the general pattern of Coca-cola production in 1969 and Buchanan makes the point that 'the penetration of the world by a commodity like Coca-cola represents a good index of Americanization' (Buchanan 1972, p. 21). In effect, all these aspects of foreign dependence make Latin America part of the Third World. They also help to make it an entity. All its constituent countries, except Cuba, depend upon similar trade partners and suffer from similar trade problems.

---

*Oil is a major exception. In October 1973 the old cartel of the international oil companies was apparently replaced by OPEC, a cartel of thirteen oil-producing nations. In effect the price of oil was fixed by the producers rather than the consumers. The OPEC cartel has held firm – despite the need to avoid a glut of oil by reducing production in 1975. Sampson (1975) argues that the new cartel has held firm because the producers (especially Saudi Arabia) could afford to reduce production and because the old cartel of the major oil companies – with their global system of allocation, control of world-wide markets, refineries, and tied filling stations – under pinned the new cartel. As supporting evidence, Sampson quotes U.S. Senator Church's report in January 1975: 'the primary concern of the established major oil companies is to maintain their world market shares and their favoured position of receiving oil from OPEC nations at costs slightly lower than other companies'. To maintain this favoured status the companies are now engaged in ensuring that expensive oil will always find markets.

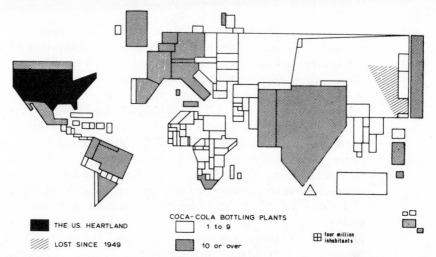

THE US. HEARTLAND

LOST SINCE 1949

COCA-COLA BOTTLING PLANTS

1 to 9

10 or over

four million inhabitants

Fig. 4.6. An index of Americanization. American products have been exported to most parts of the World. Penetration of Coca-cola is a good index of Americanization. The map shows the pattern of Coca-cola production in 1969. (Source: Buchanan 1972, p. 21.)

Many underdeveloped countries rely for the bulk of their export earnings on primary products. Yet, as Helleiner (1972) points out, prospects for agricultural exports are constrained by low income elasticities of demand for agricultural raw materials in the developed countries; modest population growth rates in their principal markets; low price-elasticity of demand for most tropical agricultural commodities; the production of cheap and often qualitatively superior synthetic substitutes by rapid technological change; and limited market access for agricultural exports of underdeveloped countries because of agricultural protection in richer countries.

The severity of these problems is emphasized by Lacarte's (1973) contention that the rapid expansion of exports is a fundamental key to development of employment in the developing countries. Yet trade restrictions relating to basic commodities, the granting of subsidies, the imposition of quotas, and the use of escape clauses and international agreements for the unilateral limitation of trade in certain products all militate against the rational international division of labour, reducing the exports of developing countries and thus their ability to stimulate employment.

Many writers, assuming that the developing countries are locked into the world capitalist economic system for one reason or another, see the solution to such problems in tinkering with the mechanics of the system. Arguments for lowering tariff walls in the developed world to give greater freedom to the manufactured exports of developing countries, for price support programmes, and increased flows of concessionary aid and technical assistance all exemplify this approach. Their utility as redistributive strategies is discussed in Chapter 7, but it should be emphasized here that they offer no simple solutions. Price support programmes, for example, would benefit some developed countries whilst penalizing developing countries which are major importers of raw materials (such as India and Pakistan), since few commodities are entirely produced in underdeveloped countries. Because of such difficulties, some groups of small countries have begun to organize themselves into producer-cartels and regional federations (McConnel and Conkling 1973) in order to strengthen their bargaining position within the political and economic system. On a broader level, the developing nations as a whole have used the platform of the United Nations to call for a 'New Economic Order'. At the Sixth Special Session of the General Assembly, four main concerns were expressed. (1) the desire for greater control over raw materials and the terms of trade; (2) the need for greater influence in the international monetary system; (3) the desire for more aid with fewer strings attached; and (4) the need for curbs on the multinational corporations (*New Internationalist* 1975b).

A satisfactory response from the rich and powerful élite clearly comprises something more than lip-service to these demands. But past experience suggests that promissory statements, global conferences and token concessions are the most that poor nations can expect unless a new philanthropic or egalitarian philosophy emerges as a counter to the seemingly boundless selfishness of the capitalist dynamic that hinges on the search for profits. Unfortunately, there are few signs of such a philosophy in the West. On the contrary, the developed nations have already filed over 200 pages of reservations to the UN Plan of Action associated with the proposed New Economic Order. It is no surprising, therefore, that an increasing number of people in the poor countries of the world are seeking paths to 'development' which lie as far as possible outside the capitalist economic system. These include the use of 'alternative technologies' which are held to be more relevant to conditions in developing countries than the sophisticated, 'prestigious', and resource-consuming technology of the West, and the adoption of the model of rural self-sufficiency exemplified in the 'ujamaa' system of Tanzania. Such alternatives stand in direct contrast to the idea of development as a trade-based process, and to pursue them is by no means a straightforward matter of national strategy. As the recent experiences of Vietnam and Chile have shown, the difficult of actually breaking out of the world economic system is a major, and sometimes insurmountable, obstacle.

REGIONAL INEQUALITIES

So far we have focused attention on international inequalities, though many of the arguments relating to matters already discussed in this chapter could, in general terms, be readily adapted to the inter-regional scale. It is, however, necessary to examine more explicitly some of the inequalities found at selected intra-national scales resulting from the operation and evolution of the dominant economic system. Chapters 1–3 demonstrated that not only are nations unequal in economic and social well-being but so too are regions and cities within them. Inter-regional and interurban inequalities are generally most pronounced in 'dual economy' developing countries where development tends to be concentrated in one, occasionally more, dominant metropolitan centre (core area or enclave) with the hinterland (or periphery) both lagging behind and also exposed to change in ways dictated by the core area. Stöhr (1974) postulates that the cost and revenue surfaces for urban-industrial development in developing and developed

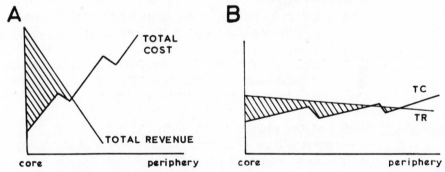

Fig.4.7. Possible relationship between distance from core area and total revenue and total cost in: (A) newly developing countries, and (B) developed countries. (Source: Stöhr 1974, p. 26.)

countries may approximate to those shown in Fig. 4.7A and B and he argues that 'the graphs give an explanation in economic terms of why industrial activities are much more concentrated in newly developing countries — such activities usually extending wavelike over only a short distance from the major metropolitan centre and rarely residing in secondary or lower-ranking cities' (p. 26). As the realities of economic space are generally accompanied by, and related to, equally marked

spatial bias in the geography of transport, political power, the appl
cation of technology, capital, and entrepreneurial talent, it is readil
apparent why countries passing through the early stages of economi
development are often viewed in terms of Myrdal's model of circula
and cumulative causation (Myrdal 1956, 1957a, 1957b, Keeble 1967
Friedmann 1973).

Some writers argue, however, that such gross regional inequalitie
are eliminated, or at least radically reduced, as a result of the diffusio
of the twin processes of industrialization and urbanization into th
periphery (see below). Fig. 4.7B suggests one reason why it is easier t
create peripheral growth centres in mature industrial economies, if th
gap to be bridged between the revenue and cost curves is indeed muc
smaller as a result of more widely diffused information and transpor
systems, national education programmes, existing regional urba
centres, and past experience of coming to terms with development
But it is now recognized that a new and much more intricate circula
and cumulative feedback process sets in as the largest and most im
portant metropolitan complexes in advanced economies increasingl
dominate activity in the rest of the systems of cities operating in th
metropolitan core countries of the world economic system (Pre
1974, Westaway 1974, Parsons 1972, Berry 1972a). This sectio
focuses on the inter-regional inequalities of the complex advance
industrial countries and, in particular, examines the persistence of suc
inequality in advanced urban-industrial societies within which, acco
ding to classical economic theory, the inequalities should have bee
reduced to minimal proportions as a result of the creation of hig
levels of economic development and associated factor flows of labou
and capital.

All but the smallest countries are divided into regions for a variet
of purposes and in a variety of ways. There is an extensive literature o
the problem of defining a region, the value of the regional division
commonly in use, and the advantages and disadvantages of regiona
analysis. As our concern is with the broad spatial inequalities within
nation state we are able to bypass most of these problems of definitio
and use the word 'region' simply to refer to a geographic scale slotte
in between national and local scales. It should be noted, however, tha
the spatial variations in social and economic inequalities are such tha
the range discerned in particular nation states will in large part depen
upon the scale of regional sub-division adopted (Keeble 1967, Stöh
1974).

Clearly regions have not benefited equally from the sustained hig
level of economic activity experienced since World War II, nor indee

from the impact of the forces of industrialization and urbanization that have swept over the now industrialized world in the last century or more (Perloff *et al.* 1960, Coates and Rawstron 1971, Barlow Report 1940). Every advanced industrial country, capitalist and socialist alike, is aware that it faces the problem of regional inequalities (Robinson 1969, Wright 1965), whether expressed in terms of imbalance between town and country, between older and more modern industrial regions, or between urban areas of different size, economic function, and environmental quality.

What are the economic characteristics and situations producing such inter-regional and interurban disparities in welfare levels in advanced industrial countries? Why does the supposed free flow of factors of production, particularly labour and capital, fail to slow down economic growth in the metropolitan congested regions and effect a quickening in the 'backward/depressed/underdeveloped' regions? Until recent years economic theory recognized the existence of regional inequality but concerned itself with the reasons for its persistence. This approach involved a tacit neglect of geographic space (expressed in terms of the spatial patterns of production and incomes, of the diffusion of technology and innovation, of agglomeration economies, of the friction of distance, of locational preferences, of rates of population increase, and of the size, age, and distribution of capital stock, etc. — most of these items are regarded by Richardson (1973a) as basic requirements of a more satisfactory regional growth model) and retarded the investigation of questions of regional economic development. Consequently the theory of spatial development is not yet as refined as that for micro-economic or macroeconomic theory (Stöhr 1974). Richardson (1973a, p. 14) prefaces his critical review of regional development theory as follows: 'the state of the art of regional growth theorizing is very primitive. This partly reflects the limited time and effort put into it compared with the vast literature on growth theory in general'. It also reflects a too-heavy reliance on growth theory and insufficient analysis of the characteristics of particular regional economies. For our purpose we must ruthlessly select some of the economic realities which underlie regional inequalities and encourage the reader to seek further guidance and illumination in the literature (see, for instance, Brown 1972, Richardson 1969, 1973a, Nourse 1968, Smith 1971).

Specialization. The hallmark of the market system is specialization. We are so accustomed to living in a system containing an extreme division of labour with its sharp differentiations among and within the fields of production, distribution, and consumption that we need to remind ourselves in the present context of the degree to which activities a specialized. The geography of economic activity exhibits extren regional and local differentiation: some areas are characterized as cc mining areas, some specialize in agriculture, some in chemicals, some textiles, some in steel production and heavy engineering, some have much more diversified industrial structure, some rely heavily on tertia and quaternary employment, and so on. Some areas are more develope than others, either because they possess natural advantages (coal, iro good harbours, centrality, proximity to trade routes or to fast-growir metropolitan areas, etc.) or because they have been 'favoured' in terr of capital investment, political power, entrepreneurial skills, transpo networks, and the fruits of innovation.

Where one lives therefore matters a great deal in terms of incom employment, and general quality of life, for unbalanced region growth is a feature of the free market economy and represents th aggregation of innumerable decisions, taken perhaps over a long peric of time, in a basically *laissez-faire* system. If the individual is willing move and knows where to go, his opportunities increase. If he is relu tant to move, then they are circumscribed by the place in which l lives. Some places are good, some bad, and some indifferent. Person income is not always related to degree of diversity in employment b in general places characterized by a high degree of specialization economic activity are less secure and more restricted environmen in which to work than are diversified places. In most advanced indu trial economies, opportunity for employment varies considerably ov the country from a high degree of limited and narrow specialization i a declining group of industries in some places to highly diverse emplo ment in flourishing manufacturing and service industries, notably in th metropolitan complexes. Lack of varied opportunity for employmer restricts the local social environment, and it can also lead to the su pression of many talents, which may remain for ever latent and wastec

According to Rawstron and Coates (1966), if a worker decided i the mid 1960s to stay in any of the following places in the Unite Kingdom – and there were many more like them – it meant that h was severely limiting his or her employment opportunities: Bradfor where 31 per cent of employment was in textiles, mainly woo Sheffield (30 per cent in metal trades); Stoke-on-Trent (34 per cent i ceramics); Kettering–Wellingborough–Rushden (36 per cent in clothin mainly footwear); Luton and Dunstable (32 per cent in vehicles Holland, Lincolnshire (32 per cent in agriculture); Dundee (21 per cer in textiles, mainly jute); or Barrow (40 per cent in shipbuilding c marine engineering). These are not necessarily bad places in an absolut sense. Their restricted opportunities may provide reasonable security, tolerable prospects, and adequate income. But they are bad in a comparative sense, because they cater inefficiently for the wide range of potential talents of their inhabitants. As a class of town, they may expect to lose population to areas with better opportunities and to attract population only on a limited and selective basis.

In contrast, because opportunities are excellent, there is no general incentive on grounds of employment to leave Greater London, though other centrifugal forces do operate in a small way. London offers the best opportunities for many reasons. Employment in manufacturing approximates to the national average and is extremely diverse, and this diversity contains a higher proportion of expanding trades than elsewhere. The most rapidly expanding sector of all in the national economy is the service or tertiary sector, and of this London has more than its fair share. Moreover, a great deal of employment classed as manufacturing in London is office employment which in effect augments the expanding tertiary sector. Finally, security is high and incomes are above the national average in the Civil Service, whose better-paid jobs are concentrated in London. The employment structure makes people want to remain in London and induces others to seek work there. Thus people with a wide range of aptitudes and skills are drawn from the rest of the United Kingdom and from abroad (this argument is developed in Coates and Rawstron 1966, 1971; see also Chisholm 1964).

There is an almost infinite number of examples of industrial specialization transmuted into geographic specialization; for example, automobile manufacturing focused on Detroit, consumer goods industries requiring economies of scale located close to the major market areas, and the concentration of decision-making organizations of major public and private firms in the information centres of the world's economic system. One of the best known examples is the classic nineteenth century one of the spatial concentration of cotton textile production in Lancashire. Such specialization of production in a limited space was characteristic of developments on or close to many European and American coalfields. Indeed, geographic and industrial specialization was often carried a stage further: in Lancashire, for example, the industry was concentrated in the southeast and absent in the west (even though the raw cotton was imported through Liverpool), and, furthermore, within the southeast there emerged specialized spinning, weaving, and finishing districts (Smith 1953, Jewkes 1930). The recent history of the Lancashire cotton area is one of dramatic, long-term collapse of a once great industry. Much of the 'mushroom growth' of settlements and many of the mills remain but the main industry and *raison d'être* of the area have had to change — slowly and painfully.

Yet the basic cause of regional inequalities does not lie in the industrial composition of the regions in question. Williamson (1965) has shown that whilst regional dualism in the industrial sector does play a minor role, its significance has been grossly exaggerated in much of the current development literature. Richardson (1969) too observes that analyses of industrial structure in almost all cases fail to support the hypothesis that a region's growth is explicable by its industrial composition. Recent growth of North American cities is, however, said to be related in part to the 'industry mix effect' as the cities which are growing most rapidly are those fortunate enough to have a large share of their workers in the nation's rapid-growth industries (Berry and Horton 1970); and Graham (1964) explained recent changes in the geographical distribution of total personal income by state and region in terms of differing industrial structures. In regional terms, however, the tremendous differentials in agricultural productivity and significant regional differences in economic structure, that is, the relative importance of agricultural and manufacturing employment, would appear to be more crucial factors than is 'industrial mix' (Graham 1964). Of pre-eminent importance in the spatial development of the economic structure is the question of economies of scale.

Agglomeration economies. As the economic system becomes more sophisticated, increasing returns to scale within the firm, external technological economies, and economies of scale in the supply of urban services give rise to agglomeration economies which are best developed in urban areas which have the comparative advantages of initial advantage, market size, complex information systems and linkages, accessibility, high rates of innovation, and well-developed traits of adaptability and flexibility giving an ability to absorb change and development. Industrial activity, establishments supplying public utilities, and other services requiring a high population threshold for viability will cluster around certain focal points which are selected because they have special locational advantages. Areas with problems of unemployment, relatively low wage levels, outworn environments, low welfare levels, and conservative attitudes towards change are unlikely to be selected very often without government intervention.

Regional disparities are in part related to the fact that the ability to take advantage of external and scale economies differs between:

(1) employment sectors: in agriculture, for instance, the returns are

restricted because of the limits to which capital can be substituted for its major production factor, land.

(2) places of varying size: Berry (1967) cites work suggesting the emergence of new metropolitan forms accompanied by more extreme types of specialization. The United States, it is argued, is gradually becoming a set of metropolitan regions, each with a population of 300,000 or more located within two hours' commuting time of a core area on modern expressway systems (Friedmann and Miller 1965). Duncan (1960) sees the 300,000 figure as marking a transition point at which 'distinctly metropolitan characteristics' appear, and Thompson (1965) asserts that areas of this size appear to have reached scales necessary for self-sustaining growth. Urban areas outside these metropolitan complexes are at a disadvantage in the market-place for service industries, offering fewer scale economies than either the big cities or smaller ones favourably located near the great centres of population and their well developed economic infrastructure.

(3) places at different levels (stages) of development: Hawley (1956) Schnore and Peterson (1958), and Pickard (1959) have shown that the major trends in population distribution in the United States can be summarized as processes of concentration, structural change, and decentralization, making possible the division of the country into a set of metropolitan regions. Yeates and Garner (1971) in their study of the North American city show how the trend in urban growth was successively oriented towards arable agricultural land, water power sites, junction points in the transportation network, mining settlements, major metropolitan areas, and resort and retirement cities. They stress the changes in initial advantage associated with the coming of the railroads because it was in the period 1870–1920 that the basic features of the present-day pattern of cities was established (see also Pred 1965). Borchert (1967) too places particular emphasis on evolutionary stages in changing industrial and transportation technology and changes in demand for specific natural resources. He also concludes that the present metropolitan patterns of the United States were established in all major aspects by the 1920s. In his studies of the Upper Midwest, Borchert has traced how the processes operate at the regional scale by analysing the progressive shift of people from farm to non-farm occupations, from farms and small trade centres to large urban areas, and from built-up city areas into neighbouring suburbs and countryside (Borchert 1963). In this evolution, the general welfare of a community is related to the role it plays in the wider regional system and to the stage of development (or decline) of the area itself and its region in the national and indeed international system. Some

areas become 'fossilized' as they are bypassed by change and development. Williamson (1965, p.41) concludes that 'regional dualism [is]
more prevalent in a traditional sector, (for example) agriculture, and
one in which technology is more localized by regional resource
development'. He points out that in Yugoslavia, Spain, and Brazil in
the late 1950s and in the United States around 1900 regional income
inequality in the agricultural sector was approximately two and a half
times that of industry. In stark contrast, regional dualism in Japan
(in 1959) was more severe in industrial than in agricultural production.
Stöhr (1974) explores how availability of external and scale economies
changed in the course of four periods of differential spatial development in the United States: Period 1, up to 1820, Pre-industrial; Period
2, 1820–70, Incipient industrialization; Period 3, 1870–1920, Full-scale
industrialization; and Period 4, 1920–present, Post-industrial. In Period
1 external and scale economies were insignificant, during Periods 2 and
3 they increased steadily and levelled off in Period 4 'owing to the
emergence of external diseconomies in the most highly developed
areas (particularly in the major metropolitan centres) and to a shift in
demand towards the service sector with its limited ability to make use
of scale economies' (Stöhr 1974, p.20).

Impact of industrialization on regional disparities. This 'levelling off' in the
availability of external and scale economies in the post-industrial phase
of advanced industrial economies will be accompanied by a reduction
of regional inequalities if, as a result, average *per capita* incomes of
regions do indeed move closer together in a mature industrial-urban
economy. Empirical investigations into the long-run relative *per capita*
income behaviour of regions in the United States do, in fact, point to
a clear trend towards regional *per capita* income equalization since
1880 (Keeble 1967, Richardson 1969). Table 4.3 shows regional
income *per capita* as a percentage of the national average in the period
1880–1957 (Perloff *et al.* 1960). The convergence process is indicated
by the reduction in the range of regional incomes from 50 to 211 per
cent of the national average in 1880 to 70 to 119 per cent in 1957.
High income regions (Far West, New England, Middle Atlantic) were
apparently pulled down towards the national average, and low income
regions (Southeast, Southwest, and Plains) were, rather belatedly
pulled up, but equalization was far from complete and it is noteworthy
that the rank of multi-state regions (and States) according to *per capita*
income changed very little over the period. Nevertheless, Williamson
(1965) shows that the trend towards inter-regional income disparities
was strongest during and immediately after the American Civil War

Table 4.3

Regional income per capita in United States, 1880–1957, as percentage of national average

Region	1880	1900	1920	1930	1940	1950	1957
New England	141	133	124	129	127	109	113
Middle Atlantic	140	138	133	143	133	118	118
Great Lakes	102	106	108	110	112	111	109
Southeast	50	48	56	50	58	68	70
Plains	90	97	87	82	81	94	90
Southwest	61	68	81	64	70	86	86
Mountain	166	145	102	86	84	96	92
Far West	211	163	135	131	132	120	119

Source: Perloff *et al.* 1960, p. 27.

and disparities diminished rapidly between 1935 and 1960.

In a major empirical investigation, Williamson (1965) examines the statistical evidence relating to the existence and stubborn persistence of regional dualism at all levels of national development and throughout the historical experience of almost all developed countries. In order to explore the 'North–South problem' Williamson selects twenty-four countries which together span the 'development spectrum' from mature economies such as the United States and Sweden to developing countries such as India and the Philippines. Table 4.4 ranks these countries according to Kuznets' (1963) seven levels-of-development classification. The coefficient of inter-regional disparity (Vw) measures the deviation of regional *per capita* income from the national average and is weighted by the relative magnitude of regional population: the higher the Vw the greater is the inter-regional income disparity. The range of Vw values is from 0·700 in Brazil to 0·058 in Australia.

Williamson suggests that inter-regional income disparities are relatively small in mature economies and rise sharply in the middle income group of countries. The lower income groups are poorly represented in the list but inter-regional disparities are probably smaller than in groups 3 and 4. Williamson concludes that (1) poor but developing countries are characterized by increasing regional disparities, while more developed ones exhibit decreasing disparities: 'the pattern of regional inequality is in the form of an inverted 'U' reaching a peak in the middle income class' (p. 15) (Fig. 4.8, after Keeble 1967, p. 265); (2) inter-regional disparities increase as the country is disaggregated into smaller units; (3) intra-regional inequalities increase as one moves

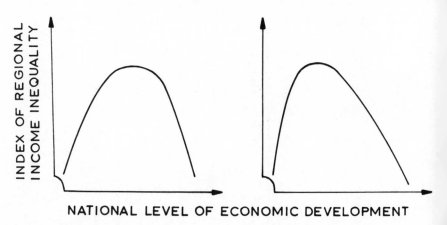

INDEX OF REGIONAL INCOME INEQUALITY

NATIONAL LEVEL OF ECONOMIC DEVELOPMENT

Fig. 4.8. Possible relationships between indices of regional income inequality and national development. (Source: Keeble 1967, p. 265; after Williamson 1965

Table 4.4

*International cross-section analysis of inter-regional
income disparities for 24 countries (in late 1950s)*

Country and Kuznets (1963) group classification by *per capita* product	Size (in square kilometres)	Coefficient of inter-regional disparity
GROUP 1 (highest *p.c.* product)		
Australia	7 704 112	·058
New Zealand	268 674	·063
Canada	9 960 486	·192
United Kingdom	244 180	·141
United States	7 827 929	·182
Sweden	449 045	·200
Average		·139
GROUP 2		
Finland	337 125	·331
France	550 783	·283
West Germany	245 330	·205
Netherlands	33 281	·131
Norway	323 913	·309
Average		·252
GROUP 3		
Ireland	68 896	·268
Chile	741 763	·327
Austria	83 835	·225
Puerto Rico	8 896	·520
Average		·335
GROUP 4		
Brazil	8 515 990	·700
Italy	304 247	·360
Spain	506 351	·415
Colombia	1 138 600	·541
Greece	132 726	·302
Average		·464
GROUP 5		
Yugoslavia	247 493	·340
Japan	369 445	·244
Average		·292
GROUP 6		
Philippines	299 401	·556
GROUP 7		
India	3 164 647	·275
TOTAL AVERAGE		·299

Source: Williamson 1965, p. 12.

from rich to poor regions; and (4) developed small states have been most successful in spreading the fruits of economic growth across their regions.

Williamson's over-all conclusion that our past and current system of social and economic organization does not necessarily perpetuate inter-regional growth and income differentials once they come into existence appears to lend weighty support to the spatial diffusion aspect of neo-classical economic theory: that is, that the expansion of efficient capital, labour, and commodity markets into undeveloped or under-developed regions will decrease regional economic inequalities in the country as a whole (see also Tachi 1964). In arguing that there is a consistent relationship between regional dualism and national economic development — 'rising regional income disparities and increasing North–South dualism is typical of early development stages, while regional convergence and a disappearance of severe North–South problems is typical of the more mature stages of economic national growth and development' (p. 44) — Williamson is confronted by the fact that in the mature industrial countries there is deep and widespread concern about regional inequalities and their persistence. The clue to unravelling this paradox is provided by a telling sentence in Williamson's paper (and one that has been neglected by many commentators): 'It should be made clear again, however, that we have made no attempt to measure regional concentration of population and urbanization, but only have measured regional variation in *per capita* income levels weighted by the distribution of population' (Williamson 1965, p. 16).

Convergence of regional *per capita* income may not, in fact, be accompanied by regional convergence of opportunity, economic power and quality of life. Such convergence, or spatial equalization, will not take place if the owners of wealth, controllers of capital, key decision makers, the entrepreneurially talented and technically innovative, are concentrated in particular regions, most probably the metropolitan core regions. Each of these elements may be spatially biased and each is likely to limit factor flows between regions and thus outweigh the effects of equilibrating factor movements. The end result would be an unacceptable regional distribution of welfare. Indeed, 'the mosaic of regions at different levels of development' would then be subject to stresses in a system which favours those areas which already hold an advantageous position and harms those regions with lower levels of economic development (Myrdal 1957b).

Two case studies of spatial bias. The coefficient of inter-regional disparity (V_w) scores for the United States and the United Kingdom are relatively low

One might infer, therefore, that as a result of their long period of industrialization and urbanization these two countries have 'solved' the regional problem. Is this so? As a partial answer to this question attention is focused on, first, a study of the poor in the world's mightiest economic nation and, second, a study of the role of the Celtic lands in the national development of Britain — the world's oldest industrial state.

Poverty in the midst of plenty. For 25 million Americans the daily fight for survival is an enduring fact of life. Only 8·4 per cent of the non-poor are blacks compared with 31·7 per cent of the poor. In contrast, two-thirds of the poor are whites but only 12 per cent of the white population is poor. The poor are in greatest need of medical care but get least. There is a greater incidence of poor health among low-income groups because of uneven distribution of health services. The poor face a vicious circle of poverty, poor development, illness, poor medical care, poor employment or unemployment and underemployment, physically demanding jobs, poor health, low income, etc. The poor live in shanties and shacks in rural areas and in decaying neighbourhoods of great and small cities.

The economic and social structure virtually guarantees poverty for millions of Americans. Most of the poor remain poor because access to income through work is currently beyond their reach. Acceptance by the federal, state, and local governments of an unemployment rate means that not everyone can work who wants to work, wages will be lower because of less competition for labour; young people, people with low educational attainments, and members of minority groups subject to discrimination will be particularly handicapped in their search for employment. Low wages are related to: (1) spread of automation; (2) migrants from the agricultural sector, more young people, and more middle-aged women looking for jobs and adding to the supply of low-wage job candidates; (3) immobility of labour and capital resources; (4) discrimination in hiring, with non-whites and females the main sufferers; and (5) the fact that nearly one in five of poor under 65 male and female family heads left school after only barely attaining the accepted level of functional literacy.

Where are the poor? Two-thirds of the poor live in urban areas but the risk of being poor is greater for those who live in rural areas (20 as against 14 per cent). Twenty per cent of Southern families are poor, only 9 per cent elsewhere. Half of all poor families live in the South, two-thirds of all poor non-white families live in the South, two-fifths of all poor white families live in the South. Another focal point for poverty is the inner core of the major cities, from which it is often difficult, time consuming, and expensive to reach well-paying jobs in outlying areas. In many American cities the story is the same: there are no jobs where the poor live, the poor cannot afford — or are not allowed — to live where the jobs are opening up, and there is no (public) transport between these two places.

This description of the lot of 25 million people in the richest nation on earth is not drawn from such books as Michael Harrington's *The other America* (1963) or Harry Caudill's *Night comes to the Cumberlands* (1962), but has been constructed from *The U.S. President's Commission on income maintenance programs* (1969). It is a dramatic illustration of inequality in the world's most technologically advanced and affluent nation.

Morrill and Wohlenberg (1971) highlight certain vital characteristics of the American economic system which confront the potential worker and affect his potential income. These are, and we quote (pp. 73 ff.):

(1) For the most part, the creation of job opportunities is concentrated in the hands of rather few investors and employers. The location of these jobs will be where the most satisfactory profits can be obtained, not where people happen to be. There is no reason for the locational preferences of employers and people to coincide.

(2) The rational employer cannot be expected to pay more for labor (or other inputs) than he has to in a competitive labor market. If a portion of the labor force is not competitive, it will be allocated wages that society considers to be poverty level; some may be allocated no job or income at all.

(3) The demand for various products, efficient production processes, and the transport system are constantly changing; the rational employer cannot be expected to remain in inefficient locations or maintain uneconomic levels of employment.

When these characteristics are expressed at the regional level in terms of general imbalances in demand and supply of labour the result is generally one of regional inequality. Such inequalities are also related to regional variations in industrial mix, rate of technological change, productivity changes in different employment sectors, imperfect mobility of labour, economies of scale, accessibility, and other economic as well as social factors.

Dividing the United States according to the spatial pattern of poverty, Morrill and Wohlenberg discern seven regions — Metropolitan America, Metropolitan Periphery, Urban South, Inland Hills and Mountains, Agricultural Interior, Agricultural South, and Appalachian Coalfields. Metropolitan America, the most favoured region, is the largest market within the country, and has average to high levels of schooling, low levels of farming, very high labour-force participation, and average to low levels of non-white population. These dominant characteristics are associated with low levels of poverty and

Metropolitan America is prosperous, with only a minor poverty problem when measured in proportional rather than absolute terms. In contrast, the region of most severe poverty is the Agricultural South. Its outstanding poverty-associated characteristics are high or very high levels of black population, high or very high unemployment, and low or very low levels of educational attainment.

In general terms, Morrill and Wohlenberg conclude that the relative poverty of non-metropolitan America is dependent upon the essentially regional character of resource allocation (especially in agriculture, forestry, and mining). In rural, small town, and even small city America there is an inability to attract activities to offset the relative decline in the capacity of agriculture to support a population. Moreover, lower-density peripheral regions — already left behind in the process of metropolitanization — are at a competitive disadvantage with respect to the growth centres of the modern economy.

In contrast, poverty in the relatively prosperous metropolitan sphere is seen to be the result of problems of economic and social structure. 'Even the richest cities contain surprising numbers of the poor, because of (a) racial discrimination and its effects on black family structure; (b) low educational achievement of part of the population; (c) the persistence of industries paying poverty-level wages; (d) growing numbers of the elderly, and (e) the shortage of adequately paying jobs relative to the numbers needing them' (Morrill and Wohlenberg 1971, p. 119). These city poor are, of course, spatially concentrated in well-defined neighbourhoods (see below).

Any real change in the basic structural problems in American society — discrimination, differential power, income distribution, and the matching of labour supply and demand — 'will require a new attitude toward the functioning of the market in the economy and a different approach by the more affluent toward the poorer and weaker' (Morrill and Wohlenberg 1971, p. 138). But structural change must be accompanied by a re-ordering of the space-economy. The continuing concentration of activities in the largest metropolises must be checked, but how? 'At the root of the problem is that the investor or employer who chooses a metropolitan least-cost site does not bear the immense social and economic costs of congestion, crime blight, racial conflict, pollution; the employees do' (Morrill and Wohlenberg 1971, p. 143).

The periphery under long-term industrial and urban attack. Britain is the oldest industrial state, and throughout this century more than 80 per cent of its residents have been classified as living in urban areas. If industrialization and urbanization do effect an equalization in regional well-being, one might reasonably expect such a desirable result to be present there. Perhaps surprisingly, therefore, we find that regional imbalance has been a matter of serious concern for at least four decades. Hammond (1968), Coates and Rawstron (1971), Manners *et al.* (1972), and many other writers (for example, Hunt Report 1969) have described some of the regional inequalities within this small country in which the processes of urbanization and industrialization have been operative for longer than anywhere else in the world. And the fact that successive British governments have intervened to counter-act what they regard to be unacceptable regional differentials is itself indicative that the diffusion model of social and economic change, as applied to the study of national development, has not operated satis-factorily enough in the United Kingdom. The model suggests that, once the peripheral regions are brought into the national network of commercial flows and transactions, inequality might temporarily increase but thereafter equilibrium will be reached and economic integration will be achieved — to the advantage of all parts of the country.

Hechter (1975) in his analysis of the British Isles tends to suggest (Hechter stresses that his findings are 'merely suggestive' at this stage) that the expectations of the diffusion model were not upheld with respect to long-term trends in aggregate regional inequalities. The Celtic lands (taken to be Scotland, Wales, and Ireland, equals peri-phery) gained much by association with the premier industrial power of the nineteenth century (England, equals core). Indeed, between 1851 and 1911, when the rate of English development was unequalled the Celtic lands kept pace with it. But, Hechter argues, a satisfactory level of equalization has not occurred because (1) industrialization took a different form and had different consequences in the periphery it was geographically confined to a highly limited and relatively un-changing number of counties and these counties might be visualized as industrial enclaves in non-industrial hinterlands; (2) these industrial enclaves were oriented to, and dependent upon, English and inter-national markets: the periphery developed regional economies pro-viding the metropolitan core with primary products and a labour supply and market for its own industrialization; (3) cosmopolitan life-style emerged in the core and the social and cultural gap between core and periphery grew steadily wider: thus acute cleavages of social, economic and political interests arose between the periphery and core and within the periphery itself as a result of the uneven wave of industrialization sweeping over territorial space; (4) the dualist structures emerging in the core and within the periphery itself limited the spatial diffusion of industrialization; and (5) this led to excessive specialization of production, geared for export, in the periphery and to the development of a more diversified and more resilient industrial structure in the core, which area also controlled decision-making, credit, capital, economic policy, and trade (both inter-regionally and internationally: for a discussion of external control and regional development in Scotland see Firn 1975).

Hechter concludes that the disadvantageous position of the Celtic fringe relative to England did not change substantially over the period 1851–1961. *Per capita* income of Celtic countries and many other regional inequalities persisted despite the spread of industrialization. Moreover,

the very economic backwardness of the periphery contributes to the inevitability of residential and occupational segregation. As an impoverished and culturally alien region there is little incentive for members of the core group to migrate there in force. Typically the periphery has a declining population, an over-abundance of the elderly, and a disproportionate number of females, all of which reflect the lack of adequate employment opportunities which is both a result of peripheral backwardness and a cause of further economic disadvantages (Hechter 1975, pp. 42–3).

At this point Hechter reminds us that the vicious circle of regional underdevelopment is lucidly discussed in Myrdal's *Rich lands and poor* (1957a). Our case studies have demonstrated some of the reasons for regional inequalities in advanced industrial countries and indicated that these 'mature' metropolitan societies have failed to solve the 'regional problem'.

Regional problems in developing countries. If regional problems persist in both the oldest and the most affluent of the metropolitan countries, it is not surprising that they exist in the Third World. It is surely unreasonable to expect a poorer country both to develop its economy and at the same time avoid all the major spatial inequalities associated with economic growth, it being almost inevitable that inter-regional inequalities will widen. Even if emphasis were given to development of the agricultural sector, the 'spin-off' in the towns would reinforce existing urban–rural inequalities.

Two aspects of the 'regional problem' in developing countries are of particular concern. The first of these is the spatial imbalance itself. Modernization is concentrated in urban areas, particularly the most populous urban areas (often the capital or main port), and the more inflexible traditional economy of the rural areas changes much more slowly. The hinterland becomes more backward, more subservient and poorer (relatively if not absolutely) as the 'haves' with the political power and economic wealth are concentrated in the towns. The control centres may exhibit symptoms of 'hypercephalism', as in Latin America, as the economic rewards of 'modernization' are reaped, or rather heaped, in a tiny portion of a nation's total space and in the hands of a minority of its urban residents. Social and political consequences of this two-sided unequal economic distribution may be immense, especially as many under-developed countries are attempting to industrialize on a weak and unstable social and political scaffolding. More than two decades ago, Kuznets (1955, p. 26) wondered whether 'the underdeveloped societies (could) withstand the strain which further widening of income inequality is likely to generate'. This is still one of the most important questions in the contemporary world (see Chapter 6).

The second aspect concerns the role of overseas capitalism in the primate-city nature of Third World economic structures. In many small states foreign investment is almost entirely focused on the capital, and the rural hinterland is simply a market to be exploited. Even in Nigeria, the most populous state of Black Africa, three-quarters of the capital invested in medium- and large-scale industry in the mid 1960s was provided by foreign investors (64 per cent from Britain, 9 per cent from the United States — Hakam 1966). Foreign firms employed 60,000 people in Nigeria. Most of the foreign investments relate to activities dependent upon imported raw materials or goods in various stages of processing, and at the same time the activities are largely market oriented. In consequence, foreign firms favour locations such as Lagos–Ibadan and Port Harcourt; and about three-fifths of foreign-owned industrial investment was sunk, in the mid 1960s, in the two major coastal areas of heavy urban concentration of population. A further 12 per cent was invested in the Kano-Kaduna area, which offers the advantages of local demand, raw materials, and the 'natural' protection of distance from southern competitors (Hakam 1966).

Are these features of spatial imbalance and dependence upon foreign investment of a temporary nature? It is too early to say, but there are few reasons for optimism. Referring again to Nigeria, Logan (1972) considers that manufacturing has led to some import replacement but has not effected any restructuring of the space economy. On the contrary, it has consolidated the organizational and spatial structure originally imposed by the colonial power. Thus managerial and production units are strongly localized in the port cities of Lagos and Port Harcourt, in Kaduna and Kano in the north, and in wholesale distribution outlets strategically scattered throughout the nation. Hay also concludes that there was no evidence in the early 1970s that th desperately underprivileged states of the north have succeeded in overcoming the poverty of their educational and health services. Each state has competed with every other for the favour of foreign investors, but 'there is no evidence that this is leading to any major new distribution of regional income, *per capita* incomes, or employment' (Hay 1974, p.27). The 'regional problem' has not therefore been solved, neither has manufacturing brought any real economic independence to Nigeria. Inasmuch as manufacturing increases the dominance of a few cities, it has reproduced the metropolitan/periphery relationship which already exists at the international level within Nigeria itself — a two-tiered spatial imbalance which is perhaps even more evident in scores of countries smaller in area and population than newly oil-rich Nigeria.

Underdevelopment in the developed world. Let us assume that a system of regions can be equated with a system of centres (cities) and that such a system is already in existence in a country. The regions will vary in economic size as a result of initial advantages, for example, in resource availability, proximity to major markets, presence or absence of successful innovators, etc. These advantages lead to the establishment of industry in the regions which have an initial multiplier effect resulting from the demands of employers and employees. This in turn attracts other industries to serve these demands and an upward spiral

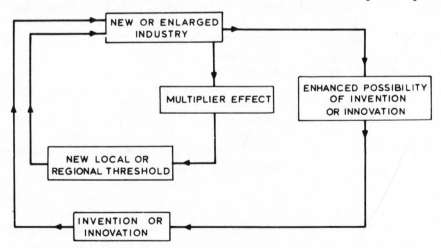

Fig. 4.9. The circular and cumulative process of industrialization and urban-size growth. (Source: Pred 1965, p.165). Redrawn with permission from the *Geographical Review* Vol. LV, 1965, copyrighted by The American Geographical Society.

of growth is entered. As a result of the more complex networks of inter-personal communication there is a greater probability of invention and innovation leading to new or enlarged industrial activity. This gives rise to the circular model of cumulative causation shown in Fig. 4.9 (Pred 1965).

When transport innovations bring previously unconnected regions together into a national system, some of the regions possess greater initial advantages and they assume a dominant role in the system. The position of a region within the emerging hierarchy of regions will therefore depend upon the magnitude of its initial advantage — some will lag behind while others will forge ahead to become metropolitan regions.

The most important regions (centres) within the system will interact with each other to their own advantage, attracting flows of wealth, employment, decision-makers, and political power commensurate with their economic power. These attributes will tend to assure the continuing dominance of the favoured regions. Less important regions (centres) are excluded from this higher level of interaction and their contacts are confined and are generally in the direction of the more important components of the system, that is, they will be dependent upon higher-order regions. In the case of regions with valuable resources, development may be initiated by a more important region. This will be of benefit to the region being developed, but even greater benefits will accrue to the region calling the tune, and naming the price. In other words, a 'colonial' type relationship now exists between the less and more important regions (Berry 1961b, 1972a, Kraenzel 1955, Pred 1974). This arrangement can best be described as a core and periphery system.

A number of metropolitan cores have developed in some countries (United States, Australia, and Canada), but in many others a single centre is dominant. Johnston (1973) considers the best explanation of why 'primate' cities occur in many countries is the 'colonial' (Rose 1966) or 'gateway' (Burghardt 1971) model. In countries settled from overseas, administration, commerce, and secondary industry were highly concentrated in the port of entry — the 'link' between the mother country and the extensively farmed and/or minerally exploited hinterlands. Clarke (1972) considers 28 of 37 primate cities in tropical Africa are 'peripherally' located and 22 are ports. This spatial pattern he relates to the extreme political fragmentation produced by the colonial impact, together with the 'islandic' character of the modern economy. Vance (1970) postulates a general cartographic model of an urban development process in which the central place pattern of the 'mother country' is eventually matched by that of the colony. This model suggests that rank-size/central place hierarchy and primate distributions are not mutually exclusive: some countries may indeed have an amalgam of the two (Johnston 1973).

Whichever urban system is present in a given country, the subservient position of the peripheral regions, which may consist of a mixture of predominantly agricultural or specialized industrial regions, is partly accounted for by the nature of the tasks allotted to them by the metropolitan core complexes. These 'primary' producing areas will tend to have an adverse balance of trade. This produces a flow of income out of the area, results in adverse multiplier effects and leads in turn to a further fall in regional income and employment. This cumulative process is best illustrated by reference to an underdeveloped agricultural region in the system. An increase in income in the metropolitan regions raises the demand for primary goods and income is bolstered in the agricultural region. However, given that the marginal propensity to consume manufactured goods is greater than that for agricultural goods, the demand for manufactured goods will increase relatively more than the demand for agricultural products. This is analogous to an increase in imports into the agricultural region and a worsening of the balance of trade. The result is an outflow of capital and labour to regions where reutrns are higher and, contrary to the postulates of classical economic theory, there is unlikely to be a compensating downward adjustment of wages (in developed economies at least, wages are only flexible upwards in practice) to attract capital searching for cheap labour (Nourse 1968, Richardson 1969).

In addition to the problem of inflexible wage structures the out-migration of labour from underdeveloped regions is selective. It is the young, the most able, and the most ambitious who tend to leave, and their departure worsens the age and sex distribution and makes the region less attractive to employers. Those who remain in the underdeveloped region will tend to be poorly educated and may have value systems and social customs which again deter would-be employers from coming into the region. The general air of pessimism and depression confirms the employers' judgement, as do the low tax revenues. These, in turn, produce a poor infrastructure and dependence upon the central government for almost all forms of social investment. The cost of such investment may be so high that the investment itself is not forthcoming. These factors together act against the underdeveloped region and increase the gap between the 'haves' and the 'have nots'. Myrdal (1957b, p. 12) finds appropriate words for this situation in the Gospels: 'For unto everyone that hath shall be given, and he shall have abundance: but from him that hath not shall be taken away even that which he hath'.

Many of these underdeveloped regions (centres) are, in reality, geographically as well as economically peripheral in the regional system. Others are peripheral just in an economic sense, for they are contiguous to the metropolitan complex (the Appalachians, for instance, squeezed between Megalopolis and the industrial Midwest). But their initial advantages dictate the type of development that takes place and they are unable to compete with the unassailable initial advantage of the nearby metropolitan regions (UN 1954, Perloff and Wingo 1961).

The dominance of the major metropolitan complexes and their ability to call the tune has been accentuated in recent decades by the increasing centralization of government and the development of major job-providing organizations, in both the public and private sectors (Pred 1974). These organizations have grown to a massive size (for example, the Post Office and National Coal Board in the United Kingdom; the New Zealand government employs 20 per cent of the country's labour force; Sears, Roebuck of Chicago with 380,000 employees; Imperial Chemical Industries (I.C.I.) of London with 142,000 employees in the United Kingdom and 60,000 abroad). They are taking an increasing share of employment in most developed economies and their locational decisions play a vital role in the operation of the regional system. As a consequence of their size it has become necessary for the organizations to hive off their administrative functions; I.C.I., for instance, has sixty plants in eight product groups in the United Kingdom alone. The administrative functions are generally located in the major metropolitan complexes in order to take advantage of their specialized information channels and linkages. Inter and intra-organizational multipliers accrue therefore to these places giving rise to further growth and in the process ensuring that the non metropolitan producing areas will become more dependent upon the metropolitan core.

After analysing the location of the headquarters of the 1000 larges United States multi-locational organizations whose primary functio was manufacturing (Table 4.5), Pred (1974, p.62) concludes that 'th current degree of spatial concentration (of the headquarters) does no begin to approach the level of concentration prescribed for nationall functioning units by classically based city-system models'. It is o tremendous importance none the less: weighted by sales or jobs cor trolled, New York's headquarters account for about 40 per cent of th headquarters activity of major firms in the United States. Compar tively few headquarters are in backward, lagging, or depressed region

Table 4.5

Headquarters location and job control in U.S. of 1000 largest U.S. manufacturing organizations (Top 1000) and 300 leading non-industrial corporations*(The 300), 1972. Only metropolitan complexes with 200,000 jobs in total job control column are listed here: full details are given in Pred (1974), Tables 7, 8, and 17.

Metropolitan complex	1970 population (nearest 000)	Headquarters location of			Jobs controlled by (in 1000s)		
		Top 1000	The 300	Top 1000 + The 300	Top 1000	The 300	Top 1000 + The 300
New York	16894	255	72	327	5802	2706	8508
Los Angeles	8452	46	22	68	711	188	899
Chicago	7612	99	27	126	1297	876	2173
Philadelphia	5317	33	17	50	394	274	668
Detroit	4200	20	7	27	1683	153	1837
San Francisco	4174	27	10	37	316	332	648
Boston	3389	22	7	29	209	110	319
Cleveland-Akron	2743	41	9	50	790	103	893
Pittsburgh	2401	24	3	27	528	12	540
St. Louis	2363	19	6	25	415	97	512
Dallas-Fort Worth	2318	22	8	30	229	51	280
Houston	1985	16	7	23	177	36	213
Minneapolis-St. Paul	1814	22	13	35	334	150	484
Cincinnati	1611	9	6	15	149	157	305
Hartford	809	7	9	16	118	147	264

*The 50 organizations with the greatest revenues or assets in *each* of the following categories: retailing, utilities, transportation, commercial banking, life insurance, and diversified financial. Source: Pred 1974, Table 7, 8, and 17.

These regions lose skilled jobs, high wages, stability, and the intra-organizational multiplier effect. Parsons (1972, p.103) suggests that the policies and geographic distributions of the giant manufacturing corporations in the United Kingdom 'are not wholly compatible with balanced regional growth', and goes on to forecast that unless the British government intervenes to change these operations 'one may expect this force for regional inequality of development to continue and to curb the alleged aims of regional development policies.'

URBAN INEQUALITIES

Most of the world's cities are the result of *laissez-faire* development based on the belief that unplanned and unregulated development dictated by economic, technological, and demographic forces will result in an environment suitable for economic man. Urban dwellers therefore live with and in cities produced by basically unregulated market and social forces and an unbridled and burgeoning technology (Henderson and Ledebur 1972). In effect, the pricing mechanism produces an 'economic city', with countless simultaneous and successive decisions effecting a market-oriented allocation of resources. If the citizens were equal in social and economic as well as in physiological terms, then their quality of life would depend upon the economic function of their city in the wider market system.

The market system has channelled investment to produce a great variety of economic cities — highly specialized and diversified, rich and poor, large and small, booming and declining. The well-being of the average citizen will reflect the general prosperity of his city: Phoenix is a 'better' place to live than Calcutta, Lagos is better than Kano, and Paris is better than Marseilles. Thus the position and importance of a city in the international and national systems of cities is a vital consideration in an assessment of the welfare levels of urban dwellers (Thompson 1965, Richardson 1973b). In general, inhabitants of Western cities enjoy an affluence and material prosperity unparalleled in history. On the other hand, urbanites in 'peripheral countries' are less well off, though their lot is generally superior to that of their fellow countrymen in rural areas. Even in the developing world 'bigness' counts, for there is said to be a positive association between the rate of growth in gross domestic product *per capita* and increasing primacy (Mera 1973).

Inequalities also result from changes in the economic base of the city. The economic city is not a static entity fixed for all time, but a system in flux, a creation of 'dynamic motion'. Within the city some sectors may decline and die as investment is withdrawn or withheld while others grow and prosper as investments pour in. Such intra-urban change may result from functional change through time; for example, a mining town may lose its collieries, a port may be unsuitable for large tankers, a city may suffer through poor air transport links or it may lose its status as a regional capital. Adjustment to the changed situation will not occur overnight, and in the meantime poverty levels will rise as unemployment spreads through the town in a cumulative manner but produces greater effects in some neighbourhoods than in others. Whether the city is booming or declining, spatial change within it will occur as a result of the ageing of older property areas, an influx of poor rural families or immigrants from overseas, labour-shedding as a result of automation, development of new suburbs or satellite towns on the fast road or rail commuter routes, and the movement of offices and industry to the suburbs (Bourne 1971, Manners *et al.* 1972, Goddard 1975). In the changing city, those without access to personal transport, skills, and opportunities will be 'left out' by the market system, for the latter is geared to serve the prosperous rather than the needy.

Similarly, if the economic base of the large city (that is, its economies of scale, localization economies, and urbanization (external) economies) is weakened through competition or diseconomies of scale (perhaps mirrored in deteriorating environmental quality, high taxation, flight of the rich beyond the city and concentration of the poor within, the political boundaries of the city, rising crime, ageing infrastructure, and tarnished image), then the capitalist market system accentuates the already unequal allocation of resources by allowing the costs to be borne by individuals, certain neighbourhoods, and the public welfare programmes. Local or central government is unlikely to intervene effectively enough to avert a fall in the quality of life enjoyed by many city dwellers, a fall which continues to the level at which the area is once again able to compete in the market system.

Pressure to 'decentralize' some of the economic functions of the largest metropolitan cities raises the question whether such decentralization can be justified, and whether the need to act in the interest of the minorities, the aged, and the poor remaining in the central cities will not seem much more urgent as a national goal (Pred 1974, Pahl 1971). Within the metropolis the 'distribution of manufacturing has already decentralized considerably and assumed a Babel-like disorder of enormous proportions' (Pred 1964, p.170).

Spatial inequalities and territorial injustice exist in every 'economic city'. A city contains human resources ranging from the most talented

and aggressive to the most marginally employable, and occupation:
stretching down from the directors of multi-national corporation:
through their managers and research staff, workers in the mass pro
duction units requiring a narrow range of skills, to the most menia
jobs in the service trades. These differences are compounded by, as wel
as related to, ethnic, religious, and racial characteristics, life-cycle, ag·
and sex structure, health, education, vocational training, endeavour
perseverance, and sheer opportunity.

The unequal distribution of income is one result of this plethora o·
conflicting pressures and interlocking attributes of city life. This, ir
turn, produces unequal competition in the market-place. It is necessar·
to stress that this basic inequality is not simply a result of the economi·
forces alone, but emanates from a complex interplay of social and
political as well as economic forces. Economic reality for certair
groups is, for instance, influenced by the extent of discrimination, botł
social and political. Relationships within a city are of great complexity
but a common result of the unequal distribution of income is residen
tial segregation and the creation of ghettos. Such features within a city
are the spatial expression of deep-seated economic and sociologica
realities. They bear witness to the basic fact that the extent to whicł
benefits accrue in the market system is a function of income, wealth
education, health, race, and so on. The market mechanism is designec
to discriminate through its rationing function against those who hav·
purchasing power inferior to that of other consumers in the marke
(Henderson and Ledebur 1972). If this is allied to racial, ethnic, reli·
gious, class, or caste discrimination, which excludes those discriminatec
against from access to jobs and other forms of income, then ar
'apartheid situation' will exist in the city (for example, see studies o·
residential segregation in Belfast, Birmingham, Kuwait, and Detroi
carried out by Poole and Boal 1973, Jones 1967, 1970, Hill 1973, anc
Bunge 1975 respectively). Within the ghetto the process of cumulativ·
circular causation may operate in a similar fashion to the one depictec
in Fig. 4.10 (Henderson and Ledebur 1972).

In the intra-urban situation, as in the international and intra
national, the market mechanism results in the exclusion of som·
individuals from participation in market activity because of their failur·
to conform with social, educational, or other standards established by
the institutions that control market behaviour and participatior
(Henderson and Ledebur 1972). Conversely, the market mechanism
works in favour of the wealthy who also tend to cluster in space
choosing desirable locations in terms of positive attributes (exter
nalities) such as quality of physical environment, access to commute

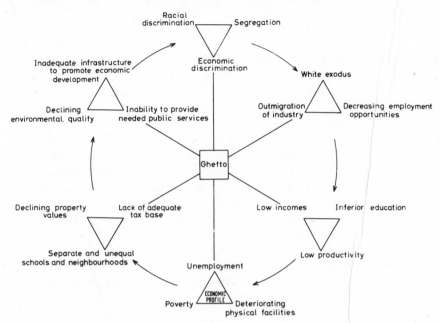

Fig.4.10. The circular and cumulative process of socio-economic relationships in the ghetto. (Source: Henderson and Ledebur 1972, p.164.)

services, proximity to suppliers of luxury goods, and security of investments in property, and avoiding areas accumulating negative attributes (externalities) such as pollution, crime, poverty, disease, poor schools, and inadequate health and recreational facilities (Thompson 1965, Harries 1974, Cox, Reynolds and Rokkan 1974). The institutions of the economic city, for example banks, estate agents, mortgage companies, lawyers, are geared to help the affluent attain their supposed 'needs' and maximize their advantages (Harvey 1974b).

Clearly people compete to live in certain socio-economic environments. Once they are established in the area of their choice, that is, in areas which accord with their own 'mental map' of the city, they will act to maintain its character to protect their status, family position, and financial investment. Their actions produce conflict over 'goods' which they themselves do not produce — such 'goods' are generally termed externalities (Cox, Reynolds and Rokkan 1974). The actions of others produce benefits or costs, that is, positive or negative externalities. In the 'economic city' of capitalist society one of the more important positive externalities for which households compete concerns property values. The value of its homes and its land are indicative of the socio-economic status of a neighbourhood and thus of its

inhabitants, who often view their property as a major speculative invest
ment as well as a home, and they will act to protect their capital by
fighting for positive externalities and against negative externalities
(Harvey 1973) — a feature which accords with the objectives of the
estate agents, banks, insurance companies, and building societies, as
well as with those who raise local taxes on property rated by its
monetary value.

These institutions are in a position to alter the status of a neighbourhood. It can be raised by channelling investment into domestic
properties and by developing positive externalities such as well-equipped
schools, rigid controls on industrial development and pollution, access
to the main commuter links, and so on. On the other hand, a
neighbourhood can go downhill as property investment finance is
withheld and as negative externalities are allowed to accumulate in the
area — the public incinerator, the demolition scars of 'slum redevelopment', the ageing schools, the serried ranks of cars left by commuters
from another area, and the children playing in the streets for want
of a safer place in which to burn up a portion of their abundant
energy.

In the conflict for these externalities, the competitors do not begin on an equal
footing. Those with wealth and power are better able to manipulate the socio-
economic and political systems which distribute — sometimes unintentionally —
the externalities . . . [and they] dictate the form of the urban residential mosaic,
allocating other groups to areas outside that which their social and economic
superiors normally visit (Johnston and Herbert 1976, p.8).

Third World cities. Are these or similar features being reproduced in the Third
World as a consequence of the penetration of the capitalist ethic? This
is an enormous subject and space is too limited to do justice to it here.
We have seen how transfers of capital and technology to underdeveloped countries are generally limited to narrow sectors and tend to
be concentrated in the modern, industrializing urban areas. Such transfers often accentuate the dualistic nature of Third World countries,
and many cities are divided into a capital-intensive, firm-centred and
labour-intensive, bazaar-centred economic structure (McGee 1971).
In the firm-centred sector productivity is high and the possibilities for
employment are limited by labour-destroying innovations; and labour
is what poor countries have in embarrassing abundance. Traditional
industries are smothered, agriculture is 'organized' more efficiently,
and more people are added to the already swollen ranks of the unemployed. Possibilities for employment are much greater in the bazaar-
centred economy even though returns are much smaller and the

end-product may be described as 'shared poverty' (Wertheim 1964) or 'subsistence urbanization' (Breese 1966).

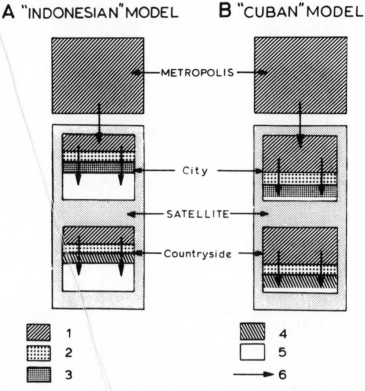

Fig. 4.11. Two static models of an underdeveloped country subjected to different degrees of penetration by the capital-intensive sector. In the 'Indonesian' model (A) penetration is only partial, but in the 'Cuban' model (B) almost the entire economy has been Westernized by the capitalist sector. Key to numbers: (1) Metropolitan capital-intensive production/appropriation; (2) Indigenous capital-intensive production/appropriation; (3) Government sector; (4) Peasant cash-crop production; (5) Bazaar-peasant sectors, and (6) Capital intensive penetration. (Source: McGee 1971, p. 88.)

These two systems are not mutually exclusive. But the capitalist system is able to produce goods to satisfy the demands of the favoured few — Mercedes, air conditioners, refrigerators, French wines, hi-fi sets, contraceptive pills, and clothes from London, Paris, New York, and Rome. It also produces (and advertises to the point of market saturation) cigarettes, Coca-cola, Lactogen, and transistor radios, for the many who have to face the daily task of survival. McGee (1971) reminds us of the danger of over-generalizing about the Third World. It is not the homogeneous entity we often suppose it to be (see Buchanan 1964). Its constituent countries are at different stages of development — or underdevelopment — as a result of their varying historical experiences of capitalism, their indigenous socio-economic structures, and the interaction of the one on the other. In Indonesia, for instance, McGee regards the infiltration of the still largely traditional urban/rural sector by the capital-intensive sector to be only partial (Fig. 4.11A), whereas penetration in Cuba, before Castro, was such that almost the entire economy had been Westernized by the capitalist sector (Fig. 4.11B). These are the two poles of the Third World. How far a country moves from one to the other will be decided in its cities, for they are the launching pads, the enclaves, and the advance-guards of the penetrative forces. Their inflated tertiary sectors bear witness to the form of economic development, and the existing inequalities within Third World cities are gross, nakedly paraded and shamefully manifest.

CONCLUSIONS

We conclude this chapter by focusing attention on one geographer's attempt to draw together the many strands of life in a city which epitomises the modern industrial world — Bunge's study of Detroit (1975): the model could also be applied at the inter-regional and international scales in the context adopted in this chapter. Bunge characterizes the socio-economic patterns of Detroit as three distinct but functionally interrelated cities: the City of Death with approximately 130,000 job-holders, the City of Need with 830,000 job-holders, and the City of Superfluity with about 30,000 job-holders (Fig. 4.12). Assuming that all men are created equal, Bunge (1975, pp. 149–50) considers

any departure in the condition of men from this truth is a measure of the degree of biological breakdown among the species *Homo sapiens*. The extreme irregularity of the income map of Detroit reveals extreme pathology — the map depicts a region of super-abundance adjacent to a region of brutal poverty. Between these two zones is an intermediate zone in constant danger of falling into poverty.

Bunge argues that in the Cities of Need and Death people lose money to others by paying a 'machine tax' for the privilege of using the machinery necessary to life itself. In the City of Death people lose additional money to others because they are often runted in mind and spirit and thus not worth as much as a man raised normally — a 'death tax' on the weak, the sick, the old, and the children. This death tax is collected by overcharging for food, housing, schooling, and loans, and

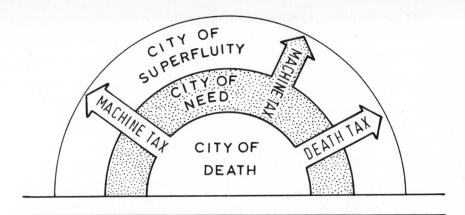

Fig. 4.12. Income flows between the Cities of Death, Need, and Superfluity. (Source: Bunge 1975, p. 153.)

in many other more subtle ways. The City of Death is a deteriorating city: 'its homes, its streets, its schools and its children's teeth fall apart as the money is sucked out' (p. 162). The biggest of the three cities, that of Need, contains the solid union members of Middle America. It keeps pace, generation by generation, with the needs of the machines: its children are trained as 'factory fodder' to levels needed to operate the machines. The City of Superfluity contains few people but an abundance of wealth and power. Here the owners of the machines live in a commuter culture marked by an extreme separation of work from home.

Why then is the most powerful of the three Cities the greatest distance from the city centre and the powerless City located in the most convenient position? Because the spatial configuration of the Total City is the product of population density per square mile of housing which, together with the division of labour and its concomitant occupational structure, governs land values, rent per unit area, and transport costs. The boundaries of the three Cities are located at the distances from the centre where one form of 'rent' gives way to another (Fig. 4.13). The highest paying unit, the City of Death, dominates the centre and crowds out the other Cities.

Who is to blame for these fierce inequalities? Is it the rich, the powerful, and the influential in the City of Superfluity? No, answers Bunge, it is the machines which have run amuck: 'machinekind is un-bridled, wild and out of control . . . Members of the so-called power structure are as much entrapped by machinekind as anyone else, be-cause the machines own them' (p. 179). What then powers the three cities? The threat of the slum is seen as the engine of fear that drives the entire city. Its levels of living set the levels of fear for all people who might sink to a more impoverished state because of misfortune of one kind or another.

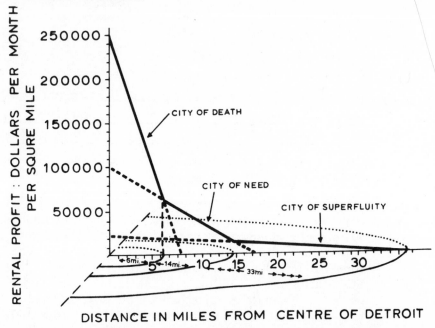

Fig. 4.13. The relationship between rents per square mile and the relative locations of the Cities of Death, Need, and Superfluity. (Source: Bunge 1975, p. 173.)

There is abundant evidence that suggests that this same engine of fear powers the Metropolitan Cores of the world capitalist system, the metropolises of all parts of the world, and, indeed, all communities in which some are richer than others and are thus afraid to contemplate basic changes in the prevailing socio-economic system, for fear that the gap between the 'haves' and the 'have nots' might be narrowed to the point of discomfort, apprehension, loss of face and, above all, loss of control. In the meantime, a minority of nations, a minority of international companies, and a minority of individuals wrestle with the problems of gross affluence, while the majority of the world's population live in almost unimaginable poverty and deprivation. 'Fair' and 'free' market forces have resulted in benefits accruing to those strong enough to seize them — whatever the initial source of their strength. 'Free trade', 'the profit motive', and 'the cult of superiority' have produced gross inequalities between nations, between regions, between towns and within them. The fruits of the system are often bitter and most certainly are unevenly distributed in space at all these scales.

5   Location and livelihood

In the first section of this book, we showed how places — countries, regions, towns, suburbs etc. — vary on a wide range of indicators of social well-being. Some of the reasons for such variation have been outlined in the previous chapter; our focus here is on the question: to what extent does a person's location within a spatial system influence his social well-being? So this chapter is about the role of one variable — distance — which many geographers (for example, Abler, Adams, and Gould 1971) have suggested lies at the heart of their discipline. Distance is usually measured in miles or kilometres, but, as has been previously argued (Johnston 1973), this is but a surrogate for the costs and time involved in moving from place to place, and the influence that these two factors have on flows of information and the perception of opportunities.

In all economies based on market exchange, individuals and households must trade their labour to obtain money with which to buy their levels of living. Investigation of spatial patterns in living standards therefore involves the study of spatial variations in wages and prices. Much of the present chapter is concerned with the geography of incomes and costs, and the extent to which these are influenced by spatial variables. As we have already shown, however, the level of a household's social well-being also involves aspects of life and livelihood which are not bought and sold (at least directly), and later sections of the chapter look at spatial influences on these.

THE GEOGRAPHY OF INCOMES

Different places have different income distributions, at least in part because of their various positions in the international division of labour, as was indicated in Chapter 4: where the high income occupations are concentrated, so too are the high income earners. Thus the mean incomes by standard regions and major conurbations within the United Kingdom varied from a high of £1632 in the south-east of England to a low of £1317 in Ulster, according to the 1971–2 income tax returns. (Data are from *Board of Inland Revenue, 1975*, Tables 63–84.) Averages conceal much of the variation, however, so in Fig. 5.1 we have graphed the percentage of declared incomes in each region that were in each of 24 income groups as a ratio to the national percentage in that

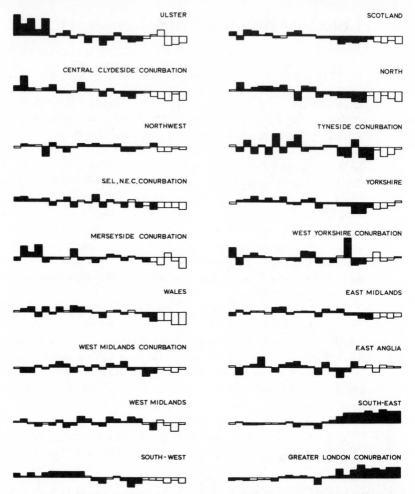

Fig. 5.1. Inter-regional income variations in the United Kingdom, 1971–2. Income categories are arranged from the smallest incomes (less than £420 p.a.) on the left to the largest (more than £10,000 p.a.) on the right. The length of the bar above or below the central line indicates the amount by which the percentage of the regional income-earners in a given category deviates from the national percentage in that category: above the line indicates a greater percentage in the region; below the line a greater percentage nationally. Shaded bars indicate income categories in which the regional percentage is significantly different from the national percentage

income group (that is, 1·0 indicates that the region has the national percentage). Simple tests of statistical significance have been applied to indicate where the major deviations from the national pattern are and these are indicated in the diagram. The clearest picture to come from this is one of incomes increasing to the south and east. The Celtic fringe countries, the North and Northwest of England, Yorkshire, and the Southwest are all characterized by above average percentages in the low income groups and below average proportions in the high income groups. The reverse is the case in Greater London and the Southeast, whereas in the Midlands and East Anglia variations from the national income distribution are in general much less pronounced. Such a pattern fits in well with our discussion in the previous chapter, which associated higher incomes with the location of control functions and growth industries within a space-economy.

If the occupational structure of an area's population is the major determinant of the income distribution there, then this should be testable by relating the two measures. Lankford (1972) has done this for the United States, using data for the period 1930–67. From all of his analyses he concluded that the educational level of a population was the best predictor of its mean total income: presumably better-educated people are in higher-paid jobs. He also found that the location and, less importantly, the size of a place were positively related to income levels, and that over the period 1930–60, the larger increases in incomes were recorded in the rapidly-growing places outside the older industrial core regions of the United States.

Of most interest to us here is Lankford's finding regarding the relationship between income levels and the size and location of a place. This suggests that, even when we have standardized for occupational structure, differences in incomes still occur; in other words people living in different places are paid different wages for the same work. Evidence for this is given in Table 5.1, which shows regional variations in Britain in the wage rates paid in selected industries. Such data are not completely unambiguous, for there is a wide range of skills within each of the broad occupational groupings indicated in the table, but they do suggest the operation of some spatial variables. More detailed data from the United States are unambiguous on this topic, however. For seven occupations – four female (keypunch operator grade B, general stenographer, receptionist-switchboard operator, and typist class B) and three male (automotive mechanic, labourer [material handling], and janitor-porter-cleaner) – Hoch (1972a) found that the major determinants of variations in wage rates between metropolitan areas were city size and location in the southern region: large cities paid more for the same job, within any region, and for a given city size lower wages were paid in the southern region.

In a perfectly competitive labour market, wages are determined by the operation of laws of supply and demand. The larger the number

Table 5.1

Regional variations in average hourly earnings: selected industries, 1971
(in new pence)

Region	All Industries	All Manufacturing	Coal/Petroleum	Paper, Printing	Vehicles	Public Administration
South East	71·27	73·99	90·07	88·98	84·49	59·89
East Anglia	62·53	64·46		72·28	66·66	53·29
South West	64·84	68·67		75·27	76·76	54·35
West Midlands	73·60	76·82	61·67	76·16	95·82	58·19
East Midlands	65·64	67·35	71·06	70·38	73·69	56·00
Yorkshire	64·46	65·58	67·53	71·20	71·64	55·68
North West	68·54	70·11	84·61	78·96	78·16	53·63
North	68·40	72·62	62·91	77·35	82·42	53·23
Wales	70·05	74·65	83·24	73·30	79·02	50·60
Scotland	67·15	69·66	76·31	72·04	85·48	55·35
Ulster	62·03	65·70		69·74	74·13	50·10

Source: Department of Employment 1973, p. 55.

of people looking for jobs relative to the number of vacancies, the more an employer is able to operate a buyer's market, and to keep wages down. Where there is a shortage of labour relative to demand, a seller's market will be operating, with workers able to push up their prices. Labour markets are not perfectly organized in this way, however. Many jobs are unsuitable for the available labour force, so that one job cannot always be substituted for another: if it were, all jobs should pay approximately the same wage. Furthermore, the increasing power of trade unions protects workers from the vicissitudes of the market, especially when the buyers of labour have the upper hand because of an over-supply.

Wage rates should change over time according to fluctuations in the supply of, and demand for, labour, and the form of this relationship was outlined in a classic paper by Phillips (1958). From a study of wage rate changes in Great Britain between 1861 and 1957 he established a general trend, universally known now as the Phillips curve, of a negative exponential relationship between unemployment levels and rates of change in wages (Fig.5.2). The higher the percentage unemployed, the lower the increase in wages, because as unemployment

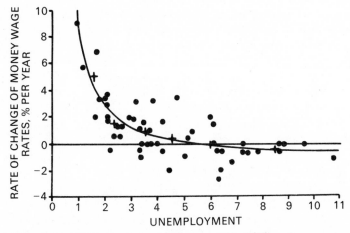

Fig.5.2. The relationship between unemployment level (%) and wage-rate change in Great Britain, 1861–1963. (Source: Phillips 1958, *Economica*, 25 p.285.)

increases, the labour market becomes more favourable to the buyer. The early 1970s have shown marked deviations from this general trend, as both unemployment has increased and wage rates have soared, in Britain and elsewhere. Many reasons have been suggested for this unprecedented inflation, among them the power of the trade unions and the increasing prices of raw material imports: for our purposes here, we will treat the early 1970s as abnormal, since high prices were sustained for only a few raw materials, notably oil.

In any country as a whole, and also in the international system, wage rates are strongly influenced by the operation of the laws of supply and demand. But a national economy, especially a large one such as the British or the American, does not act as a single labour market. Rather, it is the sum of a large number of local, at least partly independent labour markets, within each of which the laws of supply and demand are operating independently. These local markets exist because, just as labour is not completely mobile between occupations, so it is far from completely mobile between places. The distance an average person can, or is prepared to commute each day limits his or her choice of jobs, unless he or she is also prepared to move home. This distance varies considerably, according to personal tastes and incomes, and to the available transport facilities: researchers have suggested, however, that countries such as Britain and the United States can be subdivided into 'daily urban systems' or 'labour market areas' which cover most of the national space-economy (Berry 1973, Hall *et al.* 1973, Johnson, Salt, and Wood 1974).

These separate labour markets within a given country are not completely independent of each other. National wage bargaining by unions, for example, may well establish wage minima, but in many occupations local labour forces may be able to negotiate with employers to obtain payments above these levels. This will be because they are in favourable sellers' market situations. In other words, the Phillips curve trend should be separately applicable to every labour market area. Attempts to apply this have, in general, not been very successful in predicting changes in wage rates. Examination of data for Houston, Los Angeles, Portland, San Franciso, and Seattle, referring to the period 1961–72, found that only for San Francisco could more than half of the variation in wage movements be accounted for by variables reflecting unemployment and price changes in the relevant cities. Indeed, in none of the five cities was the change in wage rates significantly related to the change in unemployment rates; the important determinants were the rate of change in prices and the difference between local wages and the average wages over all five cities, two time periods earlier. In other words, local wages tend to rise in accord with local prices and to bring rewards up to the perceived regional average – which presumably also continues to rise (Marcis and Reed 1974) Similar work with a larger sample of eastern U.S.A. cities has also found little relationship between wage-rate changes and unemployment

King and Foster (1973) suggest that this is because of the need to incorporate measures of the degree of interdependence between labour markets (that is, to what extent labour is mobile between cities). Their conclusion seems to be that we are unable to translate the Phillips curve, which works well at a national level, into a viable model to account for inter-regional wage differentials, despite its inherent logic.

Attempts to relate wage changes to supply:demand ratios in Great Britain have similarly met with difficulties of interpretation, as well as of data collection. Thus Pullen (1966) found little evidence of a good fit to the Phillips curve, for either Britain as a whole or for various regions, although this was not true for one data set he had on regional income levels. Webb (1974), however, found very strong correlations between rate of change of earnings and several independent variables, in combination: rate of change in demand for labour, rate of change in prices, and either unemployment level or level of unfilled vacancies. Of the last two, the level of vacancies was more important in explaining changes in earnings than was the unemployment level: earnings tended to increase by three percentage points during the period 1959–70 for every increase of one percentage point in the unfilled vacancies. Over 80 per cent of the variation in half-yearly earnings-rate changes could be accounted for in the analysis of Britain as a whole, and the average percentage accounted for in analyses of separate regions exceeded seventy. The shape of the Phillips curve was not the same in each region, however, the rate of change being greatest where demand was greatest (that is, where vacancy and unemployment rates were on average low).

Incomes should be highest, therefore, where the supply of labour does not match the demand for it. This general proposition has been tested against New Zealand data (Johnston 1976e), and found valid. Information on (1) the income distribution for each occupational category, and (2) the occupational distribution in each area was combined to predict what the income distribution would be in each area if there were no inter-area variations in wage rates for the same job. Comparison of the predicted and actual income distributions for the areas showed that the large, growing cities had greater-than-predicted proportions of their wage-earners in the high income brackets, whereas 'provincial' New Zealand contained greater percentages of low-income people. This finding is clearly in line with our arguments here. Large, rapidly-growing cities, to which migrants are flocking, are usually those which offer the highest wages because labour is in relatively short supply there: to stay in a small town is generally to forego the high wages, because there are more competitors for the few jobs.

Our argument so far has been that two variables influence spatial differences in incomes: the nature of the jobs performed in a place and the ratio of supply:demand for employees in those jobs. Three further variables can be suggested, however (Hoch 1972a, 1972b, 1974a). The first is that labour is more productive in large cities, since the latter are presumed to be efficient locales: higher incomes thus reflect greater productivity, and can exist even when occupational differences have been standardized. The second is that costs of living are higher in larger cities (see below), and higher wages result because workers (and their unions) demand compensation for their greater costs. Finally, and following on, the quality of the environment in large cities is often poor relative to smaller places (see below again), and the higher incomes paid in the former are 'compensatory payments' for workers having to live in such conditions.

Disentangling the relative contribution of these five variables to the geography of wage differentials is an excessively difficult task. Hoch (1972a) has indicated that *per capita* incomes in New York are 35 per cent above the national average, and he estimates that of this, 9 per cent reflects cost-of-living differences, 8 per cent results from the differences between New York and the nation as a whole in occupational structures (New York has a greater than average proportion of high-income jobs), and the other 18 per cent encompasses the compensatory payments. The latter presumably cover productivity differences and different supply:demand ratios as well as the compensation for a poor environment. Clearly further investigation into this topic is needed, for the differences are substantial and major elements in the geography of opportunity and affluence (Rawstron and Coates 1966).

JOBS, VACANCIES, AND UNEMPLOYMENT

If, as we have suggested, wage levels are partially determined by supply and demand functions for labour in local markets, then the distributions of jobs and vacancies are crucial determinants of levels of living; it is the converse of these distributions — unemployment — which has been most frequently investigated in a geographical context.

Unemployment figures for any place can be divided into a series of components. At a macro-time scale, there are cyclical trends which reflect general economic considerations; these booms and slumps are particularly reflected in certain key industries, such as construction, and so may be magnified in some places relative to others, depending on the local industrial structures — often this is termed 'demand deficient' unemployment. Over shorter periods, there are seasonal fluctuations reflecting trends in labour demand for certain industries, such as tourism in parts of south-western England (Cliff *et al.* 1975); this component can be very marked in some places (Campbell 1975), with consequences on levels of living unless 'out-of-season' alternative employment can be found (as for seaside landladies in some British resorts which were the sites for new universities in the 1960s). At the micro-time scale, there is frictional unemployment, which arises through the sometimes voluntary, sometimes forced, process of changing jobs. Finally, there is structural unemployment, resulting from the lack of demand for particular skills in a given place at a certain time. This differs from any of the others — notably cyclical and seasonal unemployment — in that it is likely to be permanent, the result of certain industries becoming obsolete. It also contains a category often known as concealed unemployment, the best example of which is that group in the population which, knowing that no jobs are available, do not seek work and so are not officially classified as unemployed — the housewives.

Many large cities, as we saw in the preceding chapter, have fewer specialized economic functions than their smaller counterparts, and are thus less open to the consequences of a major recession in a particular industry. In Britain, for example, certain industries are much more sensitive indicators of national recession than are others. For twenty-three major industries, during the period 1949–64 an increase of one percentage point in the national unemployment rate led to an increase of the following percentage points (Thirlwall 1966):

Most Sensitive Industries		*Least Sensitive Industries*	
Textiles	7·758	Insurance/Banking/Finance	0·129
Leather/Fur Goods	2·437	Gas/Electricity/Water	0·214
Clothing/Footwear	1·506	Mining/Quarrying	0·217
Shipbuilding	1·406	Professional/Scientific	0·222
Timber/Furniture	1·342	Vehicles	0·247

The industries in the former group are very much associated with 'one-industry towns', as in the textile-producing districts of Lancashire and Yorkshire, and so it is not surprising that certain places suffer more in periods of recession than do others (see also Estall 1966). Thirlwall (1966) estimates that half of the inter-regional variation in British unemployment rates can be accounted for by the inter-regional variations in economic structure, which is a further example of how the 'control centres' of capitalism are insulated from its major economic vicissitudes.

Some of the major reasons for spatial variations in unemployment

have already been indicated, most notably the decline, temporary ‹
permanent, of certain industries located in certain places. As v
stressed in the previous chapter, much of the pattern of job oppo
tunities, at all spatial scales, is a consequence of the internation
division of labour in a capitalist society. Thus structural unemploymer
is likely to be greatest where industries are declining, as on the coa
fields of many countries in recent years. Separating out the variou
components from a single unemployment total is a difficult analytic
task, but examination of British data suggests the general validity ‹
the above hypothesis. At the time of the 1966 census, male unen
ployment increased by 0·7 per cent for every tenfold increase in cit
size, whereas for females unemployment levels fell by 0·46 per cer
for a comparable size increase (Vipond 1974). Holding this relatio
ship constant, unemployment was on average 1·9 per cent higher fc
males and 1·0 per cent higher for the females in towns within th
development areas, suggesting that structural unemployment is greate
there. (An alternative interpretation is that workers in developmer
areas take longer to find a new job, which again suggests a clear in
balance between supply and demand.) The city size variable sugges
that structural unemployment is greater in small towns, a function
probably, of the absence of several comparable employers in suc
places.

Spatio-Temporal Trends. The analysis of the unemployment pattern at on
point in time throws light on its spatial correlates. There should als
be spatial variations in unemployment trends since different labou
markets in a country are not independent. A rise of wages in one fc
a particular occupation can lead to demands for comparable rises i
others, so that certain regions may be 'inflation leaders'; a decline i
employment in industries in one place could lead to unemploymen
elsewhere, because of economic linkages. London is often regarded a
an 'inflation leader' in Britain because of its under-supply of employee
for certain occupations, such as secretaries. It may also be an 'ur
employment leader' in certain circumstances. The complexity o
modern industrial processes means that the transition from raw m:
terials to finished products involves many steps and stops in the pr‹
duction chain. Most factories take as their inputs the outputs of othe
factories, and in turn pass their outputs on for further processin
Such linkages are often between nearby factories, to encourage eff
ciency in the flows of goods. But many flows will be between labou
markets, and will be paralleled by inter-market flows of growth an
decline impulses. Thus, in an economy as a whole it is possible t‹

identify 'lead' industries, those in which growth generates growth in others, through demands for inputs, and 'lag' industries, those whose growth is dependent on expansion elsewhere in the economy and are unlikely to experience much autonomous expansion. Placing these industries in their spatial context, we can suggest that there should be groups of labour markets which experience common employment trends because of the strong links between their industries, with, in each group, a separation of the labour markets into those that 'lead' and those that 'lag'.

Two groups of researchers have produced a considerable volume of research on inter-regional linkages in unemployment trends in recent years, attempting to identify groups of labour markets with common experiences, and hence common temporal patterns of economic vicissitudes, which will be reflected in level of social well-being indices. Within the United States Jeffrey (1974) has identified seven regional systems among the unemployment trends for the period 1960–5, referring to 140 separate urban areas. Some of these seven systems involve groups of towns with similar industrial structures, which might be expected to have parallel trends of business prosperity and depression (an example is the group of five 'automobile-manufacture cities' – Detroit, Flint, Lansing, Saginaw, and Dayton); others comprise cities which are spatially clustered but have different industrial structures, suggesting very obvious geographical patterns to local fortunes. Similar patterns have been noted in work on southwestern England (Cliff *et al.* 1975), in which attempts have been made to identify whether any particular city 'leads' within its group, and is thus the source of the impulses which lead to either prosperity and low unemployment or the converse, recession.

The transmission of economic growth and recession impulses operates at the international scale also, as was made clear by the worldwide effect of the 1929 Wall Street crash and the 1973 rise in crude oil prices. The 'industrial revolution' spread out from its original core in Britain in a radial fashion through Europe (Casetti, King, and Williams 1972), while at the same time places increasingly far away were being drawn into the British 'food-producing' orbit (Chisholm 1962, Peet 1969). For the latter, many countries – the tropical 'sugar islands' of the Caribbean, the temperate pastoral lands such as New Zealand, and the prairies of Canada and Australia – came to occupy niches in an economic system based on the reciprocal exchange of British manufactures for colonial food and raw materials. The economies of the 'far-flung outposts of Empire' were integrated with Britain's, and rose and fell in concert with the latter; the well-being of the colonial populations varied accordingly.

Within countries, these foci of economic impulses have been identified in recent years as 'growth poles' (Darwent 1969), places which experience some form of spontaneous growth that influences the economic fortunes of other areas. (Most research workers seem to be optimistic, as there is no parallel literature on 'decline poles'!) Growth in the larger centre is beneficial to centres nearby since it offers opportunities for manufacturers in the latter to sell components to factories in the growth centres and also to make goods for sale to the consumers in the enlarged local market. Thus settlements close to large towns are more likely to grow than are those which are more isolated from a growth pole, and so have a harder task finding markets for their products (Johnston 1969a, 1969b); one result is that the inhabitants of towns benefitting from the 'trickle down' effect of expansion in a nearby centre are likely to become more prosperous, and Odland, Casetti, and King (1973) have shown that, among 244 small settlements in part of the American Midwest, retail sales increased more rapidly during the period 1948–67 in those near to the main centres of Chicago, Indianapolis, Cleveland, Cincinnatti, Columbus, and Detroit and also, secondarily, in those close to other, though not as important, large urban centres. Thus, within an urban system prosperity is likely to be greatest in the larger cities with the more diverse economies and this prosperity is often shared with nearby towns, which receive some 'overspill' of the large-city's growth and participate in its general economy (Keeble and Hauser 1971, 1972).

Combating the Phillips Curve: Migration. Although labour markets are in many ways closely linked, unemployment and wage level variations between areas are frequently maintained because of their spatial independence. As clearly indicated, workers are limited by their commuting range as to the jobs which they can take. This may occur even within a single large city. In London, for example, many new manual service jobs are being created annually in the central area, in hotels, office blocks, and so on, but the people eligible for these jobs are being moved, through 'redevelopment' schemes, to new housing in outer suburbs. In Chicago and comparable American cities, industries have moved to the outer suburbs in great numbers but residents of inner-city ghettos — notably blacks — are often prohibited from taking jobs in the suburbs because of the time, cost, and, sometimes, the sheer impossibility of the necessary 'reverse commuting'.

Because of the spatial separation of jobs and unemployed the logic of the Phillips curve is that the regional variations in unemployment and wage-rate differentials will increase. Wage inflation will be great where labour demand exceeds supply, and low where the converse holds. People, of course, will react to this by moving; employers may move jobs to where labour is cheap, and workers may move to where jobs are plentiful and wages high. At the world scale, the former reaction has occurred with companies transferring certain of their processes to 'cheaper' places (as, for example, with the tourist boom presently occurring around the Mediterranean and the movement of labour-intensive industries to places like Mexico and Taiwan), and the latter with the great out-pourings of migrants from Europe to the 'brave New Worlds' of America and Australasia whilst Asians and Africans seek the better wages of Europe. In several cases, rather than 'export' their industries, countries 'import' workers — in Europe in 1965, 2·8 million workers from Greece, Italy, Portugal, Spain, Turkey, and Yugoslavia were employed elsewhere, most in West Germany, France, and Switzerland (Magee 1971) — subsequently sending them 'home' during periods of economic recession ('exporting their unemployed'!). Within countries, too, firms may set up branch factories in regions where labour is relatively cheap, and also less likely to move to other jobs. Migrants are attracted to the apparently better and securer levels of living: in the United States, movement between labour market areas between 1955 and 1960 showed net flows towards areas of low unemployment and high median incomes (Schwind 1971); in Britain, similar factors operate, although it is the higher-paid who are apparently best able to discover and move to the attractive opportunities (Johnson, Salt, and Wood 1974).

If the factors of production — land, labour, and capital — were all perfectly mobile, spatial variations in wage levels and unemployment would be removed. Jobs would move to where labour was cheaper, changing the supply:demand ratio in favour of the worker; workers would move to where wages were higher, changing the ratio in favour of the seller, the employer. An equilibrium would result. Disturbances to it would occur, as some industries grew and others declined, and as population growth rates varied, but these would be minor. However, the factors of production are not very mobile, despite efforts, such as those of the European Economic Community, to increase their movements. At the international scale most governments regulate migrations, acting to preserve their *status quo* in the international economy rather than to produce a better-regulated total system: they do not even, it would seem, allow flows of one factor to compensate the lack of flow of others (Freeman 1973). And, of course, many people, for one reason or another, do not want to move, because of the capital —

real, social, or psychological — which they have invested in a particular place. Of those who wish to move, the worst-off may be least able to, because of constraints of cost and ignorance: in New Zealand it is the professionals who have the nationwide job-information systems (Keown 1971); in Britain the unemployed are apparently relatively immobile (Johnson, Salt, and Wood 1974), and the movement of jobs may be of little benefit to populations in recipient areas if the key workers are brought in from outside. Much migration today in the 'developed' countries, and also between countries, is what has been called an 'inter-metropolitan circulation of élites' (Taeuber and Taeuber 1964); highly paid professionals move from city to city, and country to country, in pursuit of career advancement, whilst the poorly paid unskilled are either trapped in their 'deprived' home areas or they drift to something slightly better, but rarely to security and prosperity. In an Australian case study, Holmes (1971) has shown that long-distance commuting may be an initial reaction to a local decline in jobs, given the availability of opportunities within travelling distance, but doubts whether this will produce a long-term equilibrium, except where the formerly independent settlements are engulfed by suburbanization. In general, then, inequalities remain.

SPATIAL VARIATIONS IN LIVING COSTS

Our discussion so far has indicated that where one lives is a partial determinant of how much one is paid for a certain job, and of the security of that job. The geography of money incomes, however, is only one aspect of the geography of real incomes. What one can buy with £1 in one part of Britain, for example, may cost only £0·80 somewhere else, so that the person in the latter place is as well-off as the resident of the former, even if he is paid 20 per cent less. In part this follows from our Phillips curve analyses: if labour costs more in X than Y, then goods produced in X may be more expensive — but goods are generally more mobile than people, and are often sent in search of the highest prices. Further, many goods have standard prices over an area either because of regulation, which makes life easier for the seller, or because transport costs form such a small proportion of the total cost that a spatial pricing policy is unnecessary.

To assess whether the differences in money incomes between places mean differences in real incomes requires analysis of spatial variation in prices. This is often attempted, albeit in a small way only, in comparisons of the costs of standard 'baskets of goods' (that is, the same products) in different capital cities (many newspapers undertake such regular surveys), and it became an issue during the 1975 debate on Britain's continued membership of the EEC. Such comparisons are fraught with difficulties: different countries have contrasting cultural norms towards certain items (the amount of fish which is eaten, for example), and climatic variations lead to different demands for clothing, shelter, and home-heating. To say that residents of country X are better off than those of country Y is to invite criticism, therefore, because of different attitudes to, and needs for, various items. Large-scale contrasts can be drawn, of course, between the quality of diet which can be bought by unskilled workers in, say, Canada and Colombia, and when we are dealing at this scale perhaps further detail is unnecessary; the contrast between poverty and plenty is all too obvious, as is its relationship to the international division of labour.

Within countries many of these difficulties are not so apparent, though this may be less so in large countries with great climatic variations, such as the United States and the Soviet Union. In New Zealand, for example, it is possible to compare living costs between the large (metropolitan), medium-sized (provincial), and small cities. The consumers' price index, which is calculated quarterly, is based on the prices for six groups of items, weighted in the following manner, in line with observed family expenditure patterns:

Food	30·09%	Apparel	10·91%
Housing	17·99%	Transportation	9·44%
Household Operation	11·21%	Miscellaneous	18·15%

The base for the index is June 1965 (=1000), and Table 5.2 shows the changes in the components of the index, by size of place, to 1972.

In Table 5.2, columns A and B for each group of centres show the relevant indices for that group in 1965 and 1972; columns C and D show the relevant indices for that group relative to the national pattern. Thus in 1965, column C shows that the four metropolitan centres were above average in every component of the cost of living except household operation (fuel and light, furnishing, domestic supplies); the ten provincial centres were not above average in any category; and household operation was relatively very expensive in the small towns, whereas housing was cheap there. Over the seven-year period, living costs increased by about 51 per cent in the metropolitan centres, and 49 per cent in the provincial and small towns. The greatest increases were in housing, transportation, and miscellaneous costs.

For Britain, a recent survey conducted by the Association of University Teachers (1975) shows similar spatial variations in basic living costs (Table 5.3) for towns with universities. As would be

Table 5.2

Changes in the cost-of-living index : New Zealand

	Four Metropolitan Centres				Ten Provincial Centres				Eleven Small Towns			
	A	B	C	D	A	B	C	D	A	B	C	D
Food	1000	1430	1011	1446	1000	1450	985	1429	1000	1435	995	1428
Housing	1000	1572	1061	1669	1000	1555	951	1478	1000	1528	907	1386
Household operation	1000	1405	996	1400	1000	1374	993	1365	1000	1406	1026	1442
Apparel	1000	1461	1004	1468	1000	1424	1000	1424	1000	1437	987	1419
Transportation	1000	1621	1000	1621	1000	1551	1000	1551	1000	1533	1060	1534
Miscellaneous	1000	1606	1001	1608	1000	1606	996	1599	1000	1598	1063	1603
Total	1000	1508	1015	1530	1000	1494	985	1472	1000	1487	983	1462

Source: New Zealand Department of Statistics 1974, pp. 17–20. For key to columns, see text.

expected, London came out as the most expensive place in which to live, mainly because of its much more costly housing and the higher travel expenses incurred in large-city commuting. University teachers living in London received an extra weighting of £213 per annum on their salary (in 1974), but this clearly did not compensate them for their much higher living costs relative to colleagues in, say, Hull. Which group, then, has the highest real income?

Housing Costs. The data just discussed have indicated not only that housing is a major expense but that its cost varies considerably from place to place within a country. Furthermore, the last few years have been a period of very rapid inflation in property values in many countries, and this could well be accentuating the spatial variations in this component of the cost of living.

Housing markets operate in very much the same way as labour markets, being spatially independent, since for most people a house in one place is not replaceable by a house in another. Thus variations in the price of housing should reflect the supply and demand situations, the expensive areas being those where supply does not match demand — which are likely to be the rapidly growing places. Over a reasonable period of time, the construction industry might be expected to react to these variations by providing more housing where it is in most demand. It is not in their interest to provide a supply which will match demand, however, since this will reduce prices; profit-maximizing strategies will lead to relative shortages in order to maintain the inflation of prices where demand is greatest.

Each housing market is, in effect, a mosaic of sub-markets. It can be divided, for example, into various tenure and quality groups, and an additional variable can be added — location within the urban area. The classical models of urban land value patterns (for example, Alonso 1964) are built on the assumption that housing provides not only shelter but also a base for movement, for the daily and weekly journeys of a household, to work, to shop, to play, etc. All other things being equal, it is assumed that people wish to minimize transport costs, so that they will pay more for housing in accessible locations. If we assume that all journeys focus on the city centre, then the most expensive property will be in the city centre; the further out one goes, the cheaper property will become (Fig. 4.13).

Not all journeys do terminate in the city centre, of course, and so the property value pattern of an urban area is usually multi-modal rather than uni-modal. The city centre is likely to be the most dominant node, however, and this has been observed in many empirical

Table 5.3

Regional variations in living costs : United Kingdom, 1974

Region and University Town	Annual Costs (£) of			
	Mortgage[a] 3-Bedroom House	Mortgage[a] 4-Bedroom House	Food, Fuel[b] Light, Power	Fares[c] to Work
South East				
London	1305	2458	676	180
Canterbury	1023	1846	669	53
Guildford	1129	2306	669	115
Oxford	952	1540	669	39
Reading	1058	1836	669	93
Southampton	1023	1682	669	37
Brighton	1070	2035	669	72
South West				
Bath	1047	1800	646	97
Bristol	952	1682	646	86
Exeter	918	1741	646	59
West Midlands				
Birmingham	717	1317	636	86
Keele	659	1270	636	31
Warwick	906	2223	636	96
North West				
Lancaster	752	1388	631	95
Liverpool	741	1270	631	92
Manchester/Salford	741	1459	631	118
North				
Durham	729	1234	619	43
Newcastle	800	1718	619	51
Yorkshire				
Bradford	670	1305	614	80
Hull	705	1035	614	47
Leeds	705	1764	614	45
Sheffield	659	1670	614	37
York	683	1411	614	58
East Midlands				
Leicester	741	1494	596	34
Loughborough	776	1564	596	26
Nottingham	741	1317	596	51
East Anglia				
Cambridge	1047	1623	583	25
Norwich	789	1564	583	81
Colchester	918	1518	583	103

Table 5.3. (continued)

| Region and University Town | Annual Costs (£) of | | | |
	Mortgage[a] 3–Bedroom House	Mortgage[a] 4–Bedroom House	Food, Fuel[b] Light, Power	Fares[c] to Work
Wales				
Aberystwyth	1011	1670	657	38
Bangor	694	1141	657	56
Cardiff	812	1435	657	82
Lampeter	859	1411	657	6
Swansea	800	1635	657	47
Scotland				
Aberdeen	1176	1836	653	73
Dundee	1234	1940	653	38
Edinburgh	1141	1587	653	52
Glasgow	1047	1447	653	81
St. Andrews	977	1764	653	38
Stirling	683	1141	653	45
Ulster				
Belfast	NK	NK	691	40
Coleraine	NK	NK	691	63

Source: Association of University Teachers, *Regional Costs Survey, 1975*, (1975), pp.6–11.

a Mortgage repayments were based on a 75% loan, at 11%, repayable over 25 years for average-priced homes in areas where university staff live.

b Amounts spent on food, fuel, light, and power were estimated from the regional tables in the Government's *Family Expenditure Survey*.

c Annual costs of fares were established from questionnaire returns provided by AUT members.

studies (see Johnston 1973). In different cities, the slope and altitude of this distance/property value gradient may vary according to their size. The larger the city, the greater the range of accessibility for different locations, and so the higher the price which might be asked, and paid, for the 'better' locations.

So far, we have suggested that property values are greatest in the larger and the more rapidly expanding urban areas: such variation, it would seem, is probably more a consequence of differences in land values than of the costs of housing itself. Data published by the Nationwide Building Society for British regions (Table 5.4) illustrate the nature of these spatial variations very clearly: in 1974, the average downpayment required for a mortgage in Greater London was three times that for the Northern region, and involved a much greater proportion of the borrower's annual income. In New Zealand, the average price of a building plot in the Auckland urban area, in 1973, was $6290, whereas in Greymouth, a small town in the South Island, it was only $1789. Over the preceding eight years, land prices increased by 193 per cent in Auckland compared to an increase in house costs of only 133 per cent. Analyses have shown (Johnston 1976d) that the spatial variations in house and land prices among New Zealand towns are closely related to their size and growth rates.

It is possible to suggest reasons for spatial variations in housing costs, therefore, but these deal only with relative and not with absolute differences between places (Harvey 1973). Housing and land are used by many people not just as basic components in the provision of a home but also as investments. Housing, for example, is treated by some as a status symbol, and the price of the 'desirable' is inflated accordingly. It is also used by many as a source of capital gain, particularly in periods when other forms of investment — notably industrial stocks and shares — offer poor returns. Thus land price inflation in Britain and elsewhere in recent years can be explained by the activity of speculators (Davidson 1975), aided by the estate agents and financial institutions whose businesses thrive on high turnover rates for property, at high prices. Only a model of the housing market which includes the actions of these people, many of them quasi-monopolists because of the locational uniqueness of their properties (Johnston 1976d), can account for the phenomenal rates of price inflation recorded in Table 5.4.

The various groups involved in the operation of land and housing markets manipulate them for their own ends, and these involve profit (Harvey 1974b). By reducing supply in different areas relative to demand, they can engineer price increases, and in doing this they are often aided by government actions aimed at other ends. Planning legislation in many countries is aimed at preventing urban sprawl, minimizing the effect of noxious land uses, and promoting orderly urban development. But, by restricting the amount of land available for development, it strengthens the sellers' market and encourages speculation and price rises (Boal 1970, Goodall 1970), just as the ban on new office building in central London during the mid-1960s encouraged a boom in office rents (Marriott 1967).

In the residential market, sub-markets are formed by the policies of lending institutions, regarding who they will advance a mortgage to and where (Harvey 1974b, 1975, Ford 1975). Supply:demand ratios can be altered considerably by 'red lining' policies, which determine the areas in which agencies are prepared to invest money; by

Table 5.4

Mortgage costs in the United Kingdom

Region	% Increase Sale Price 1965–1974	% Increase Average Income of Mortgagees	Downpayment Needed			Downpayment as % of Income		
			1969 £	1974 £	% Increase	1969	1974	% Increase
North	126	76	1011	2865	183	64	85	32
Yorks/Humberside	132	89	802	3322	314	54	118	98
East Midlands	132	78	1007	4409	338	64	157	145
East Anglia	151	95	1249	5669	354	75	175	133
Greater London	146	94	2002	8644	331	93	206	122
South East	140	78	1814	8097	346	90	226	151
South West	157	84	1340	5075	279	81	167	106
West Midlands	135	93	1238	5195	320	75	165	119
North West	123	82	1010	3150	212	62	106	71
Wales	120	66	1145	4464	290	67	157	134
Scotland	111	80	1287	4815	274	70	145	107
N. Ireland	116	131	1008	3734	270	66	106	61

Source: Department of the Environment 1974, pp. 45–7.

'gentrification' policies in which the actions of a few individuals ma stimulate redevelopment in an area, perhaps with the aid of governmer grants (Ambrose and Colenutt 1975, Hamnett 1973); by plannir policies which determine acceptable densities for different areas an which decide whether public money will be invested, for improvemer of dwelling conditions, for example (Duncan 1974); and by the dec sions of public housing managers to allocate their 'problem' famili to particular estates or even streets (Baldwin 1975, Coates and Silbur 1970). The consequences of such zoning — implicit or explicit — a almost always associated with an increase in housing demand by are relative to supply, and thus with rising prices. By restricting mortgag availability to certain areas, prices are usually enhanced there; b making certain areas unacceptable for mortgages private landlords a able to exploit them by charging high rents, or private financie are able to exploit the inability of certain groups to obtain mortgage by charging them high interest rates and prices (Harvey 1975). Eac separate area becomes a quasi-monopoly, with the expected cons quence for housing costs.

Spatial variations in housing costs result from different supply demand ratios, especially for land in separate market areas; therefor in general, costs are greatest, and increase fastest, in the largest, mo rapidly growing cities where public restrictions on urban developmer are strict but the property market is largely in the hands of the privat sector. The inequalities which these patterns produce are comple Those already owning property prior to the onset of rapid inflatio receive unearned capital gains relative to the rate of inflation; thos buying later must pay relatively high prices; those moving for jo opportunities are probably going from a low- (slow growth) to a high cost housing market, with consequent falls in their living standard because of the greater expenditure on housing. This further inhibit the mobility of labour to which we have already referred.

Food and Consumer Goods Prices. The data in Tables 5.2 and 5.3 suggest tha spatial variations in prices for food and other goods normally bought i shops are not great. Nevertheless, such variations clearly do exist: a the time of writing, one of us had on his desk a paperback book with recommended United Kingdom price of 80p and a New Zealand pric of $2.75, although the exchange rate at the time was approximatel UK £1 = NZ $1.80. A number of factors create such price difference The costs of producing a good may be standard, although this is un likely if it is produced in several places because of variations in the pric of labour, raw materials, and overheads (Smith 1971). For a goo produced in one place, however, an element in its final price is the cost of transporting it to the retailer.

At the international scale, all of these factors come into play. Many countries are small, dependent on overseas suppliers for raw materials and finished components, and can sell only small volumes of many goods. Thus their factories are unable to benefit from the economies of large-scale production, and their goods are expensive relative to those produced by the larger, wealthier countries. But often they are unable to import goods at cheap prices, and more intermediaries are often involved. Their small markets mean that the economies of scale are not enjoyed in moving the goods to them, so that transport costs are great. (Many countries, for example, consume insufficient oil to make visits to their ports by supertankers worth while, so their oil imports are carried by the relatively more expensive smaller tankers (Couper 1972).) In other words, many countries are sellers' markets with regard to imported goods, so that their living costs are relatively high. And often, too, they are disadvantaged with regard to their exports; producers of temperate-zone agricultural goods, in particular, frequently have to pay the transport costs of their products to the buyers' market. Thus such countries often pay transport costs on both imports and exports, to the detriment of their standard of living and the benefit of that of their trading partners (Johnston 1975b).

Within countries, many goods are sold at standard prices, although there are some variations from this practice such as the arbitrary basing-points on which c.i.f. steel prices are based (Warren 1966). Under such a standardization system, the consumers living near to the production point tend to subsidize, although probably only very slightly, those who live further away. But free markets do operate for some commodities, in very much the same way that they do for labour and housing. The greater the supply of a commodity in a place relative to the demand for it, the lower its price should be, and vice versa. Warntz (1959) investigated the validity of this notion in a pioneer work on the geographical variation of prices for four farm products — wheat, potatoes, onions, and strawberries — among the states of the conterminous United States. The average price paid to a farmer for a bushel of wheat over the whole country during the 1940s, for example, was $1.51, but farmers in North and South Carolina, far from 'the wheat belt', received $1.71 and $1.68 respectively for bushels of their product, whereas the average price paid in Idaho was only $1.39. For each of the four commodities, Warntz showed that between 52 and 76 per cent of the variation in the price received by farmers could be accounted for by just three factors: the supply of the commodity in the area, the demand for the commodity in the area, and the timing of the supply in the area (the date of harvest) relative to the timing of the supply elsewhere. He concluded that the universal effect of an increased demand, all other things being equal, was a higher price, so that, for example, of two states producing the same amount of onions, that with the largest local market for those onions would have the highest price paid to the farmer. Similarly, holding demand constant, an increase in the supply led to a depression in the price.

Warntz's findings suggest a clear spatial pattern of price variations which, if it applies to sufficient commodities, could strongly influence living costs within a country. Another way of looking at this pattern, therefore, is to inquire about the cost of a certain diet in different parts of a country, a task which has been attempted for Guatemala by Gould and Sparks (1969). They defined a basic minimum diet, providing the necessary calories, protein, and vitamin C levels, and, from data on prices for forty different foodstuffs at various Guatemalan markets, estimated the cost of this basic diet, comprising a combination of foods from those available, at each of the twenty-four towns. Various constraints were added to different solutions (for example, that one-third of the protein came from animal sources), but the general pattern of prices remained much the same. The main cities — Guatemala City, Quezaltenango, and Escuintla — stood out as the highest-cost centres, with the basic diet there costing 12·4, 12·8, and 13·2 cents daily, compared to the national average of 10·2 cents; the transport costs of bringing food in to these centres of demand were clearly important in causing such a price differential, one which applied not only to the large towns but also to the smaller ones in their vicinity, with which they were in competition for food supplies.

Even for standardized products — deep frozen, canned etc. — retail price maintenance is rare and shopkeepers are able to vary their prices in order to attract custom. Two variables apparently influence the amount of price-cutting — the type of retail organization and competition. The latter operates in a spatial context, again according to the laws of supply and demand in separate markets.

In the food-retailing industry, three types of store can be identified: the large supermarket, which is usually one of a chain of such stores; the independent grocer who is a member of a chain group for buying and advertising purposes, and who may operate his shop as a supermarket; and the wholly independent shop, usually a family business. In terms of use of land and labour, the first of these is usually the most efficient and the last the least so. A consequence of this is the amount of price-cutting which can be undertaken, and a survey in Melbourne

(Table 5.5; Johnston and Rimmer 1969) showed that the various supermarket chains were able to offer more 'specials' per week (goods sold below the manufacturers' recommended price) than were stores in the buying chains. These organizations are able to benefit from the economies of large-scale operation, notably buying in bulk and by-passing the independent wholesalers. Similar patterns, though less marked in some countries, occur in the retailing of other goods.

Table 5.5

Food store types and 'specials' offered according to
newspaper advertisements:
Melbourne, 6 August 1966.
The initial letters refer to different supermarket chains and
grocer groups.

NUMBER OF 'SPECIALS' OFFERED

I SUPERMARKET CHAINS

A.	43	B.	34	C.	32

II INDEPENDENT GROCERS IN BUYING AND ADVERTISING GROUPS

A.	36	B.	23	C.	14
D.	22	E.	20		

Source: Johnston and Rimmer 1969, p.41.

Supermarkets and other large stores depend on very high levels of turnover for their survival, and so are not usually found in small towns and areas of low population density (Cohen 1972). Thus where one lives can well influence the cost of goods. Small-town residents have only relatively expensive local shops to buy at, if they are not prepared to pay the costs of travel to larger centres — and as Table 5.2 suggests, transport costs are increasing more rapidly than most others. (This pattern is the reverse of that found in the Guatemalan study, because there foodstuffs were locally produced near small towns rather than 'imported'.) This was found to be so in a survey of the Athlone area in the Republic of Ireland (Parker 1974a). The prices of ninety-seven different items were investigated in a sample of shops representing centres of three different sizes and three types of establishment — supermarkets, grocers affiliated to buying chains, and independent grocers. Supermarkets stood out as the cheapest places at which to shop and, as these were only to be found in the large and medium-sized centres, this led to the conclusion that 'lower prices are charged for grocery products in larger centres compared to medium-sized centres, and in medium-sized centres compared to small centres' (Parker 1974a, p.87). Furthermore, only the supermarkets among the three shop types were likely to offer the whole range of goods surveyed, so residents of small centres also suffered from limitation of choice of goods. A similar study in Northern Ireland (O'Farrell and Poole 1972) found no clear-cut relationships, however; the main conclusion was that stores in the west of the province were on average cheaper, because, it was suggested, shopkeepers are discouraged from charging high prices by the low incomes of their customers.

The geography of prices in shops is also influenced by the amount of competition in the area, in the same way as the pattern of wheat prices to farmers. The greater a shop's monopoly over its customers, the less concerned it need be about price-cutting. Thus isolated stores, whether in separate settlements or different parts of a town, may be more expensive than those with direct competition in the same shopping centre. (One gets no cut-price petrol on the British motorways, for example, because there are no competitors to the single selling points every 40–50 kilometres.) In the Athlone survey just referred to, it was found that 'the larger the centre the cheaper are the supermarkets, the affiliated grocers and the independent grocers . . . probably due to the intensity of competition which decreases from large centres through medium-sized centres to small centres' (Parker 1974a, p.87): thus supermarkets in Athlone charged an average £17.31 for the ninety-seven items, whereas supermarkets in the medium-sized centres charged £17.52. The absence of spatial competition was also shown to be conducive to higher prices in a parallel study of variations within the Dublin urban area (Parker 1974b). Isolated grocers' stores were, on average, more expensive for a standard set of twenty items than were stores located in centres with other grocery stores, and within the three types of retail organization a shop was on average more expensive if there were no similar shop within 0·2 miles.

Although there are marked place-to-place variations in the costs of many consumer goods, it must be recognized that these differences are often slight compared to those reported for farm prices and basic foodstuffs sold in market places (from the work of Warntz and of Gould and Sparks). The reason for this is given by Galbraith (1975) who identifies two separate price-fixing mechanisms, that of the market system and that of the planning system. In the former, the market is characterized by a large number of buyers and sellers, no one of whom either buys or sells a sufficient proportion of all the goods sold to be able to influence their price. This is the classical perfect competition of economists, in which supply:demand ratios at a particular market determine the price. In the planning system, however, the ratio of buyers to sellers is very different and one group can dominate the market and impose its price. Usually this is the case with consumer goods produced by large firms, sometimes with a spatial monopoly but more frequently in competition with two or three other producers — only this 'competition' rarely involves prices, as purchasers of motor cars are aware. Dealers who retail these products usually have a little flexibility, as they balance volume of sales against profit margin to produce an acceptable total income, but price variations under this system are usually relatively slight. Occasionally the monopoly or oligopoly is in favour of the buyer, as with the small number of firms who purchase wool at the annual auctions in New Zealand.

The greatest spatial variations in prices, at least within an individual country, thus refer to the goods sold in the market system. Farm products form a major component of these, thus creating considerable revenue differentials for farmers — which might be balanced by lower production costs; possible large fluctuations in the prices of farm commodities, as happens in the international market where over-supply depresses prices, which can lead to further over-supply merely to maintain income levels; and higher prices for buyers where supply is low relative to demand, a consequence which is particularly disadvantageous to the poor residents of large cities.

It is interesting to note that differentiation between a market system and a planning system may be developing in Britain with regard to regional variations in wage rates. Hart and MacKay (1975) have shown that there has been a considerable reduction in the variations among twenty-eight areas in the earnings' rates for fitters and for labourers working for members of the Engineering Employers Federation. Over the period 1914–68 there was a fairly stable regional hierarchy, with the highest earnings' rates in London, Coventry, Derby, and the West Midlands. The growth of national wage bargaining has resulted in earnings in other areas coming closer to those paid in the 'wage leader' areas, where unemployment has tended to be relatively low: in other words, it is suggested that strong union pressure can lead to considerable reduction of spatial variations in earnings' rates, as the labour market becomes characterized by a few buyers and a single seller.

ACCESS, COST, AND REAL INCOME

Our information on spatial variations in costs is too sketchy for any firm statements about the geography of the cost of living. We have plenty of fragmentary pieces of evidence, however, which suggest that where one lives can be a significant influence on one's real income, on what can be obtained for one's money income, and what facilities are generally available. In general, the greater the demand relative to the supply, the greater the price, which in a spatial context suggests that incomes and costs are both higher, the larger the place. Whether the extra income balances the extra expenditure is far from clear, however.

So far, we have looked only at goods which are priced and widely sold, such as food and dwellings. In increasingly leisure- and culture-conscious societies, however, there is a much wider range of 'goods' which go to make up the 'quality of life'. For many of these — theatres, restaurants, museums, art galleries, and 'night life' in general — the large city offers a greater range of opportunities. Indeed, many people are unable to gain regular access to such facilities because of both the transport costs involved and the time. Smaller settlements, on the other hand, may have much easier access to rural areas and much less pressure on available open space. Again, it is difficult to strike a balance, and one could argue that people have the choice of where to live. For all facilities which are financially based, however, the larger cities increasingly seem to be benefiting. In professional sport, for example, as the participants demand ever-higher wages so it is only the large cities, with the guaranteed large audiences, that can afford to support facilities. Relatively small towns, such as Carlisle in recent years for example, find it very difficult to raise the revenue to support a first division soccer team in England, and cricket tests in Australia are only ever held in the five metropolitan centres (with Perth but recently added to the list of places). The decline of the small-town cinema is another example of this evolving pattern (Bertram 1970).

Access to certain leisure facilities used on a short-term basis may be better in some places than others, therefore, as also might access to tourist centres. In Britain, for example, package tours to the Mediterranean are very popular at present, and are generally cheaper than holidays of a comparable length 'at home'. But these package tours are based on a few regional airports: the further one lives from one, the more expensive the holiday.

All of these differences in real income operate at every spatial scale. Internationally, it is only the countries with a large enough affluent audience that can attract major cultural and sporting items like theatre groups and orchestras, world title fights, and Olympic Games; small countries offer insufficient financial returns to cover the cost of a visit unless, as with Mohammed Ali's world heavyweight contests in Zaire Malaysia, and the Philippines, world TV rights can be sold as well

Thus cultural impoverishment is a possible consequence of small size and relative isolation. Within cities, too, there is generally a far from equitable distribution of, for example, parks, cheap supermarkets, doctors' surgeries, fire stations, and a host of other facilities, provided both by private enterprise and by local governments. Many people are unprepared, if not unable, to travel far for such facilities, and thus are deprived if the distribution does not match their requirements. A great proportion of parents are not prepared to let children travel far to a playground, so infants in some areas never play on swings and slides; others may not be able to visit doctors frequently because surgery hours do not fit their time schedules (Palm and Pred 1974). Elderly people, too, are frequently confined to very limited areas, and so are unable to visit many facilities that they might wish to use (Golant 1972).

Patterns of relative location to facilities provided only at certain points can markedly influence levels of real income among residents of a city or a country, therefore. Girt (1973), for example, has shown how a person's access to a surgery in a rural area is related to his propensity to consult a doctor, and the large Chicago Hospital Study has indicated the relative deprivation of social groups who are forced, by the constraints of the system, to travel long distances for hospital out-patient visits (de Visé 1973). Where a birth control clinic is sited can influence who will use it (Fuller 1974), as can the location of a polling booth (A.H. Taylor 1973). Summing together all the costs and benefits of various locations is probably an impossible task. We can identify inequalities in most distributions, but as yet we find it hard to produce a total map of all inequality. Awareness of a problem, however, is at least part of the battle towards its removal.

Health and Security. Many aspects of one's social well-being are neither traded in the market-place nor consumed by attendance at publicly provided facilities. Health and security are continuous features, influenced by a range of characteristics over which the individual may have very little control. With these, as with everything else discussed so far in this chapter, where one lives can have a strong influence on the nature and extent of those characteristics, and hence on components of one's quality of life.

The aetiology of diseases is immensely varied. Different physical environments may be particularly favourable to the development of certain diseases; drinking supplies of soft water, for example, are closely correlated with high mortality levels from cardio-vascular disease (Howe 1972). An obvious environmental hazard to health is

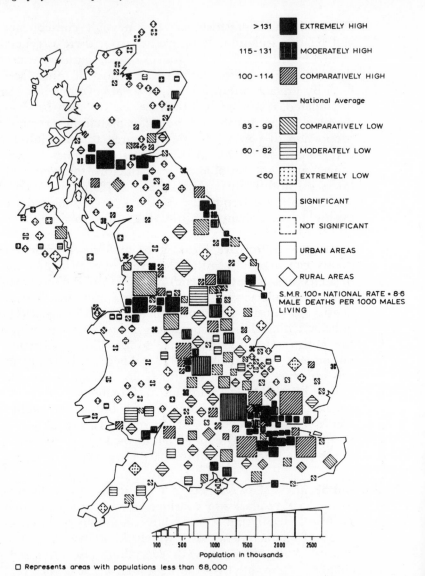

Fig.5.3. Standardized Mortality Rates for deaths from cancer of the trachea, lung, and bronchus among males, 1959–63, in the United Kingdom. (Source: Howe 1970, p.110.)

pollution, and a map of standardized (for age) mortality rates for cancer of the trachea, lung, and bronchus among males (Fig.5.3) suggests a clear relationship with both urban size, where hydrocarbons from petrol burning are concentrated, and centres of heavy industrial activity (Howe 1970).

Aspects of the man-made environment are also causally related to disease development and transmission. The higher the population density in an area, the greater the probability of contact with a person carrying an infectious or contagious disease, so that many urban settings, notably those in which sanitary standards are low, are very open to epidemics. Other diseases are largely man-induced. Some, such as cancer from smoking, are unlikely to show any spatial variations in cause or effect, unless the incidence of smoking is variable, perhaps related to the frustrations of certain environments (urban?) relative to others. Several complaints are consequences of various forms of pollution, particularly air pollution, and so are more probable in the heavily industrialized areas and in large cities, where fumes from the high densities of traffic are often a major cause of pollution and disease, assisted by the climatic modifications wrought by the mushrooming of the built environment (Hoch 1972b). Urban residents are more likely to suffer some debilitation, if not actual sickness, causing absence from work and demands on the health services, than are the inhabitants of smaller settlements and rural areas. They may also be more prone to the mental illnesses induced by the stresses and frustrations of high density living. In all, then, life expectancy rates may be lowest in the largest cities (Lave and Seskin 1971), and life less healthy while it lasts.

The relationship between population density and disease transmission is similar to one which suggests why crime rates are generally higher in the largest settlements. Why a particular individual indulges in crime does not concern us here (though see the next section); what is of interest is why certain environmental situations may be more conducive to crime than others. Of course, we have problems in defining crime. To most of us, it is a relative concept — 'what the other person does' — and collected statistics on crime reflect the definitions of the groups who hold power in a society (Smith 1975b).

A crime occurs when a person likely to submit to a certain temptation yields to a contact with the relevant object. The spatial pattern of crimes thus reflects the distributions of potential criminals and of criminal opportunities. The more opportunities per unit area, therefore, the greater the crime rate is likely to be, especially since the majority of crimes are committed close to the miscreant's home (Baldwin and Bottoms 1976, Pyle 1974). An analogy has been drawn between the relationship of crime rates to city sizes and densities and the collision of particles in matter (Kyllonen 1967). The larger the number of

particles (persons), the greater the number of possible collisions (con
tacts leading to crime). With three persons in a place, there are six
possible crimes involving one person in some way affecting anothe
(1-2, 1-3, 2-1, 2-3, 3-1, 3-2); with five persons there are twenty
possibles, and with seven, forty-two. The number of potential oppor
tunities increases with the square of the number of individuals, les
that number (that is, potential crime rate = $(N^2 - N)$), so bigger citie
should have more crimes per unit of population. But population den
sity is also important. We have already noted that most crimes occu
close to the offender's home, so that the fewer the opportunitie
within a given radius, or, more generally, the lower the population
density, the smaller the number of potential criminal contacts. So
crime rates should be positively related to both urban size and den
sity, and Haynes (1973) has combined the latter two variables (P^2/A
where P = population and A = area) to show the validity of this hypo
thesis in American cities (Fig. 5.4). Note that his data refer to rates
bigger places should have more crimes simply because they are larger
but crime rate data show that they have more crime than their popu
lation size alone would suggest.

Not all crimes can be causally related to the size and density of the
place in which they occur, for there are many other causal influences
like a greater cultural predisposition towards crime in certain areas
such as the American Deep South (Harries 1974). And it is argued
that the correlations between P^2/A and crime rates do not indicate
causal relationships, only that the 'criminal classes', those permanently
or temporarily alienated from society, are more likely to live in large
cities, being attracted by their anonymity and marginal life styles
Most murders, for example, are committed by a close relative of the
victim. City size is unlikely to affect the murder rate, therefore, bu
density might; the higher the density, the greater the contact, or the
harder it is for individuals to retreat into seclusion (Hall 1966), and
murder could well result from the frustrations of too much contact
The is shown in Hoch's (1974b) detailed analyses of American data
for seven major crimes — homicide, rape, robbery, assault, burglary
larceny, and auto theft. Of these, only the homicide rate is not asso
ciated with the size of the place, which appears to have most influence
on the robbery and auto-theft rates. The design of the urban environ
ment may be crucial, too: Newman (1973), N. Taylor (1973), and
others have shown that certain urban layouts, because they are no
overlooked or 'policed' by families in their homes, are more conducive
to crime than are those where the ownership of all space is clearly de
fined and protected (see also Cybriwsky and Ley 1974, on the

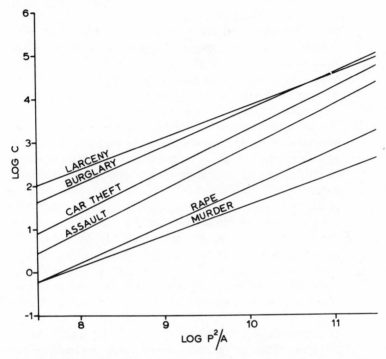

Fig. 5.4. The relationship between city size and density (P^2/A) and crime rates (C) in American cities, 1960. (Source: Haynes 1973, p. 164.)

types of places where parked cars are likely to be 'stripped').

The role of spatial variables as an influence on these two aspects of social well-being — health and security — is far from certain, therefore. Much more detailed research is needed to chart the extent and nature of the possible relationships. But there is plenty of evidence that, whether or not place is a causal influence, where one lives can clearly affect one's life chances, one's level of health, and one's liability to be the object (or subject?) of a crime.

SOCIO-SPATIAL MILIEUX

The vast majority of people live in social groups, and need frequent social contact with their selected peer group in order to sustain them. As urban areas have grown, and developments in transport technology proceeded, so the range of contacts available has widened. Many people no longer live in very tight, localized communities, but even in the large cities, there are still those who, through choice or the lack of it, live most of their social life in very confined areas. Young children and their mothers, and old people are among those who are usually very restricted in their spatial range; members of closely-knit minority groups, such as immigrants, often choose to remove most of the city from their regular contacts; some groups, such as blacks in South African and North American cities, are constrained by a variety of legal and quasi-legal constraints to living in certain areas only.

The kinds of social contact that people want involve others with whom they have a community of interest, who share the same likes and dislikes, and enjoy the same life styles and conversational topics. Community is most likely to develop between people of similar occupational and educational levels, income, and age — as well, of course, as kinship; apathy, even antagonism, is likely between people of different groups. The residential areas of cities reflect these desires, being the result of a sorting and sifting of people of different categories into spatial groupings with their peers, which will allow the development of some form of community, if the individuals concerned so wish. This sorting process is far from perfect, however. As noted in our section on housing costs, homes are financial investments for many people, who will do all that they can to protect both those investments and the social environments which are conducive to financial gain. Thus households and groups are in conflict for locations, and also for other 'goods', such as access to desired facilities like shops and schools, doctors and open spaces, and distance from noxious elements such as industries and 'undesirable' residential uses (such as blocks of flats for students). Spatial separation of social groups results from this conflict (Cox 1974); it is based on knowledge of social inequalities and a desire to perpetuate them by forbidding access to society's 'goods' for those unable to pay the high price.

Geographers and sociologists have done a lot of work in the last few years mapping the complexity of the urban residential pattern, understanding how it has come about, and evaluating its effect on levels of social well-being (Johnston and Herbert 1976). Such work has shown that, because of the complexity of the division of labour and the consequent social stratification, the various social groups in a city often overlap considerably in their spatial distributions, at least at certain scales. Thus, whereas individual streets may be almost exclusively occupied by members of a particular 'class' and age grouping, a school catchment zone may combine several different types of residential area.

Analysis of the spatial patterning of residential areas suggests two ways in which it affects inequalities between groups, in addition to the variations in housing costs and land values that we have already discussed. The first of these shows how certain social problems are concentrated into certain areas. This largely results from the association of such problems with certain groups within the population: poverty is a characteristic of the lowly-paid, who live in the cheapest housing, for example. A group of researchers has mapped the distribution of ten social problems in Belfast, by a network of 200 m x 200 m squares (Boal, Doherty, and Pringle 1974), and from analysis of these maps suggested that there are two basic spatial patterns of social malaise in that city. The first represents the patterns for the rates of male, female, and juvenile unemployment, and male juvenile crime (by place of residence). The areas with the highest rates are in the western sector of the city (Fig. 5.5), where families are on average larger, birth rates

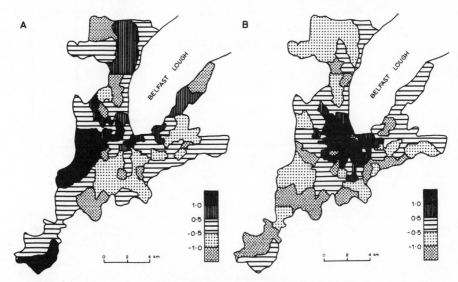

Fig. 5.5. Areas of social malaise in Belfast, showing (A) the areas — those with positive indices exceeding + 0·5 — having high rates on the relevant variables for the first malaise pattern (see text), and (B) the inner city areas — those with positive indices exceeding + 0·5 — where death rates are high and many children are in care. (Source: Boal, Doherty, and Pringle 1974, p.82 and 84).

higher, the proportions of males in semi-skilled and unskilled occupations higher, and the proportion of households living in public housing greater, than elsewhere in the city. The second pattern reflects the spatial patterns of illegitimate birth rates, of the proportions of children in care, and of death rates for those aged 25–65, including deaths from bronchitis. It is most marked in the inner city areas (Fig. 5.5), where most of the housing is rented from private landlords, population densities are high, and the average age of the population is relatively high for the city.

Such patterns as these, indicating a clear-cut spatial concentration of various aspects of social malaise, are to a considerable degree self-perpetuating. A team of research workers in Liverpool has suggested that a cycle of poverty operates in such areas; their arguments are developed from the provocative writings of Pahl (1970). In its most basic form, this cycle reflects the interdependence of unskilled work, low incomes, poor living conditions, and poor educational opportunities; these are all interrelated, so that, for example, people with poor educational opportunities are likely to go into unskilled, perhaps irregular work, with consequences on income, where they can afford to live, and educational opportunities for their children. Expanded, the cycle suggests further relationships between the four basic components and mental and physical health, leading to the sorts of social

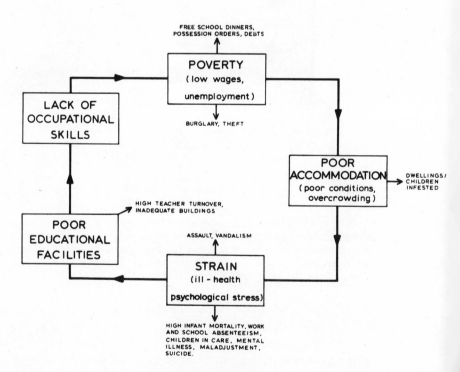

Fig. 5.6. The cycle of poverty (after Raynor *et al.*): the boxes show the main causes of poverty; the arrows show the major consequences of these causes.

malaise mapped in the Belfast study (Fig. 5. 5). This expanded cycle, and the consequent symptoms of malaise, is shown in Fig. 5.6 (from Raynor *et al.* 1974, p.46). Its interpretation is clearly that people who live in areas characterized by at least some of these variables, which tend to be the inner areas of cities, have social and physical environments operating against their chances of improving their quality of life.

Where, because of the overlapping of social groups, there is population mixing, examples of neighbourhood effects on behaviour can be found. In brief, a neighbourhood effect is the result of a person's attitudes and activities being influenced by his or her local social environment. Many people, to gain the respect of their peers, will conform to what they perceive as group norms so that, for example, if the general attitude in an area is towards children attending university if at all possible, then most parents will tend to adopt this attitude, even if it is somewhat alien to their general social background. An excellent example of this is provided in research by Wilson (1959) into the educational attitudes and performances of high-school pupils in the San Francisco area. The various schools studied were classified according to the average status of their catchment areas: in grade A schools, 65 per cent of fathers had attended a further education college, compared to only 35 per cent in grade B, and 14 per cent in grade C. One of the resulting tables (Table 5.6) shows attitudes and performance

Table 5.6

Neighbourhood type and education

School Type[a]	% Aspiring to a college education			% Achieving a median grade of A/B		
	A	B	C	A	B	C
Father's Occupation						
Professional	93	77	64	66	50	18
Other White-Collar	79	59	46	50	28	18
Self-Employed	79	66	35	51	35	11
Manual	59	44	33	35	13	11

[a] For key to school type, see text.
Source: Wilson 1959, pp. 839–42.

decreasing both along the rows and down the columns. Thus, for example, the children of manual workers have higher educational aspirations, and perform better, if they are in the 'hothouse' atmosphere of a grade A school, in which middle-class achievement-motivation i likely to be great, and, conversely, the children of professionals do les well at a grade C school. Many other factors can influence these tw variables, notably parental aspirations and the amount of home en couragement (see Kelsall and Kelsall 1971), but even when surrogate for these were held constant, Wilson was able to show a definit relationship between school type and aspirations/achievement: no only did grade A schools motivate working-class pupils, but grade (schools failed to motivate students from middle-class backgrounds.

The spread of attitudes through a neighbourhood population is, i its pattern, very similar to the spread of a disease; the greater the pro portion of the population with a certain attitude, the greater the likeli hood that they will 'infect' the others (Johnston 1976f). The attitud which is spread may be considered a 'good' one, such as having educa tional aspirations, but it could be 'bad', such as one which draws peopl into criminal activity. In their research on Sheffield, for example Baldwin and Bottoms (1976) found higher offence rates amon members of a particular socio-economic class in areas where that clas was a high proportion of the total population than in other areas wher the class percentage was low (Table 5.7). The implication of this i

Table 5.7

Crime rates and neighbourhood structure
(offenders per 1000 population)

Percentage of area population in social class IV/V	Socio-economic class of offender	
	IV/V[a]	III
< 15	31	7
15 - 24	48	14
25 - 34	56	21
35 - 44	68	33
44 <	85	67

[a]Class V is the lowest on the British classification.

Source: Baldwin and Bottoms 1976, p. 125.

that the greater the class homogeneity of an area, within the 'lowe classes', the more likely an individual is to become aware of, and involved in, a life of crime, since there are more potential offenders living there. Alternative interpretations would suggest that such 'high risk' areas are more closely patrolled by the police, and so their offenders are more likely to be arrested, but the investigators found no support for this position.

We have seen, then, that the social stratification which is created out of the division of labour produces an unequal distribution of income and wealth between social groups, which in turn is reflected in the conflict for residential areas. Certain groups are privileged, in that the social-spatial milieux in which they can afford to live are safe, healthy, and provide the type of socialization for their children and social contact for themselves which adds up to a satisfying social life and allows the perpetuation of the class system. Other groups, however, must live in relative deprivation, where schools are poorly staffed and equipped, health is bad, morale often low because of poverty and unemployment, and a cycle of poverty ensures that the next generation continues in a similar relative, if not absolute, position. This is not to argue for neighbourhood environmental determinism, however. Some do 'drop out' from the higher status, privileged classes, and people do escape from the cycle of poverty, either individually or as groups like the Latin American squatters who build their own 'slums of hope' in which attitudes vary markedly from the 'slums of despair' where social malaise is rife (Johnston 1972). As we have seen, these processes of inter-class mobility may be aided by some mixing of the populations, giving the members of a local minority a different reference group which they may try to emulate or aspire to. But neighbourhood effects can work both ways, accentuating the 'goods' as well as the 'bads' in society, as the sad story of the growth of religious intolerance among Ulster children indicates (Fraser 1974).

CONCLUSIONS

Distance is a barrier; it takes time and money to cross it, so that it inhibits the flow of information, especially that which involves personal experience rather than propagation through the telecommunications of mass media. Because of this barrier, people living in different places have different levels of accessibility to jobs, to housing opportunities, to shops, police stations, hospitals, reference groups, and so on. Some of these variations in accessibility produce spatial variations in monetary values, in the price which labour can command, and which is asked for housing and various consumer goods. They can also produce variations in what we call real income, the sum of the various components which comprise a level of living. Residents of certain places must pay extra costs to attend certain facilities, because of the travel involved; if the distances are too great, they may have to go without altogether.

Residents of other places may be more prone to ill health or to criminal attack because of the nature of their environment, and the career chances of their children may be influenced by the general set of attitudes in the locality.

Many of these variations are associated with settlement size and its location relative to other settlements (settlement and country may be used synonymously here, perhaps even along with neighbourhood). But they do not all operate in the same direction: large settlements tend to produce higher wages, for example, but also higher crime rates. Hence it is not possible to come to any general conclusion about the benefits of one place relative to another on the whole gamut of components of social well-being. We must confine our attentions, at least at our present state of knowledge, to the various components as individuals. In this way we can see how spatial variables operate to create, amplify, maintain, or dampen social inequalities, as the many examples given here illustrate.

Governments play two major roles in most societies (Buchanan 1974). The first is that of the 'protective state' and involves them in the maintenance of law and order, according to society's prescribed rules. The second, that of the 'productive state', gives governments a much more active part in the provision of goods and services which are either absent or not available to all in the workings of the private sector. Of these two roles, the latter is becoming increasingly dominant, even in countries which do not overtly accept the concepts of the 'welfare state' or a 'mixed economy'. The nature of the 'public goods' provided by the productive state — what, where, and how — depends on the ideology of the government involved, the resources available to government (this largely depends upon the territory's position in the international, or inter-regional, or intra-urban division of labour) and the administrative structures employed to disburse the public goods.

All governments — at all scales — operate in what Cox (1972) calls legally bounded spaces. Within these *de jure* spaces public goods and services are supplied to individuals (for example, unemployment benefits, maternity grants, etc.), to groups (for example, old people's homes, special schools for the physically and mentally disabled), and to the community at large (for example, fire services, street lighting, water supply, and public parks). Clearly the level of such services varies from space to space and location thus becomes an independent variable affecting individual consumption of public goods (Smith 1976). Several features of such variability have been examined in the previous chapter, particular attention being given to the distance variable. In this chapter, attention is focused on the way in which the territorial partitioning of the world, a nation, or a city influences the quality of life of the individual. Once again we examine the statement that where one lives affects what one gets and how much one gets.

The nation state is the principal agency of social and economic planning and (especially in the Communist bloc, Western Europe, and the West in general) accepts responsibility for establishing schemes leading to an improvement in material welfare, cultural opportunities, and, more occasionally, political equality. Such measures can be taken only within the historically defined territories of nation-states (Eisenstadt and Rokkan 1973). However, it does not follow that all parts of the state will benefit equally. Indeed, in most Western countries considerable power is delegated to, or acquired by, smaller legally bounded spaces within the national space. And inequalities often arise through the actions of these 'local' governments (be they related to states or provinces within a federal state; counties or départements within a unitary state; municipalities or special purpose districts; school boards or water authorities, and so on).

Local governments have exercised greater power and influence over individuals' quality of life as the multiplication of public goods and services has proceeded apace. The situation is well summarized in a frequently quoted passage written by Teitz (1968, p. 36):

> Modern urban man is born in a publicly financed hospital, receives his education in a publicly supported school and university, spends a good part of his life travelling on publicly built transportation facilities, communicates through the post office or the quasi-public telephone system, drinks his public water, disposes of his garbage through the public removal system, reads his public library books, picnics in his public parks, is protected by his public police, fire, and health systems: eventually he dies, again in a hospital, and may even be buried in a public cemetery. Ideological conservatives notwithstanding, his everyday life is inextricably bound up with governmental decisions on these and numerous other local public services.

Such complexity of life demands that we consider political, social, and economic problems in a locational context. Yet, 'in recent decades spatial relations including physical distance, contiguity, distribution, and empirical and theoretical questions pertaining to geographical scale and the areal aggregation of locations have received only casual treatment by most analysts of conflict behavior' (Cox and Reynolds 1974, p. 19).

If, as Cox and Reynolds argue, much, if not most, political conflict in an industrial-urban society is associated with geographical externalities, then the partitioning of space for political/administrative purposes is a key element in the structures designed not only to provide public goods and services, but also to resolve such conflict. This is particularly apparent at the international and metropolitan levels. The apportionment of externalities (unpriced benefits or penalties) between countries is patently unequal (see Chapter 4), and accentuates the inequalities already fossilized in the partitioning of space, there being a great range among states in terms of size, population, resources, and location (in relation to markets, trade routes, access to the sea, and so on). The extent to which a country receives positive and negative externalities is also related to its position in the world economic system. (Regional groupings can be viewed as attempts to internalize positive benefits.)

Within states a major consequence of rapid urbanization is the proliferation and growing awareness of externalities (or neighbourhood effects, free-rider costs and benefits, third party effects) arising from the actions of others and affecting the individual or community in a 'positive' or 'negative' manner (as discussed in Chapter 5). In complex urban societies, such as Megalopolis, Tokyo, London, Paris, and Chicago, individuals and groups have had to turn to government for the resolution of the conflicts produced by the existence of these externalities (Wolpert 1972, Cox and Reynolds 1974, Cox 1974).

Political institutions are needed, therefore, to offset the tendency of the market mechanism to favour the affluent states and the affluent groups within states, regions, and cities (Harvey 1972). Assuming, for the time being, that a government is determined to counteract the perpetuation and promotion of disequilibrium and inequalities by the capitalist system, its response either will be channelled through the institutions operating within existing legally bounded spaces or it will create new legally bounded spaces to meet the needs of the situation (Stetzer 1975). In this chapter, therefore, we examine the evolution and restructuring of legally bounded spaces at the international and local levels and analyse some of the major consequences of the way in which space has been partitioned for political/administrative purposes. First we examine the partitioning of the world into unequal units and, paying particular attention to the emergent states of the Third World, we discuss some of the consequences, in terms of inequalities, of their inheritance and their position in the economic system. Secondly, we concentrate attention on local legally bounded spaces and here we pay particular regard to the Developed World, for two reasons: first, local governments have established a position of considerable influence over the allocation of public goods and services in advanced industrial countries and, secondly, the provision of public facilities and services is on a much grander scale in the metropolitan areas than in the periphery — the 'productive state' is in fact more productive in the more affluent states.

NATIONAL LEGALLY BOUNDED SPACES

The nation state has become the most prevalent organizational structure in human history. Its 'success' story in political evolution rests on the establishment of a territorially defined focus of mass identity and political action which was sufficiently large in scale to permit the societal differentiation, specialization and participation that was necessary for the massive changes engendered by industrialization (Soja 1971, p. 16).

The nation states into which the world is divided define, at any given time, the relationships between the community and its milieux (Gottmann 1973). This spatial division is complex. An explanation is not attempted here, for it would require consideration of centuries of development in various environmental settings (with particular stress on developments in Europe and the Europeanization of much of the world in modern times). For our more limited purpose, we select five aspects of the evolutionary process resulting in the political partitioning of the world.

(1) The spatial partitioning of the world into clearly defined and legally accepted bounded spaces is a modern development. In general, it has resulted from a combination of increasing population pressure and the appropriation of 'no-man's land' between settled areas, and the human striving for security, opportunity, and happiness (Gottmann 1973).

(2) The concepts of territory and sovereignty became intertwined, and a territory can now be defined as a portion of space covered by a system of laws (a jurisdiction) and a unity of purpose (sovereignty over what happens in the bounded space).

(3) The concept of 'sovereign territories' evolved in Europe and there is therefore a distinct Western 'bias' in the urge rigidly to compartmentalize political space (Soja 1971) so that the state and the nation should be coincident in their territorial extent.

(4) The practice of partitioning 'accessible space into well separated compartments endowed with self-government and sovereignty' (Gottmann 1973, p.91) spread from Europe around the world after 1815 (it had already been accepted in the United States, but in a novel [Federal] form), gathering momentum with the break-up of European Empires — first in Latin America, later (after 1918) in Europe itself, and after 1945 in Asia and Africa. Thus 'the uniqueness of the Western experiences of state formation and nation-building' (Eisenstadt and Rokkan 1973, p.25) was transferred to the Third World contemporaneously with the economic system also spreading outwards from the shores of the North Atlantic. In effect, therefore, the ex-colonial states have had to develop against a background of a more centralized, pervasive, and powerful international economy than that existing during the crucial period of European nation-building from 1500 to 1900. No surprisingly, Third World countries (and many small European ones have been unable to produce powerful 'territorial centres' of their ow1 (see below).

(5) The European nation-state was founded on the concept of national ism — for each nation a state, for each state a nation — and this concep was exported to, and superimposed on (for administrative rather tha1

state-building purposes), every continent. Scores of new states formed out of the European colonial empires simply accepted these 'accidental' old boundaries and set about becoming 'nations' by attempting to mould people of different ethnic groups into 'Nigerians', 'Kenyans', and so on. This task of reducing ethnic, religious, linguistic, racial, and caste identities was, and is, formidable. It is a major and continuing cause of inequality because so much effort must be diverted into resolving actual and potential conflicts, at the expense of upgrading the general level of welfare in all parts of the state. As Soja points out, 'some of the most critical and explosive problems in the contemporary world arise from the irregular and unstable relationships between the formally defined nation state and other organizational structures upon which it has been imposed' (Soja 1971, p. 16). The struggle for national identities is deepened by split loyalties and often compounded by a compartmentalization of economic activity in keeping with social and political differences (for example, in Lebanon, Sudan, Iraq, the Philippines, and Malaysia). Such ethnic differences can be remarkably persistent, surviving long after 'independence' (for example, the split along religious lines in Northern Ireland, the resurgence of nationalism in Scotland and Wales, of the Blacks in the United States, the French Canadians in Canada, and the traditional cleavage between Flemish and Walloons in Belgium; Soja 1971, Glazer and Moynihan 1975, Glazer 1975). Ethnic differentiation within states produces discrimination in political action and fosters inequalities — certain tribes, a particular religious group, or a caste, may be favoured while others are discriminated against. The gap between the 'haves' and the 'have nots' within the territory widens and a conflict-ridden situation simmers on, perhaps boiling over in 'civil war' (Nigeria, Northern Ireland, Lebanon, Iraq), or, at best, leading (in the short term at least) to a wastage of potential resources.

Basic inequalities of the present pattern of national legally bounded spaces. We have noted how the political partitioning of space may not coincide with the functional regions produced by the distribution of population, or of ethnic groups, or, more locally, of circulation fields of journey to work, school, shop, and leisure (on the latter see the writings of Douglas 1968, 1973, and Jones 1954). Even if such coincidence did occur it might prove to be purely temporary, for legally bounded spaces assume stability whilst functional organizations are inherently dynamic. In consequence, inequalities often result from the non-coincidence of political and other spatial patterns. Thus, for instance, 'the problems of metropolitan regional government [in the United States] in large part reflect the inadequate articulation between the functional organization of the larger region and the formal administrative structure' (Soja 1974, p.64).

This failure to change legally bounded spaces to keep in step with changing needs is also seen at the international level. Legally bounded spaces have been superimposed in some areas in almost total ignorance of the cultural structure, resources, and needs of the areas. This occurs in areas where European territorial concepts have been transferred to very different and markedly diverse overseas environments, so producing a range of political, economic, and social problems in scores of states granted independence since 1945. Colonial control and the acceptance of colonial boundaries has effected 'a freezing of dynamic local milieux and the establishment of a rigid compartmentalization of space which in most cases prevented the growth of circulation patterns conducive to the formation of cohesive trans-ethnic communities' (Soja 1974, p.65).

Of still greater importance, however, is that the basic partitioning of the land surface of the earth is characterized by gross inequality. Since the inception of the United Nations after World War II the number of member states has quadrupled. Each state has a single vote in the General Assembly (though only a handful of states have a vote, and even fewer have the power of the veto, in the Security Council). One vote, one state gives a semblance of equality. It is, however, an illusory equality as is apparent to anyone studying world maps showing the political partitions of the earth, and the distribution of population, resources, economic power, and military capability. States are far from being equal, though this fundamental inequality is not infrequently forgotten. Where one lives and how one's country is organized (both internally and by the dominant economic system) vitally influence one's expected level of welfare. For example, six states together occupy 49·7 per cent of the total land area whereas 20 states together 'control' only 1·2 per cent. Similarly, almost seven out of ten human beings live in only 14 states and their welfare is therefore determined by a handful of countries (occupying 43 per cent of available space). General global welfare levels reflect the fact that about one quarter of mankind lives in China and a further fifth lives on the Indian subcontinent. As we saw in Chapter 4, the economic system allocates far less than half of its scarce resources to China, India, West Pakistan, and Bangladesh. On the contrary, the largest share is consumed by the United States, a country with not much more than a quarter as many people as China. To a large extent, therefore, 'it is the social and economic structure of the nation and the equipment of the territory, not the extent of the land, the size of the population, or its density that determine the comfort and happiness of the people' (Gottmann 1973, p.115). Even so, the problems faced by many 'small' states are real enough and warrant further comment.

Problems of the midgets (small states). One of the great paradoxes of our time is that while great powers have become super-powers, more and more independent states have appeared that in economic strength and population scarcely measure up to an American state or even an English county (Wood 1967). As recently as the late 1950s both major parties in Britain considered many of the states which have since become independent too small in economic viability and political stability to be given full independence (Labour Party 1957, Blood 1958). Even Sierra Leone (with a population of 2 million and an area of 72,000 sq. km) was considered to be a borderline case! But by 1965 it was independent, along with countries such as Malta, Zanzibar, Gambia, Jamaica, and Cyprus. The British Government attempted to fit small colonies into Federations (for example, Singapore and Brunei in Malaysia, Malawi in the Central African, and a galaxy of islands in the West Indian). All these have collapsed, mainly through lack of contact, and too great diversity of wealth, resources, population, economic and thus political power.

Smith (1967) divides the smaller territories of the British Commonwealth of nations into two types: (1) those with a fairly dense or very dense population and small in area, for example, Malta, Singapore, Jamaica, Trinidad and Tobago, and Mauritius; and (2) those larger in area and with a very thinly scattered population, for example, the Bahamas, Botswana, Guyana, and Sabah. A large number of ex-British colonies were founded as trading posts or strategic key-points located along the ocean highways of the world. Some were also developed for plantation production of a particular crop (sugar, tea, rubber, for instance), using imported slave or indentured labour in the early stages. By no means all ex-British colonies are islands or coastal states. Many are remote, even land-locked, and far from the mainstream of cultural and economic activity (East 1960).

Granted independence, these ex-colonies are plunged into a maelstrom of problems. Many are pluralist societies, almost all are dependent upon the international trade system, most have high rates of natural population increase. They need to find a home for their surplus population and a market for their crops and for their manufactures, if any. But many doors are closed to the would-be migrants and quotas and other restrictions keep out their goods. Population growth is relentless, however, and 'specks' in the Caribbean, Mediterranean, or Indian Ocean; ports without hinterlands under their control; outposts of a lost Empire which gave them their *raison d'être*: all are often faced by an awesome set of problems. Domestic markets are small, economies of scale are limited, and an economic existence dependent upon economic specialization of a limited range of products and limited number of customers (Kuznets 1960) is a vulnerable and brittle one. Moreover, prices received for their products fluctuate alarmingly and, over-all, fail to keep pace with the prices they have to pay for Western manufactures and services, let alone Middle East oil. Opportunities for employment are limited, and if out-migration fails to match the rate of natural population increase the young drift from the rural areas to aggravate the employment situation in the towns which, given their inadequate economic base, produces severe social consequences.

This formidable list of social, cultural, and economic problems confronts the leaders of these small states with a daunting task. It is in the political field, however, that small states face the gravest disadvantage of their smallness. Wood (1967) considers that the limited pool of educated manpower and the prison-like smallness of the field of human relations engenders conflict. Small private loyalties become intertwined with the wider impersonal allegiances needed in the political system. Personal antagonisms poison public life and political parties are often based on factions held together by personal bonds rather than on intellectual convictions or class loyalties. The educated minority feel imprisoned and often leave for the metropolises of the world economic system. Benedict (1967b) too stresses the effect of social factors on political strength. The government tends to be ubiquitous, a party to every sizeable enterprise with its 'multi-stranded networks connecting members of a small-scale society' (p.53). In many states, small groups not only control the wealth and technical skill in society, but also control the internal political machinery, together with its many dependants and political clients. As the factions extend throughout the society opportunities for upward mobility are strictly limited and carefully controlled by those in power.

In such a situation inequalities are likely to be great, and the extremes of wealth and poverty are often all too visible in the urban areas of small states. These small territories also share many of the problems of their bigger neighbours. One feature of the 'dependency' in the world political and economic system which the majority of (and all Third World) states have in common is that they are totally unable, under present conditions, to develop strong and independent 'territorial centres' of their own. This is yet another major product of the way in which space has been developed and partitioned over the last two centuries.

Weakness of territorial centres. A major theme of the UNESCO-sponsored conferences on Nation-Building held in 1968 and 1970 was the relative strength of the territorial centre of the state (Eisenstadt and Rokkan 1973). Much discussion focused on Rokkan's model (p.18) of four sources of variation in the structuring of territorially defined political organizations, that is:

(1) the distinctiveness, the consolidation, and the economic, political, and cultural strength of the territorial centre;

(2) the cultural distance of the peripheries from the centre and their economic and political resources for resistance against integration and standardization;

(3) the internal strength and the external resource links of cross-locally organized sub-cultures such as churches, sects, castes; and

(4) the internal strength and external resource links of cross-locally organized economic units, such as merchant leagues, credit networks, and international corporations.

Newly emergent states of the Third World are immersed in the problems associated with the formation of the state and the development of administration (stage 1), the creation of institutions for promoting socialization leading to a territorial political identity — by way of educational penetration of the periphery, for instance (stage 2), by the institutionalization of channels of participation and the overpowering of opposition groups or regions (stage 3). Most Third World countries have not been in existence long enough, nor have they acquired the necessary skills of organization, to create 'territorial economic solidarity' (stage 4) through measures to equalize benefits and opportunities both across regions and across strata of their populations (Eisenstadt and Rokkan 1973).

It is, of course, during this fourth stage that the 'protective state' can take on the mantle of the 'productive state' and disburse public goods on a grander scale and a more equitable basis. In the meantime many Third World countries have to accept generally low levels of welfare, in addition to territorial injustice, as scarce resources are distributed unequally among groups and regions. As recognized in Chapter 4, industrial investment, trained personnel, medical services, and salaried jobs are all concentrated in the territorial centres, a situation fraught with political dangers.

Few of the emerging states today could develop effective territorial centres of their own, however. The external centres of the dominant world economy – London, Moscow, Paris, Tokyo, New York, or Washington – count for much more than the internal centres, and the strength of Rokkan's fourth dimension can be seen in most states in the way in which the urban networks are economically linked to external territorial centres. As long as centre-formation processes are weak, as long as there is relatively limited economic and cultural differentiation within each centre, as long as the social and political distances between the centre and the periphery are so great; so long will the newly emergent state find it difficult to organize its political space for the benefit of all its people. Indeed, the resources available for welfare programmes are likely to be miniscule when compared to the resources 'invested' in its armed forces (200,000 in the Nigerian army, for instance) and its bloated civil service.

Latin American experts at the UNESCO Conference laid stress on the view that the lack of commitment to the territorial centre also arose because 'the ruling oligarchies had been more concerned to protect their short-term economic interests than to develop strong, and legitimate organs of decision making' (Eisenstadt and Rokkan 1973, p.26). And most Latin American countries have been 'independent' for a century and a half! These states have had ample time to pass through to stages 3 and 4 in the Rokkan model. Why then have they failed to do so? Why did Latin American countries achieving independence within half a century of the North American colonies fail to follow a similar path of development? Part of the answer to these questions surely lies in the failure of a functional federation to emerge, even in a huge territory such as Brazil. Most Latin American countries inherited an economic system based on state monopolies in trade, strict regulation of industries, and growth of 'a parasitic bourgeoisie' without entrepreneurial spirit and with few ties of loyalty to the territory. Moreover, most Latin American countries are markedly 'monocephalic' in structure, and it is argued that this reflects a heritage of parasitism, that is, too great an emphasis on external resources and not enough on internal production. (Monocephalism also existed in the thirteen colonies of the United States. The strength of the external links was tempered by Continental expansion and the forging of internal links and domestic production on an enormous scale.) This, in turn, is reflected in the lack of an integrated railway network in the Continent: the lines focus on the ports – the links with Europe and the United States. The political and economic élites (generally one and the same) shared the same linguistic culture throughout the continent and only the poor (the least mobile) were tied to a particular region (Eisenstadt and Rokkan 1973). The recent experience of Chile demonstrates how difficult it is to change the traditional system with its gross inequalities between rulers and governed, town and country, and landlord and peasant.

The division of accessible space into political units has produced an unequal allocation with some states much weaker than others and unable, under present conditions, to function very effectively as providers of public goods and services. Some of the major reasons for inequality have been examined and the problems faced by Third World states have been emphasized, for in the underdeveloped realm the central administration must be the decision-making level which by its expenditure pattern has the greatest impact on the well-being of individuals and communities. The parameters of well-being are also set by the central government in the Developed World, but in the advanced industrial countries local governments play a significant part in the production and perpetuation of inequalities, and it is to an examination of the role of local legally bounded spaces that we now turn.

LOCAL LEGALLY BOUNDED SPACES

All but the very smallest nation states have a network of lower-tier authorities for political/administrative purposes. Such authorities may be multi-purpose ones, such as the states (50), counties (more than 3000), municipalities (c. 18,500), and townships (about 17,000) of the United States or the metropolitan (6) and county (39) councils, 296 county districts and 36 metropolitan districts of England (outside Greater London), or they may be responsible for a single function, for example, a school, a park, a forest-reserve or a sewage district, a regional hospital board, a public-transport undertaking, or a water board. Table 6.1 indicates the tremendous profusion of legally bounded spaces in the United States. Though the over-all number of units was halved between 1942 and 1972 this fall was accounted for by the disappearance of 90,000 school districts. Over the same period the number of non-school special districts went up from 6,299 to 23,885. Over-all, the density of local legally bounded spaces is greater in the US than in any other state (Soja 1971).

In many countries, such as the United States, Canada, and Australia, the power of these locally created general and special purpose districts is very considerable. The nation state is an amalgam of fortmerly independent states and the latter remain as the prime administrative units within the nation, having a considerable impact on the nature and quality of public goods bestowed on individuals and localities. A similar case can be made for non-federal countries which often work through a network of lower-tier authorities which already exist. Thus local legally bounded spaces in a unitary state have the power

Table 6.1.

Units of local government in the United States, 1942–72

	1942	1952	1957	1962	1967	1972
Counties	3 050	3 052	3 050	3 043	3 049	3 044
Townships	18 919	17 202	17 198	17 142	17 105	16 991
Municipalities	16 220	16 807	17 215	18 000	18 048	18 517
School districts	108 579	67 355	50 454	34 678	21 782	15 781
Non-school special districts	8 299	12 340	14 424	18 322	21 264	23 885
Total	155 067	116 756	102 341	91 185	81 248	78 218

Source: U.S. Bureau of the Census, *Census of Government 1967* and *1972* (after Stetzer 1975, p. 15).

to influence the services provided, and by their spatial allocation of resources they can create, fortify, or rectify inequalities. Clearly, local autonomy over how money is spent is much greater in the United States than in the United Kingdom. In the United States a far greater proportion of the money spent is raised locally, mainly from taxes levied on property (the state fixes the limits of debt held by the local units however, and this is one of the reasons for the creation of so many special districts — see below). In the United Kingdom, on the other hand, more than 60 per cent of the money spent by local authorities comes from the central government by way of rate-support grants. The central government is in a strong position, therefore, to intervene in order to even out what it considers to be gross inequality in patterns of expenditure by local authorities, and can put pressure on the local spenders to make changes in the priority they give to different services.

   In this section on local legally bounded spaces we examine: (1) why and how these spaces are created and how space is restructured over time to keep in step with changes in demand and support, organizational needs, population growth and distribution, technology (especially in transport) and availability of resources; and (2) how these local governments affect inequalities in exercising their power. This is followed by an examination of (1) how the productive state affects inequalities; and (2) how the political importance of the division of a national territory by constituency-based parliaments and representative-based federal governments is mirrored in the electoral system and (particularly) in the denial of the 'one man, one vote' principle as a result of spatial bias.

Evolution, Restructuring, and Inequalities. How do these legally bounded spaces evolve? Massam (1975) has constructed a very general typology into which case studies of the evolution of particular types of local governmental units in given areas can be placed. Underlying the conceptual framework of Table 6.2 is the awareness of continuing competition between forces working in opposite directions, towards

Table 6.2

A typology for the evolution of service districts

Time	State of the region in which districts are located	Stage of evolution
t_1	Unknown and unsettled	No spatial units.
t_2	Explored, but unsettled	Some boundaries may be shown on maps to claim sovereignty of area.
t_3	Settled in part	The settled part may be sub-divided into distinct districts.
t_4	1 Expansion of settlement	New districts defined.
	2 Density of settlement increases	Sub-division of existing districts to maintain small units.
t_5	3 Density of settlement increases	Amalgamation of small units to take advantage of economies of scale.
	4 Communication systems improve with transportation innovations	Centralization and standardization in the quality of the service.
t_6	Modification of demand and supply as values change, population density changes and distribution mechanisms change	Districts may be modified to amalgamate different functions. Districts may be kept at a level which *explicitly* does not take advantage of scale, but provides local standards of service. Affluent communities may encourage quality to dominate cost considerations of strict economic reasoning.

Source: Massam 1975, p. 130.

centralization on the one hand and decentralization on the other hand (this conflict is discussed below). Clearly, too, the actual time difference between t_1 and t_6 will vary widely between regions and between states. Even in the 'New World' it ranges in the United States from more than three and a half to less than one century (sufficient time for decision-makers to respond to technological changes by creating much bigger counties and states in the more recently settled areas). In China, the oldest nation state in the world, people have grappled with the problems of organizing local government patterns for over 2000 years (Whitney 1970), and even in England the evolution of 'local government' spans a millennium. Table 6.2 suggests that the pattern of service districts in all regions will change in a dynamic manner with the passage of time (at least up to t_6), and in response to changing demands arising from the expansion and increasing density of population and the improvement in communication systems.

Such an emphasis on changes in population and transport is common to many studies of the evolution of the partitioning of space for political purposes. Attention is focused on the spread of settlement and intensification of utilization of an area. As a result the nature of the actual decision-making process is not infrequently ignored (for example, with reference to parishes in England (Mitchell 1963) the key decisions went unrecorded and are lost in the mists of time). But, as US Chief Justice Earl Warren stated in 1964, 'legislators represent people, not trees or acres. Legislators are elected by voters, not farms or cities or economic interests . . . The weight of a citizen's vote cannot be made to depend on where he lives' (quoted by Gottmann 1973, p. 146); but it often does, as we demonstrate later in this section. Similarly, the multiplicity and spatial arrangement of local legally bounded spaces cannot be explained simply in terms of the number of people or houses, miles of tarmac, telephone subscribers, and so on — even electoral districts devised on the basis of equal population size are subject to gerrymandering. Local government units are created and changed by individuals and groups. They are neither an automatic response to population growth and redistribution nor to technological changes of any kind. Interest groups, factions, and political parties create the units for their own special interests and purposes.

In many countries local populations had great power to create their own jurisdictions, and still have in the United States (subject to state approval and legislation). In seeking an explanation for the phenomenal creation by states in the United States of new local governments within their jurisdictions (Table 6.1), Stetzer (1975) finds the models used by geographers for explaining the political organization of area (Jones

1954, Kasperson 1969, Soja 1971, Massam 1972) inadequate when attempting to explain the role of special districts (empowered by a state to render a single service within a prescribed area *within* the jurisdiction of a general purpose government) in the political system. He considers that new demands and/or 'output failures' (that is, when existing government forms cannot or will not meet all the needs of the citizens) are resolved in relation to the variety and strength of the constraints acting upon the political system and lead to the creation of special districts (SDs). The Advisory Committee on Intergovernmental Relations (1964) lists eight such constraints and to these Stetzer adds two more. The constraints are:

(1) financial limitations: legal restrictions are placed on units of local government and not on the area occupied by the unit. Thus an area can increase its debt or taxes by creating additional layers of government;

(2) limitations on power of local government: strict grants of power and the inability of local governments to establish differential taxing areas within their boundaries, encourage the establishment of SDs;

(3) areal convenience: limitations imposed by existing boundaries of general purpose districts often lead to formation of SDs which can correspond more closely to local functional areas;

(4) political compromises: new layers can be created without destroying existing ones;

(5) desire for business management: can sometimes relate service to user charges and run the 'business' as a 'social' organization;

(6) public acceptance of SDs: people prefer local organization and participation and are basically concerned with their own neighbourhood rather than the 'needs' of the wider area in which they are placed;

(7) programmes of higher levels of government: SDs are often formed to channel federal funds into specific areas (flood control, housing programmes);

(8) influence of special-interest groups: in particular, (a) citizen groups concerned with a particular function and (b) economic benefactors, either individuals or enterprises, which stand to benefit economically from the creation of a SD;

(9) desire for independence: SDs are more easily controlled than general purpose districts; and

(10) historical circumstances: especially differential interests and pressures through time; nature of settlement and its spread and growth; technological change in communications and organizational capacity. Such forces have produced and 'fossilized' many SDs.

New legally bounded spaces emerge therefore in response to new demands, existing characteristics of political space, expected support, and distribution in space of interest groups powerful enough to secure a positive legal/political response to their pressure. As a result, some districts have few resources and offer a low quality of service, whilst others are strong and their trained personnel provide a much higher quality of service (see also work on the UK by Nicholson and Topham 1972). In effect, 'the present system of district organization permits great inequalities to exist in facilities and the rendering of services. Presumably, the lack of uniformity and lack of equity meet with the approval of the district residents, the Legislature, and the courts' (Stetzer 1975, p.147).

Not all states allow local populations such freedom to create new local government units. In England, for instance, the map of local legally bounded spaces has evolved over the last thousand years or more. But during the past century or so the power of the central government has increased at the expense of local governments, and in 1974 the former carried out a major reconstruction of local government throughout the country. However, the past is not 'swept under the carpet'. Even in the major reforms of local government in the 1880s, 1890s, and 1970s most of the 'new' local government boundaries were not drawn on a 'clean slate' in relation to the supposed needs of the 'present', but followed ancient parish, wapentake, and shire boundaries. The 'new' patterns are the result of political compromise. The Acts of 1888 and 1894 did not embody many of the most important recommendations of the Royal Commission set up to advise Parliament. In particular, the number of county boroughs created was raised from a recommended handful to more than fifty by the time the Bill had passed through Parliament (Hampton 1966). Similarly, the 1972 Act recognized fiercely held traditional loyalties to existing counties and embodied a radically different structure to that proposed by the Redcliffe-Maud commissioners (Redcliffe-Maud Report 1969). Once again, 'an attitude of sacred inviolability, on the basis of which many local councils staunchly guard their own vested interests, had created a barrier of inflexibility' (Douglas 1968, p.14) — a barrier which the central government is either unwilling or unable to crush.

Faced by these barriers to change, the central government in a unitary state, rather than beat against the weight of vested interest, often bypasses the existing forms and meets a particular demand by setting up a series of new administrative bodies, each with its own structure and spatial pattern: these new units often cover a larger territory and benefit from economies of scale but they are no longer subject to local control. Functions are thereby taken from the local authorities and instead of a clearly defined set of multi-functional authorities able to co-ordinate activities, the system spawns administrative complexity, a disintegrated set of authorities, and a division of responsibility between local and central government which sometimes allows each to blame the other for 'output failures'. Though all concerned might acknowledge the need to govern all parts of the state as fairly and as efficiently as possible, the spatial political/administrative system adopted for the purpose emanates from a combination of historical factors, political compromise, and administrative convenience.

In so far as there is a time-lag between changes in demand and re-structuring of local legally bounded spaces, the system through which public goods and services are dispensed is almost inevitably antiquated. For example, the Royal Commission on Local Government reported in 1969 that 'local government in England needs a new structure and a new map' (Redcliffe-Maud Report 1969, vol. 1, p. 1). The four basic faults in the system (since 'reorganized' in 1974) were considered to be: (1) the widening gap between the patterns of life and work and the pattern of local government areas; (2) the splitting of the responsibility for development planning and transportation between seventy-nine county boroughs and forty-five counties; (3) the fragmentation of responsibility for services within the counties (the forty-five counties were divided into more than 1000 municipal, urban, and rural districts and each had responsibility for housing); and (4) the small size and limited revenue of many local authorities, making them 'too short of highly qualified manpower and technical equipment to be able to do their work as well as it could and should be done' (vol. 1, p. 2). As a result, the complex local government machinery was deemed to be 'irrelevant' and 'impotent' when faced by the problems confronting people in their daily lives, either collectively or as families and individuals. Not surprisingly, the central government often doubted the ability of local governments to manage local affairs 'within the strait-jacket of the present system'.

The pattern and operation of local government is therefore frequently inefficient because it is an outmoded relic. Citizens are thereby penalized in varying degrees. The structure is only changed when absolutely necessary and even then any reorganization is likely to relate to the existing system. New structures are unlikely to emerge from the kind of approach suggested by Senior in a memorandum of dissent to the majority report of the Redcliffe-Maud Commission (Redcliffe-Maud Report 1969, vol. 2, p. 5):

I think the right approach is to start by analysing the facts of social geography, the requirements of functional effectiveness and the conditions of democratic viability in relation to one another, to let the outcome of this analysis determine the appropriate scales of units for groups of related functions, and then to see what principle of organization best fits the needs thus ascertained and the practicalities of the transition to a new structure.

Paradoxically, the consequences of fragmentation of the political organization of space are most evident in metropolitan areas where economic advance has been most rapid. Such areas contain great inequalities, and these are in part related to huge problems of organization and the complexity of human interaction. 'An atmosphere of hostility' between the local authorities frequently leads to a lack of co-operation and co-ordination of policies and in turn this leads to a 'distorted' geographical pattern of industry, new towns, residential areas, 'overspill' areas, schools, colleges, and transport facilities, as some areas or groups are either favoured or discriminated against both by land-use planning decisions and by the local areas' ability or inability to meet its own requirements from its own tax base. The major elements of this kind of situation can be illustrated by reference to the plight of New York city.

Despite an unprecedented concentration of wealth, power, knowledge, technical know-how, and decision-making in the area labelled Megalopolis by Gottmann (1961) (that is, the northeastern seaboard of the United States), the five major metropolitan regions (Boston, New York, Philadelphia, Baltimore, and Washington, D.C.) and scores of smaller towns and cities within Megalopolis are bedevilled by a set of social, economic, and governmental problems of unparalleled magnitude. Problems of deprivation, urban deterioration, and congestion are related to human greed, selfishness, and good or bad fortune, and, of course, the operation of the capitalist system; but they are also related to the problem of political fragmentation. The superabundant concentration of knowledge and power in Megalopolis has not generated a structure of government in keeping with the needs and realities of the metropolitan area. On the contrary, the political partitioning of space is truly chaotic, and is the result, as we have seen, of historical experience, political compromise, and the self-interested actions of individuals or groups. The five major metropolitan regions are each divided into hundreds of local legally bounded spaces: in the New York Planning Region in 1960, for instance, 16 million people lived in a 6,914 square mile area divided into 1,467 distinct political units, each with the power to raise and spend money. The major consequences of such a propensity to partition space for political purposes are, according to Yeates and Garner (1971) and Wood (1961), the following:

(1) The units are on average much too small to be effective providers

of many social services, too weak to control the forces producing environmental damage, and incapable of long-term planning: matters concerning public welfare, hospitals, transportation, water supply, and air pollution require a structure with a limited number of strong authorities rather than one 'ridiculously fragmented'.

(2) The units are, not surprisingly, pursuing their own narrow interest rather than the wider interest of the region as a whole.

(3) This community-centred or 'beggar thy neighbour' form of behaviour produces a segregation of resources and needs within the region: in general, the central city areas have the 'needs' and the suburbs have the 'resources'. Part of the New York problem is therefore a general central city/suburban dichotomy problem. The central city has to provide more facilities to be used by suburbanites than the suburbs provide to be used by central city residents (see Bunge 1975, Wolpert 1972, Harvey 1972). Since local populations pay for local government-provided facilities through local taxes (usually raised on property values), as the rich leave the central areas the tax base falls; as business organizations leave the tax base falls further, and left behind in the 'twilight zones' are the biggest bills and those least able to pay them. This process may result in business interests gaining control of the city government and then attempting to increase the tax base by attracting back the middle classes and squeezing the poor out. In some respects Manhattan can be equated with the ghetto at the centre of the circular cumulative causation process depicted in Fig.4.10. The teetering of New York City on the brink of financial disaster throughout 1975 was in part a predictable consequence of the notorious spatial imbalance in the metropolitan region of public need and public provision on the one hand and resources on the other hand.

(4) The 'sacred inviolability' attitude is present in New York, as in England, and 'each body is as a rule more concerned with preserving its own autonomy than anything else' (Yeates and Garner 1971, p.461), and 'collectively the (local and state) governments are not prepared to formulate general policies for guiding economic development or to make generalized responses to the financial pressures generated by urbanization' (Wood 1961, p.113).

Similar problems occur in the Tokyo, Paris, London, Chicago, and Los Angeles metropolises and on a smaller scale in scores of 'metropolitan' areas throughout the world, not least in the burgeoning cities of the Third World. The poorest members of the 'city region' are trapped in deteriorating environments (in terms of both physical conditions and public service provision) and the richer members of the economically interdependent region flow out into 'the green and pleasant lands' beyond the administrative reach of the central city of great need and financial burden. In all such cases the political fragmentation produces a markedly inefficient situation in which the scale of the *de jure* territory and the scale of the movement network are incongruent — the more incongruent they are the greater will be the conflict between localized populations and between the administrative units and the network space (Cox and Reynolds 1974). Incongruency is most marked in the great urban centres of the world, the very places where 'conflict' can be most harmful to millions of individuals and families. The need for restructuring may be self-evident, but does restructuring take place in response to the supposed needs of all the inhabitants of the metropolis?

Once established, all local legally bounded spaces tend jealously to guard their powers and resist organizational change. They are protected by law, managed by a power structure, and staffed by a bureaucracy, all elements tending to discourage innovation and change (Stetzer 1975). In addition, they are fortified by traditional loyalties, local pride, and activity fields generated by their own actions (school catchment areas, wards equated with electoral districts, association of many English counties with cricket teams, for instance). But immense human agglomerations of high density and high average levels of economic affluence present a situation 'pregnant with organizational consequences' (Gottmann 1973; p.118; see also Wolpert 1972), and keeping such a large, affluent metropolis functioning requires more than 'good neighbourliness'. The environment must be equipped, organized, and maintained in an extremely involved and efficient manner. To provide public health, education, sanitation, long-term planning, transportation, and so on, public planning and provision is essential. As a general rule, the more complex the socio-economic structure becomes, the greater is the need for public intervention to regulate the abuses of the market system and to protect the weakest groups against the strong and powerful. But complex metropolitan areas are, as we have noted, often ones in which the political organization of space is apparently 'ridiculously fragmented'. Consideration of 'who gets what, when, and how' (Lasswell's definition of politics) therefore needs to be changed to 'who gets what, *where*, and how' (Smith 1974). As Soja (1971) points out, 'where' enters into the three main functional realms of politics:

(1) *Competition*: control over the distribution, allocation, and ownership of scarce resources (including land, money, and power) gives the ability to make authoritative decisions;

(2) *Conflict*: resolution of conflict both within and between societies

(local, regional, or national) requires the maintenance of order and enforcement of authority; and

(3) *Co-operation*: the maintenance of institutions and behaviour patterns promotes group unity and cohesiveness and thereby legitimizes the authority of the political organization by way of societal integration.

The 'where' enters the situation because the political system can only operate in space, and it therefore needs to create a geographical organization of space. It is within this structure of government and administration that competition, conflict, and co-operation take place (Harvey 1972).

How then does the political system re-process (that is, re-structure) its environmental setting? For a satisfactory conceptual framework to answer this question Stetzer (1975) turns to Easton's analysis (1965a, 1965b) of the political system. Easton sees the political system as a self-regulating one dependent on the operation of four functionally different sub-systems: (1) of inputs (perceived needs, expected support from electorate, power structure and bureaucracy, payment of taxes and size of tax base); (2) of processing and converting inputs into outputs by the governmental (including party) structures; (3) of outputs — produced by 1 and 2: these determine the amount of energy and resources that are used in establishing priorities, deciding the quality of services, planning the future, and distributing rewards; and (4) of a feedback mechanism which modifies the system and enables it to survive and gain renewed support. Easton's framework tells us how the political system operates, but why does it operate as it does? Stetzer argues that to persist the political system *must* adapt itself to changed circumstances and this adaptation may include the necessity of changing its spatial structure. But the tendency towards 'system persistence or pattern maintenance' of the existing legally bounded spaces is deeply rooted in society. This barrier to change is overcome, argues Stetzer, by the sub-system of feedback mechanism which requires adjustments in the system to ensure continuing support. Thus, at a particular moment in time the spatial system may not be 'optimal', but it will be in a state of dynamic adjustment (the 'disappearance' of more than 90,000 school districts in the US between 1942 and 1972 bears witness to the capacity of the system to re-process space). This is a vital point — the system survives so long as it gains support. It does not collapse because it produces inequalities between groups and areas, unless its supporters are determined to pursue egalitarian policies. Stetzer reports that in Cook County, Illinois, many people he interviewed were *not* committed to implementing egalitarian goals (nor orderly growth, nor public service efficiency in the county as a whole). On the contrary, they were interested in maintaining, or bettering, their own individual or group interest. It is no accident that the system produces inequalities!

Finally, one is left with the fact that in many parts of the Western world tinkering with the political partitioning of space does not necessarily resolve the clash between the forces working towards centralization and those working towards decentralization. Over time, local legally bounded spaces tend to expand geographically because of the economies of scale accruing to large units, the need to co-ordinate strategic planning (including major aspects of land use and the transport system) in response to improved communications, the awareness of great inequity between local areas in financing governmental services, and the increasing geographical range of possible 'spillover effects' and the need to internalize them (Hirsch 1970, Cox 1972, 1974). Administrative boundaries tend to be 'left behind' as the threshold sizes of many provision units (for example, hospitals, sewage disposal, pollution control) move further from the optimum size of community for local control with full participation by individuals (Massam 1975). Massam argues that productive efficiency of many aspects of public provision requires larger operating units (achieved by merging the central city and suburbia, for example). But the advantages of larger units need to be offset against the inconveniences of large-scale organizations. As units become larger there is, for example, a feeling of isolation among users and citizens, a tendency for the organization to adopt fewer outlets (thus making users travel further and thereby discriminating against some individuals and groups: Garner 1975) (see Chapter 5), a loss of local control over services and facilities, and a diminished level of participation by residents in public affairs as 'local' structures are demolished. Nineteenth-century attitudes towards local control are under great pressure as a consequence of the continuing growth of urbanized areas, the demand for high quality public services, and the increasing mobility of society in general. These pressures demand a continuing reconsideration of political spatial units.

Local autonomy and inequalities. Local legally bounded spaces have been created in recognition of the fact that despite a high degree of interdependency between groups and areas in a modern state much of human activity is localized. Spatial interaction of the individual and group is largely determined by locational attributes, especially distance and its major correlate, accessibility (Chapter 5). Political and administrative structures have therefore been developed to organize local space in response to demands from local communities whose social and economic activities require the political partitioning of space for their needs to be met. We have seen that a state is not divided to assist in the creation of territorial justice. A government (local or central) may favour not only certain groups (by the way it taxes income, property, and wealth, for instance) but also particular areas. A spatially biased system may indeed be a deliberate aim of government. Many examples of spatial bias may be cited; for instance, overt discrimination against the South after the American Civil War, action against selected nationalities in the Soviet Union in the 1920s and 1930s, the acceptance of discriminatory policies towards African areas in South Africa and Rhodesia, exploitation of the rural peasantry for the benefit of a small, privileged urban class in Latin American dictatorships, and a wide range of policies adopted in many plural societies throughout the world (including Northern Ireland). Such policies operate at different scales: there are Bantustans and African townships, and there are black city ghettos and black rural slums across the South.

Locally, a dual housing market may operate to the advantage of certain groups and the disadvantage of others. Or urban landowners (including public authorities) may place restrictive covenants on land use to protect some areas from unwanted invasions of certain groups. Similarly, mortgage companies, building societies, banks, and both public and private developers may, within the law, operate a blatantly unequal allocation of resources to different parts of the urban area, thus initiating or reinforcing intra-urban inequalities (Harvey 1973). Such inequalities arise from local government policies on land-use zoning, grading of council tenants for allocation to certain properties and estates, relocation of slum dwellers, provision of recreational space, location of schools and health clinics in relation to the public transport system, and so on. Even local government action in allocating house improvement grants in the United Kingdom may, in practice, further disadvantage rather than positively assist, as was intended by the central government, many of those most in need, as planners in the public sector and builders in the private sector concentrate on those areas where their objectives seem most assured rather than on the lower-income families and housing-stress areas (Duncan 1974). These and many other examples could be analysed in detail and some of them have already been examined in Chapter 5. In this section we discuss just two examples of the way in which local autonomy affects inequalities. Both examples illustrate the way in which inequality is accepted by the operators of local legally bounded spaces, and, supported by the full weight of a nation's law, the system of local autonomy over the way in which money is spent is thus, by its actions, a partner in the production of patterns of territorial injustice. We look first at the practice of zoning in the United States and second at the provision of public education in the United Kingdom.

Zoning to maintain inequalities. Table 6.1 shows that there are tens of thousands of local legally bounded spaces in the United States alone. Each of these territorial units instils a sense of community and separateness. Many pursue narrow local interests at the expense of the larger functional community. 'Moulded by nineteenth-century notions of the moral and ethical values of local autonomy and self-determination, much of the U.S. has become shattered like a pane of glass into a system of often competitive and mutually suspicious fragments' (Soja 1971, p.45). Most of the major northern cities find themselves surrounded (strangled?) by a resistant white collar of wealthy, autonomous suburbs determined to maintain their high-quality, low-cost schools, to keep out noxious facilities, to minimize negative externalities of all kinds, and to sustain their 'right' to provide their own rich community with services paid for by their own relatively low taxes.

Zoning is the favourite device employed to maintain the 'exclusive' and 'separate' character of political space. Toll (1969) has traced the evolution of zoning (a system of laws regulating and restricting the use of land in particular areas) in the United States. He rejects the view that the struggle for zoning was championed by reformers seeking the general welfare of the community against the powerful resistance of the rich, propertied groups. On the contrary, Toll shows that it was the ruling economic élite itself which introduced and diffused zoning laws to reinforce their power and prevent the 'invasion' of undesirable groups into their territory by controlling land use within it. Soja (1971) concludes that zoning was, and is, used to (1) protect suburban property owners; (2) discriminate against particular racial and economic groups by artificially keeping house prices high; and (3) protect local interests, thus accentuating problems of urban fragmentation with its attendant social and economic inequalities.

By manipulation of zoning ordinances, suburban municipalities can prevent free movement of certain groups in the population into suburban communities. Typically these groups are comprised of the

low-income families, the elderly, the large families, the welfare families (particularly those with a female head of household) and, above all, the racial minorities Thus much suburban zoning is now viewed as discriminatory against low income groups, racial minorities, and the like, and there can be no doubt that in many cases suburban zoning is accomplished primarily for discriminatory reasons. It is thus, extremely difficult to break down, even though the cities are anxious to achieve a better balance within the metropolitan areas as a whole. The inner city territories are in fact bearing a disproportionate amount of the nation's cost of providing welfare, education, special services, and the like. The burdens and advantages associated with a form of spatial organization set up to generate the social surplus are thus unequally distributed among the political jurisdictions. There is, in short, a pattern of allocation which is socially unjust (Harvey 1972, p. 22).

The inevitable consequence of such local government action is that within the girdle of rich, white suburban legally bounded spaces one finds central city deterioration, black ghettos, zoning, and planning based on greed or fear and 'visual pollution' of the urban and rural landscape (Bunge 1975).

Can the system producing such spatial inequalities be changed by a restructuring of politically partitioned space? Harvey (1972) observes that the forced integration of the suburbs has so far been rejected and, as the suburbs now hold the balance of political power in the country, he sees too forceful action amounting to political suicide. Moreover, he argues, like Bunge (1975), that the pricing system of many public (and private) utilities (such as water, electricity, sewage, and sanitation) systematically discriminates against the poor, giving an implicit transfer of income from the poor to the rich. Reorganization of government would mean the rich losing economic and social as well as political advantages. Noxious facilities which at present are put in the least politically powerful areas might well be distributed more evenly. Areas with poor resources and thus poor public provision of services and facilities might, given a redistribution of political power, get better services at the cost of increasing taxes in the hitherto protected suburban areas. In so far as interest groups in a city meet their objectives by exercise of social influence, wealth, and political power, a changed geographical organization of governmental and political structures would thus undermine the power base of those groups which have arranged geographical space to serve their particular interests.

The problems involved in restructuring such an unequal system are immense, therefore. Furthermore, Stetzer (1975), after a painstaking analysis of the patchwork quilt of 150 school and 196 special districts in Cook County, Illinois (main city, Chicago), concludes that the advantages of these districts outweigh the disadvantages. Many officials considered that their district was about the right size! Economies of scale were rarely considered, and the important factors in creating new units were deemed to be anticipated growth, expected support, and other governmental forms in the area. Against this background it is extremely difficult to reconcile effective local control and appropriate scale of organization. In the smaller local districts it is also difficult to internalize the benefits and costs within the same political jurisdiction, and the unequal distribution of resources within Cook County is the result of differences in location of taxable enterprises, socio-economic status, degree of development, degree of obsolescence, and so on. The crucial fact is that most of the income of the SDs comes from taxation and therefore the amount of taxable property within the district is the main determining factor in the provision of public goods.

Educational provision and inequalities. In England and Wales the provision of education for all children has been compulsory for more than a century. The central government currently provides the bulk of the money spent on educational provision but the local authorities have considerable power over the way in which the money is spent. Expenditure patterns establish that local authorities are worth treating as political systems in their own right. As Table 6.3 shows, in the school year 1973–4 the pattern of expenditure was far from being a uniform one: the Inner London Education Authority (ILEA) spent, on average, £344·56 on each secondary school child, Bradford disbursed £323·41 and Southampton £319·27, whereas cities such as Bootle, Halifax, and Wigan spent less than £221 on each pupil; that is, less than two-thirds as much as the ILEA. Taking another measure of educational provision, that is, the percentage of the relevant age group given a grant by the local authority to attend university, the range was from more than 15 per cent in Caernarvonshire, Richmond, Solihull, and Cardiganshire to less than 3·5 per cent in several working-class cities of rapid nineteenth-century growth. These and other spatial patterns in the education sector are examined in detail by Coates and Rawstron (1971).

Boaden's analysis (1971) of the factors affecting the provision of local government services in the county boroughs (large towns and cities) of England and Wales elucidates the way in which the system operates. Boaden first tests whether the local authorities are simply the agents of central government as providers of education (and of other services such as police, libraries, fire protection, and so on) or whether by their own actions they are capable of producing inequalities. He tests the following hypotheses relating to central control and rejects them. (Here we give selected items on education. It should be emphasized that Boaden is testing his hypotheses in relation to eight services, not just education.)

(1) *County boroughs (CBs) will display broadly similar levels of activity within any service area because of the operation of central pressures and controls.*

Table 6.3

Spending per pupil 1973-4

PRIMARY

Highest spenders	£	Lowest spenders	£
Cardiganshire	206·84	Cornwall	131·64
ILEA	201·22	Wakefield	131·52
Oxford	181·89	Bradford	130·46
Kingston upon Thames	178·63	Burnley	129·83
Hertfordshire	176·61	Southport	126·63
Newham	176·59	Blackpool	125·30

SECONDARY

	£		£
ILEA	344·56	Eastbourne	226·17
Bradford	323·41	Worcester	226·03
Southampton	319·27	Wakefield	224·42
Stoke-on-Trent	310·40	Bootle	220·82
Grimsby	308·94	Halifax	217·97
Norwich	307·64	Wigan	211·37

Per cent of age group receiving full and lesser value of awards at university

Highest	%	Lowest	%
Caernarvonshire	17·3	Gateshead	3·2
Richmond	15·6	Warley	3·2
Solihull	15·3	Preston	3·0
Cardiganshire	15·1	West Bromwich	3·0
Barnet	13·7	Newham	2·9
Harrow	13·6	Barking	2·1

Pupil/teacher ratio

SECONDARY

Most favourable		Least favourable	
Bradford	12·7	Isle of Wight	19·1
Southampton	14·6	South Shields	19·1
Chester	14·6	Worcester	19·2
Richmond	15·3	Blackpool	19·2
Waltham Forest	15·4	Southend on Sea	19·3
Stoke-on-Trent	15·5	Wigan	20·2

Source: Chartered Institute of Public Finance and Accountancy (1975) and *Statistics of Education* (Department of Education and Science, 1975), volume 5, table 24.

In terms of educational expenditure (rate of spending per 1000 population), Boaden finds the range is from £28,093 to £17,263, with a mean of £23,970 and a standard deviation of £2,100.

(2) *Smaller CBs will be more likely to conform to central wishes and submit to central control.*

Among the twenty smallest CBs ten spent above the over-all average on education, six were in the top quartile, and six fell in the bottom quartile.

(3) *The poorest authorities will be more likely to conform to central wishes and submit to central control.*

Five of the sixteen poorest CBs were in the highest quartile and twelve were above the over-all average in *per capita* expenditure.

Having established that CBs are not simply agents of the central government but active actors in their own right (a view supported by the work of Nicholson and Topham 1972), Boaden formulates a model relating expenditure (a measure of output, or policy) to three sets of independent variables: needs, disposition, and resources (Fig.6.1).

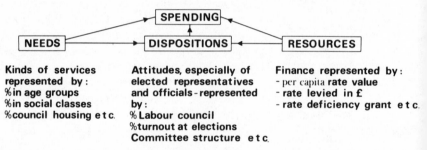

Fig.6.1. A model of local government spending. (Source: Boaden 1971, pp.21–7.

For each service (education, children, health, welfare, libraries, police, fire, and housing) operational indicators are devised for need, disposition, and resources (for a similar study in the US see Sharkansky 1970). The principal measure of output used (except for housing) is the annual expenditure per 1000 population met from local rates and central rate-support grant sources. (In housing, the main dependent variable taken is the proportion of new local houses provided by the local authority.)

In education, *per capita* spending is most obviously related to (1) the size of the school-age population (= need), (2) Labour-controlled councils (= disposition), and (3) the ability of the poor authorities to spend most (= resources; that is, other services were being given a lower priority in favour of education). Labour-controlled councils spent more on education whatever the context of need in which they found them-selves, and confirmed 'their general orientation to government activity and to education in particular' (Boaden 1971, p.52). Thus the political party in power locally does affect the level of spending and priorities, with the Labour-controlled councils most active in services with a signi-ficant impact on the over-all role of government (that is, they are bigger spenders on the bigger services), and in areas of the community supporting them (especially in the field of education). On the other hand, Nicholson and Topham's investigations (1971, 1972) of the determinants of investment in housing by local authorities and the effect on investment of size of authority found no support for the view that a local Labour majority will affect spending. They suggest, however, that the influence of the local bureaucracy is not unimpor-tant, especially with regard to the expenditure decisions of large authorities.

Though 'the central piper does not call the tune as much as is often supposed' (Boaden 1971, xiv; see also Nicholson and Topham 1972), no system of local finance seems likely to provide sufficient resources for needs to be met satisfactorily. Central equalization schemes are thus absolutely essential if severe territorial inequalities are to be avoided. Despite the activity of Labour councils, the map of educa-tional opportunity in England and Wales (including the non-CB areas which Boaden does not consider) bears a striking resemblance to the map of socio-economic status, indicating that education is being pro-vided, and encouragement being given, in a biased manner towards certain groups. In addition, of course, the higher socio-economic status groups are better able to 'opt out' of the state system and buy educa-tional privileges in the private sector (see Coates and Rawstron 1971, for the 'Geography of Opting Out', pp. 245–52).

Education — the provision of training so that individuals may realize their potential and the nation benefit from the developed skills of its citizens — is a crucial public good. If equality of opportunity is con-sidered to be a child's birthright, a facilitative environment must be produced which is spatially biased in favour of those areas where socio-economic factors operate to impair a child's educational progress. In this regard, provision of local services in the United Kingdom is more redistributive than in the United States where governmental districts divide up the city into neighbourhoods. Thus inter-governmental con-flicts in the United States tend to become intra-governmental conflicts in the more extensive and multi-purpose local authorities in the United Kingdom. Populations in local government areas in the latter are rarely homogeneous and, though demands for education may be articulated by particular sections of the population, the resources are often allocated more or less evenly across the whole area (Boaden 1971).

Inequalities in educational provision between local government areas are considerable, however, and only 'positive discrimination' (Halsey 1972) in favour of the less fortunate areas can rectify the imbalance (the favoured areas being unwilling to be dragged down to an 'average' level). Such 'positive discrimination' can only be organized by the central and local government if they recognize the strength of the following: (1) the marked social gradient in the degree of interest in education and understanding of the educational system; (2) the vicious circle of limited life chances, apathy, and bad economic and social conditions leading to limited life chances and so on for the next generation; (3) the need for positive discrimination in favour of those whose educational progress is restrained by material and cultural handicaps; (4) that variations in social conditions are more important in accounting for children staying in full-time education beyond the compulsory leaving age than are variations in standards of provision of secondary education — this means governments could make a hefty redistribution of educational resources in favour of deprived areas without lowering the proportion staying on in the more favoured areas/regions; and (5) only a fifth of school children stay on at school or enter higher education — the other four-fifths leave school at the first opportunity, though many may return as part-time student (Coates and Rawstron 1971, Boaden 1971).

Attention has been drawn to a few of the variations from place to place in England and Wales, and some of the reasons for these massiv variations have been tentatively suggested. There can be little doub that spatial inequality exists and that its removal requires much effor in the spatial levelling of educational opportunities. Territorial justic is of course a necessary prerequisite for social justice, but do we kno how to distribute resources to achieve agreed goals and how are th goals themselves to be agreed? How should we measure education output and how do we combine inputs to achieve the desired output These and other questions are not dealt with here but answers to the are vital in any programme devised to spread equality of opportunit more evenly across England and Wales. If British society adheres the equality norms of the 'welfare state', then local and central gover ments must ensure a more equitable spatial distribution of basic 'publ goods' such as primary and secondary education. There is a long way go, especially if the Regional Affairs Correspondent of *The Guardian* correct in stating: 'For all its vast bureaucratic machinery of regulatic and control, local government continues to blunder along in the da

Table 6.4

The spatial impact of certain U.S. Federal Government spending, 1969

Type of Area	Concentration Ratios for[1]			
	Defence Payrolls	Defence Contracts	Space Research	All Expenditure
Metropolitan Areas				
1 million +	0·79	1·36	1·86	1·14
1 million −	1·50	1·20	0·55	1·03
Rural Counties	0·71	0·29	0·06	0·76
Central Cities	1·66	1·25	1·50	1·50
Suburbs	1·15	1·21	2·32	0·98
Fastest Growing Counties	2·24	1·62	2·80	1·24
Slowest Growing Counties	0·43	0·75	0·12	1·15
Richest Counties	0·68	1·34	1·27	1·31
Poorest Counties	0·18	0·15	0·04	0·61
Total Expenditure ($m)	20 799	38 837	3845	197 253

[1] The concentration ratios are the same as the location quotients discussed earlier (p.73). A value of 1·00 indicates that an area received the same percentage of the federal expenditure as its percentage of the US population; a value exceeding 1·0 indicates receipt of a greater percentage of the expenditure than its percentage of the population.

Source: Evaluation Division, Office of Management and Budget, Executive Office of the President, *Locational Analysis of Federal Expenditures in Fiscal Year 1969*, Washington (mimeographed, 1 September 1970).

with no clear notion of whether its policies and programmes are meeting real needs and solving real problems'. Turning attention to local government, Ardill concludes that 'the structure of governments prevents, or hinders . . . the sensitive adaptation of national policies to local circumstances' (Ardill 1975). It is to the actions of central government that we now move.

SPATIAL BIAS IN ACTIONS OF CENTRAL GOVERNMENT

Almost all actions of central government have a spatial impact, although this aspect of decision-making and policy implementation is only rarely considered by government in an explicit manner. But, given that industry in general and industries in particular are unevenly distributed within a state, the introduction of or changes to tariffs and quotas, tax rates, subsidies, and government purchases have a spatially unequal impact (Table 6.4). Similarly, given that farmers miners, metalworkers, executives, rich and poor, and so on are no equally distributed in space, then the costs exacted by agricultura subsidies, restrictions on coal imports, subsidies for heavy industries direct and indirect taxes, and many other government actions bea more heavily on some communities than others. Or, a British govern ment may offer inducements to a private company sufficient to per suade it to establish a car-assembly plant in Scotland and, when it i threatened by total closure (in late 1975), the government is prepared at least in part for electoral reasons, to inject more than £150 millio into an American multi-national corporation to persuade it to stay i business in Scotland for a little longer, even at the cost of a greate number of redundancies in the major car-manufacturing centres i England. This example is one where the spatial consequences of decision were recognized as a major ingredient in the policy-formatio process. Perhaps the spatial bias embedded in the mean electorate size of constituencies in the countries of Great Britain in February 1974 also deliberate: England (mean electorate size 64,126), Scotlan (52,365) and Wales (57,938). Gerrymandering of territory for politic purposes 'is a political abuse . . . widely practised and generally tole ated in this country [US]' (Sauer 1948, p.403). 'The gerrymand consists in drawing boundaries in such a way that significant group form a permanent minority without means of political expressio (Pounds 1963, p.213). The practice of weighting electoral districts favour of particular areas (especially the rural areas in the US ar Australia and nineteenth-century type cities of declining populatic in the UK) is commonplace. In the rest of this section on spatial b we therefore examine, first, the political importance of the partitioning of space for electoral purposes, secondly the attempts of several governments to pursue overtly spatially biased 'regional policies', and thirdly we consider just one example of the territorial injustice embodied in the expenditure patterns of a Third World country in its provision of a basic public good.

Elections, spatial systems, and inequalities. Most discussions of the distribution of power in modern societies allocate little, if any, to the 'average citizen' (see, for example, Stanworth and Giddens 1974, Urry and Wakeford 1973). Most influence is seen to lie in the hands of a few pressure groups, and in many systems even the parliaments are thought to be virtually impotent. Nevertheless, the composition of a parliament determines the form and nature of the government in many countries, and the relative power of the various pressure groups; and since such parliaments are elected by a broad, if not universal, franchise in most countries, then elections are crucial determinants of which groups have what power.

Democracy is usually believed to involve the principle of 'one man, one vote, one value' (Dahl 1956). But in nearly every country which conducts 'open' elections, a system of spatially delimited constituencies is used to produce the governing body (Lakeman 1974). Methods of conducting elections vary considerably: the typical British and North American procedure allocates each constituency to the candidate winning most votes there, irrespective of whether these are a majority of all those cast; many European countries, and also Australia and the Republic of Ireland, have more complicated procedures aimed at ensuring that the constituency representation reflects the voters' wishes. But to many observers no one of these methods is perfect, in that parliamentary representation (the percentage of seats won) rarely, if ever, equals popular choice (that is, the percentage of the votes won, over all seats). Thus in Great Britain over eight general elections between 1945 and 1970, the Labour Party needed to win, on average, 50·2 per cent of the votes in order to win a House of Commons majority (0·2 per cent of the votes is about 80,000); in the United States, over all congressional elections between 1868 and 1970, the Democrat Party needed to win only 49·1 per cent of the votes to gain a majority in the House of Representatives. Thus the American Democrats were advantaged by the system and the British Labour Party disadvantaged (Tufte 1973, see also Rae 1971).

The major reason for the mismatching of election results in which percentage of seats won does not equal percentage of votes won lies in

the interaction between two spatial patterns, the network of co
stituencies and the distribution of voters of various opinions. (Th
latter pattern reflects the socio-economic geography of a territor
whose evolution was portrayed in Chapter 4.) If a constituency co
tested by two parties contains 100 voters, then 51 per cent of th
votes are sufficient to win it: any more votes are in excess of requir
ments, since they will win the party no more seats. Similarly, ar
votes less than the 51 per cent needed are wasted, since they too brir
no parliamentary representation. Thus a party may win 60 per cent
the votes in an election over ten constituencies containing 100 vote
each, but if it gets 90 per cent of the votes in each of three of th
constituencies and 47 per cent in each of the rest, its 60 per cent
the votes will produce only 30 per cent of the seats. This may seem
extreme example, but there are several cases, such as the 1951 Briti:
General Election, in which a party won a majority of votes in th
country as a whole but failed to obtain a Parliamentary majority.

The distribution of a party's supporters relative to the constituen
system can have a marked influence on the effectiveness of their vote
therefore. Indeed, in many cases — most but not all in the past
constituency systems have been designed by one party to disto
election results in its favour. This is 'gerrymandering', and many argu
that any elections involving constituencies must, because of the no
uniform distribution of voters with certain preferences, result in a
'unintentional gerrymander' (Dixon 1968). One party could get mo
excess votes (surplus to those needed for a constituency majorit
and *wasted votes* (not contributing to the winning of a constituenc
than another. At the British General Election of February 1974, f
example, the result in England only was

	Labour	Conservative
Percentage of votes	37·6	40·2
% of these which were		
Excess	22·5	27·4
Wasted	40·6	34·6
Percentage of Seats	45·9	51·9

The Conservative party vote was nearly 7 per cent greater than th
Labour vote, but it got 13 per cent more seats than its main opponer

The 'unintentional gerrymander' accounted for some of the bias
the English election result just outlined. But this influence is only o
of several introduced by the use of a constituency system. If th
constituencies vary considerably in their size (that is, numbers
voters), and one party's main strength is in the smaller seats, the

it gets a greater return from its votes since, for example, a party with sixty-three votes can win three constituencies with forty voters living in each, but only two if the constituencies have sixty voters each. The Labour Party was advantaged by this size bias at the February 1974 election in England: the seats it won averaged just over 61,000 voters each, compared with nearly 67,000 in the seats won by the Conservatives. And if third parties are active in a seat, or some voters abstain, then fewer votes are needed to defeat the other major party. In England in February 1974, Labour was advantaged by abstentions — there was an average of 14,370 in the seats it won compared to only 12,647 in the seats won by Conservatives — but the Conservatives were advantaged by the number of votes won by third parties (that is, the Liberals) — an average of 14,189 in its seats compared with 7,294 in Labour's.

'One man, one vote, one value' is therefore a principle apparently much violated by elections operated under constituency systems (Johnston 1976a, 1976b). This is widely recognized in the United States, where Presidents are elected by an Electoral College whose composition is determined by elections in each of 51 constituencies (the states plus the District of Columbia). It is popularly supposed that residents of the smaller states have more influence over the election of a President, since they have a greater chance of casting the 'winning vote'. (In a state with 1000 votes, each resident has a 1/1000 chance of casting the vital ballot, but in one with 5000 voters, each has only a 1/5000 chance.) But states do not have an equal voice in the Electoral College, as the number of votes each has reflects its total population. (The number of votes is the number of state senators, two in every case, plus the number of state representatives, at least one: in 1964 Alaska, Delaware, and four other states had the minimum of three Electoral College votes, whereas California had forty and New York forty-three.) Thus, although a District of Columbia voter has a greater chance of influencing his 'state's' result than does a New Yorker (New York's population was about twenty-two times greater than that of the District in 1964), the New York voter is influencing many more Electoral College votes, since the candidate with most votes in a state gets all of its College votes. As a result, Banzhaf (1968) has shown that a New York voter has 3·312 times as much power as a D.C. voter, in terms of his or her possible influence on who becomes President.

If elections were not organized by constituencies, parties and voters might act differently. Within the constituency system, however, it is clear that some voters are more powerful than others. Of itself this is an inequality since it violates what is generally considered as a basic

democratic right, an equal voice in determining a territory's gover
ment. But this inequality is magnified by the operation of the politic
system. Excess votes and wasted votes are of little value to a politic
party, which will direct its campaign to the areas where it is most like
to win votes needed for its aim — over-all victory in the electio
Campaigning involves the spatial allocation of candidates' time a
money, and American studies have shown that in Presidential electio
these are usually allocated to the 'powerful' states (Brams 1975).
addition, new voters must be wooed by more than visits and poste
and loyal voters for a cause must be rewarded, especially if their vot
are important (Glassberg 1973). Thus governments anxious to reta
power at the next election will create policies aimed at areas whe
voters are needed, and their opponents will similarly make promis
to places whose constituencies they feel they must win (Johnst
1976c, Franklin 1975). The result is that the 'productive state' does n
bestow its investments equitably in a spatial sense; political ambitio
ensure that some areas are better treated than others.

Regional policies and spatial bias. Politicians in capitalist and socialist countri
alike are acutely aware of the kind of regional inequalities highlight
in Chapter 4. They identify 'problem regions' using an array of soc
and economic indicators such as unemployment rates, *per capi*
income, selective out-migration, proportion of the labour force e
ployed in declining or labour-shedding manufacturing sectors, exte
of derelict land, proportion of old schools and hospitals, and i
adequate range of employment opportunities for school leavers. The
electorates are also conscious of the relative pecking order of regio
measured in terms of some general prosperity index. In develop
countries, regions such as the American South, the Italian South, t
northeast of England, northern Norway, Hokkaido, the Massif Centr
Siberia, and many others are perceived to be relatively 'backward',
'lagging', or 'depressed', whereas the magnetic attraction of the gre
metropolitan areas is reflected in the number of in-migrants (includi
many highly skilled professional and managerial workers) and in t
reluctance of people to leave them for peripheral areas. Such 'conve
tional wisdom' influences the actions of politicians and planners. C
grounds of 'equity', politicians pursue policies designed to reduce t
gap between prosperous and declining regions. They assume that int
vention by way of investment grants, withholding of industrial develo
ment certificates in affluent regions, public investment in infrastructu
(roads, airports, new towns etc.), employment premiums in backwa
areas, agricultural subsidies, and a rich assembly of other schemes, w

reshape the geography of opportunity to effect a more equitable spread of those activities and characteristics deemed to generate the higher incomes, rewards, and satisfactions which otherwise would tend to be concentrated in relatively small (though densely populated) areas. Such areas are generally important metropolitan areas focused on the city, often the capital, topping the hierarchical structure of the national system of cities (McCrone 1969, Manners *et al.* 1972, Clout 1975).

There are, however, many problems to be overcome in achieving a greater degree of territorial justice between regions. Not least of these is that governments everywhere are prone to seek short-term solutions to long-term needs. They are well aware that voters (or citizens, in the four-fifths of the member states of the United Nations which do not hold 'open' elections) are unlikely to be satisfied by the strength of an economic argument suggesting that all will be well in a few decades. Voters and politicians alike are more concerned with next month and next year than with the year 2000 or 2050. They want action now to eradicate inter-regional and intra-urban inequalities, they perceive that economic forces are operating unfavourably for some communities and some regions (and countries), they are aware of different kinds of problem areas/regions, and in all these matters they may seek policies designed to change the spatial order of their society, so reducing gross inequalities.

First, however, the area/region must be recognized as one deserving special government treatment. Such recognition depends upon three factors; (1) the value system of the state in which it is located: as Smith (1971, p. 446) asserts, 'there are no absolute standards that can be applied to the identification of problem regions, and no specific criteria that hold irrespective of time and place' — it follows that there are no recognized standards or criteria available for judging the success of policies adopted; (2) the extent to which the government is concerned with rewarding its supporters or improving its electoral chances in the region in question; and (3) the economic capacity of the state to divert scarce resources into declining or lagging regions. In addition, academics (including economists and geographers) are generally incapable of offering clear guidance to government on the impact of their policies over the long-term. The debate over whether to take work to the workers or to take the workers to the work is a lively one. Those who seek, on moral grounds, a more equitable spread of employment opportunities, high incomes, good health and education facilities tend to view the most prosperous region in a state — with its government offices, business headquarters, banks, prestigious universities and teaching hospitals, and so on — as a 'congested' area from which some of the elements of its affluence could be uprooted and transplanted in the periphery. Others, however, view the prosperous core region as one which by its very success is the 'engine of growth' that secures the long-term prosperity of the entire state, so ensuring the ability to transfer scarce resources to the less prosperous periphery, without killing 'the goose that lays the golden egg'. Despite several decades of experience in the field of 'regional planning' our ignorance on these matters is profound, and in such a situation it is not surprising that political parties categorize regions according to their estimation of the regions' political importance in terms of winning the next election. In the United Kingdom, for instance, Labour has had to do well in Scotland and Wales to win over-all; many French governments have had to 'mollycoddle' the rural voters (hence the emphasis on the Common Agricultural Policy in the EEC?), and in the United States the Democrats have tended to pursue policies attractive to the big city voter in the northern industrial belt whereas the Republicans have had the difficult task of retaining the allegiance of both suburban and rural voters.

The interdependency of regions within a country, and indeed the interdependency of countries in the dominant economic system, means that it is not possible to alter the well-being of one region without altering that of other regions (Friedmann 1966, 1973). This is a fundamental problem confronting politicians and planners and in part accounts for the disappointing results achieved to date by government-sponsored regional policies in many countries (see, for instance, Hansen 1972, Allen and McLellan 1970, Wright 1965, Kuklinski 1971). The government is required to operate in an area of extreme complexity, interdependency, and conflict of resource allocation. Yet in the United Kingdom

Prime responsibility for making and implementing policy rests with individual Ministries, which live and work in almost watertight compartments, co-ordinated only on the broadest scale by the Cabinet. The lack of detailed co-ordination at the centre, and the long chain of command from Whitehall to implementing agencies, prevent sensitivity of response and flexibility in applying policies and using funds. There is a growing feeling that it would be quicker, cheaper, and more effective for central government to give the necessary powers and resources to regional authorities, agree with them a package of policies and programmes, cut them free from detailed central supervision, and let them get on with the job (Ardill 1975).

To channel investment into particular regions requires not only an adequate policy-making and policy-implementing structure but also determination and clearly defined objectives. The first of these additional requirements is often lacking as a result of changing economic circumstances (balance of payments deficits, oil price rises, inflation, widespread unemployment, for instance), political pressure from prosperous areas (which not infrequently contain many marginal constituencies), and government changes (of Ministers or the whole government). The second additional requirement is generally lacking through the absence of clear, long-term policies in most countries (these are difficult to devise, as we have already noted). Though funds to finance regional policies are drawn from all parts of the country (in the form of direct and indirect taxes) to be concentrated in spatially designated zones, the goals are rarely made explicit, and policies are often justified because they will contribute to 'a balanced and prosperous environment'. Not surprisingly, such vague declarations fail to explain adequately to voters and other claimants for available funds in prosperous areas regional policies involving reallocation and redistribution of human and financial resources by central government agencies (Douglas 1973).

In their attempts to counteract powerful centripetal tendencies in the market economies of the advanced industrial countries' governments have to date produced disappointing results. The main reasons for this failure are summarized by Donaldson (1973, pp. 73–4) as follows:

(1) regional assistance is often seen as a form of charity relief rather than an aid towards an economically as well as socially beneficial regional balance;

(2) the enormous number of changes in government policy has created an unsatisfactory basis for confident long-term investment by industry and government;

(3) policies have concentrated rather narrowly on job creation through the encouragement of manufacturing industry and neglected more labour-intensive activities (service industries, relocation of company headquarters, government offices, and research establishments);

(4) there has been too little emphasis on the retraining of workers and encouraging the movement of workers between and within the regions; and

(5) the government has still not come to grips with the scale of the problem — expenditure is too low in relation to the dimensions of the problem.

In this field too, therefore, the productive state has failed to produce outputs that match its own declared policy to deal effectively with overt and recognized spatial inequalities. As a result, some regions have a lower level of well-being because of government failure. By its lack of clear objectives and determination, and inadequate structures for policy-making and implementation, the United Kingdom government has failed to remove the inequalities it recognized. One might ask whether regional policies in Western countries have been seen as 'palliatives' or as 'cures'. If governments are determined to eradicate inequalities associated with regional imbalance then, according to Carney and Taylor (1974, p. 231), they will have to 'begin to challenge both the interests of capital production and accumulation and the interests of local and national bureaucracies which have tended to stifle any radical income and resource redistributions'. The fact that capitalist and socialist countries alike are grappling with the inequalities of regional imbalance suggests that whoever owns the means of production and whoever makes the decisions, factors associated with distance, economies of scale, initial advantage, and innovation and diffusion also tend to produce a situation in which 'some areas are more equal than others.'

Spatial bias in the provision of a public good in a Third World country. After examining the spatial variations in the provision of education in the United Kingdom we concluded that there was a long way to go before such inequalities were removed. There is, however, much, much further to go before territorial equality of opportunity is achieved in a Third World country. Table 6.5 shows the very uneven distribution of primary school enrolment and success rates in Nigeria in 1970. The large disparity in enrolment between the northern and southern states is very striking, even allowing for abnormally high enrolment in the war affected eastern states produced by a backlog of over-age students. The inter-state disparities in secondary education are even greater, and those for university entrance even greater still. Thus, first-year enrolments in both primary and secondary education are about fifteen times higher in the Mid-Western State than in Kano State when weighted by population. The attainment of an enrolment rate of 50 per cent in primary education by the mid 1970s was deemed to be 'clearly impossible, and attempts to attain it in some states may lead to a serious decline in the quality of primary education' (World Bank 1974, p. 179). Despite this gloomy prediction, the Federal government announced that 100 per cent enrolment would be mandatory in all states in 1976–7.

The last column of Table 6.5 shows the estimated over-all *per capita* recurrent government expenditure in the twelve states comprising the Federation in 1968–9. In a developing country such as Nigeria the volume and pattern of government expenditures more or less dictate the pace and pattern of development (Teriba and Philips 1971

Table 6.5

Primary school enrolment, by state, in Nigeria, 1970
and over-all per capita recurrent government expenditure, 1968–9

State	Percentage distribution of primary school enrolments	Primary school enrolment as percentage of total population	Percentage distribution of total graduating (Years 6, 7 or 8)	Per capita recurrent government expenditure – all services (£0·9=100·0)
Lagos	6·5	13·4	3·6	789
Benue Plateau	4·2	3·3	5·1	156
Kano	1·7	0·9	1·8	100
Kwara	3·4	4·4	4·7	244
North-Central	2·7	2·1	2·9	156
North-Eastern	3·6	1·4	4·7	100
North-Western	2·1	1·1	2·4	422
East-Central	29·5	12·7	24·0	–
Mid-Western	9·8	12·0	14·5	422
Rivers	4·1	8·2	2·8	–
South-Eastern	10·7	9·2	5·7	156
Western	21·7	7·1	27·8	233
Total Nigeria	100·0	5·6	100·0	–

Sources: World Bank 1974, p. 251; Teriba and Philips 1971, p. 83.

Moreover, the social, economic, and political consequences of such a uneven pattern of government expenditure on public goods like educa tion are especially serious in a Federal State. Clearly expenditure is no spatially biased in favour of areas of greatest need (eight times as muc is spent on each person in Lagos State compared to Kano or Nortl Eastern States). Such spatial inequality of expenditure leads to a accumulation of inequalities; for example, the scarcity of skills is serious obstacle to development in the less-developed areas, and

it is those areas that are already richer in the possession of skills that are plannir to expand educational facilities: the Western and East Central States are going t spend proportionately and absolutely vastly greater sums than Kano, the Nortl Western and North-Eastern States. In a sense, the hollowest note in the entir planning exercise is its failure to propose measures to close the educational ga in the country or to prevent it widening unduly. Declarations about equality d not themselves reduce inequality (O'Connell 1971, p.55).

CONCLUSIONS

We have tried to show that spatial inequalities are often the result c the operation of the political system — at national, regional, and loc: levels — and that the partitioning of accessible space into legally bou ded spaces (for administration, elections, allocation of public good and so on) is often the result of the decisions of the socially, econc mically, and politically powerful who, by their actions, divide citi for political/administrative purposes, allocate resources regionall and scramble for overseas territory (as Empire builders in the conver tional sense or as 'territory' creators in the economic partitioning c space, for example, by the multi-nationals, and through the organiz: tion of international trade). Within the political territories so devise the governmental systems are allocational systems and produc explicitly or implicitly, locationally biased distributions of publi goods. There are losers in the political systems, and there is a location: bias in their distribution (Dye 1966).

Population growth, the expansion of settlement, industrializatio: and urbanization have together produced a massive redistribution c population over space, and the political organization of space is no highly complex. Urban dwellers in particular now depend upon th political system for the organization of society (locally as providers c basic services such as sewage, waste disposal, health, and educatio and nationally as regulators of the actions of individuals and enterpris and as providers of a wide range of public goods and services). Gover ment is increasingly required to rectify the more severe consequenc of the operations of the market mechanism with its in-built tendency to produce inequalities. In all these matters the political system as an allocational mechanism engenders conflict which is spatially based (between ghetto/non ghetto, central city/suburb, core/periphery); and as the 'referee', government is also involved in conflict resolution which is spatially based. In effect, therefore, the inputs, outputs, and allocational mechanisms of political systems all have a clear, yet usually neglected, locational expression, as do the attempts by the political system to reduce inequalities. These aspects of spatial inequalities have been neglected by geographers and political scientists but, as Cox and Reynolds (1974) demonstrate, spatial organization is not 'an historical aberration' but a 'logical necessity' in any society in which there exist preferences for goods which can only be satisfied through collective action.

7 Spatial engineering and social engineering

POSITIVE DISCRIMINATION

Of all the possible spatial approaches to the attenuation of inequalitie the most straightforward is the redistribution of financial technologica and labour resources in favour of the most disadvantaged territorie regions, and neighbourhoods. Usually effected by governments an centralized institutions, this approach is often termed 'positive discr mination'. In a broader context which includes aspatial policies, it part of the social engineering philosophy which, accepting that free market and mixed economies can never achieve an equitable equil brium, seeks to ameliorate the worst disparities and injustices c capitalism through piecemeal social and economic policies rather tha through the implementation of utopian blueprints. As such, it is direct product of the traditional paternalistic humanism of Wester scholarship, forming part of what Harvey (1974a, p.20) has calle 'the technics and mechanics of urban, regional and environment management'. Put more directly, positive discrimination is essentiall a way of treating the effects of inequality rather than removing it causes.

International Aid. At the broadest level of resolution, positive discriminatio takes the form of international aid. This encompasses loans, grant technical assistance, and even private investment, and may be admini tered bilaterally or multilaterally. Large-scale movements of aid bega shortly after World War II with the Marshall Plan, financed by th United States to bolster its war-torn European allies. During the 1950 and 1960s, as more Third World countries gained independence, ai became a useful weapon in Western and Sino-Soviet cold war offer sives to establish and preserve political influence throughout the world By the late 1960s the flow of resources from some donor countrie approached one per cent of their GNP, and the list of donor countrie had expanded beyond the super-powers to include smaller countrie such as Austria, Denmark, and Sweden, whose motivation in aid-givin must be seen as more philanthropic or conscience-salving than politica In addition, there is evidence of a tendency towards greater geographi dispersal of aid, which must largely be attributed to the extension o the activities of multilateral agencies such as the World Bank, th

International Monetary Fund (IMF), and the Alliance for Progress —
the regional development bank for Latin America (Friedmann, Kalmanoff, and Meagher 1966). Nevertheless, the geography of aid still
has a strong political flavour: Asia, for instance, receives less aid *per
capita* than the average for all recipient countries, yet within this region
Western strategic involvement has led to South Korea and South
Vietnam receiving above-average amounts of aid. Similarly, Turkey and
Yugoslavia receive above-average aid because of the special interest of
the West in limiting the influence of the Soviet bloc (Wall 1973).
Bilateral aid from several countries also reflects localized political aspirations and colonial ties. Thus much British and French aid is directed
towards former African colonies, whilst Japanese aid is disbursed
largely within Asia, and aid from the newly-rich OPEC countries is
mainly directed towards the three 'front-line' Arab countries of Egypt,
Syria, and Jordan. In contrast, aid from West Germany and Scandinavia
is widely spread.

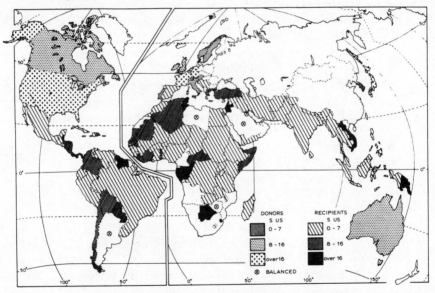

Fig. 7.1. Origins and directions of international aid: annual averages *per capita*, in $
U.S., 1968–70. Line shadings and black areas represent net official receipts from
Development Assistance countries and multilateral agencies; stippled shadings repre-
sent official bilateral flows from donor countries. (Source: Morgan 1974, p. 283.)

The flow of aid from the rich, non-communist countries of the
Development Assistance Committee (DAC) between 1968 and 1970 is
shown in Fig. 7.1. The broad pattern clearly reflects a shift in resources

from rich countries to poor countries, with the richest countries tending to be the biggest donors. Closer inspection, however, shows that the poorest countries are by no means the biggest recipients of aid. This basic shortcoming in the geography of aid, together with the continuing magnitude of international disparities in levels of living, the diminished imperative of aid-giving that accompanied international détente, the balance of payments difficulties of the United States and the United Kingdom, and the increasing disaffection within the United States with the apparent failures of US development assistance, brought about a 'crisis of aid' which prompted the World Bank to appoint a Commission on International Development to conduct a 'grand assize' on the mechanics and success of foreign aid. The Committee's report — the Pearson Report — emerged, amid much publicity, as an article of faith in a world community which refuses to tolerate 'the extreme and shameful disparity in standards of life that now exists within and between nations' and stresses that the prime purpose of aid 'is to reduce disparities and remove inequalities. It is to help the poorer countries move forward, in their own way, into the industrial and technological age so that the world will not become more and more starkly divided between the haves and have-nots, the privileged and the less privileged' (Pearson *et al.* 1969, pp. 7-10). The central theme of the report is its advocacy of a large and sustained expansion of aid to the Third World to enable developing countries to achieve self-sustaining growth by the end of the century and thus become independent of aid. Rich countries are urged to provide the necessary resources partly, as we have seen, through moral obligations, and partly through an 'enlightened self-interest' based on a desire to increase their own level of living through a fuller use of the world's resources and an increase in international trade.

These arguments rest largely on the assumption that developing countries could not supply the investment expenditure regarded as a necessary condition for material progress (that is, 'development') without intolerable reductions in already low levels of consumption. Aid, it is argued, relaxes this constraint by providing additional resources to augment investment without subtracting from consumption. *Laissez-faire* economists, however, have always doubted the desirability, the necessity, and the positive contribution to growth and development of foreign aid (see, for example, Bauer 1961, Bauer and Wood 1961, Friedman 1958). Recently, the utility of aid as a redistributive and growth-inducing mechanism has been questioned by economists whose standpoint is at the opposite end of the political spectrum (Griffin 1970, Griffin and Enos 1971, Byres 1972b). Prompted by the abundant evidence of the shallowness of the rich countries' moral commitment to aid (for example, the US 'destabilization' of Chile after it became ill-disposed towards President Allende's democratically-elected socialist government), these writers have questioned the premise that donors are selfless nations carrying the burden of aid in the interests of world prosperity. They suggest that aid is a neo-colonial mechanism whose burden falls not on the donors but on the recipients. The arguments are several. Private foreign investment may help trigger off economic development, but it is essentially done for profit and from a redistributive point of view is highly regressive in the short term. According to the U.S. Department of Commerce, U.S. businessmen invested $9 billion in underdeveloped countries between 1950 and 1965, and drew back $25·6 billion in profit in the same period. Many feel that such figures are simply a reflection of the strength of an economic empire which has been carefully buttressed by military and cultural assistance programmes designed to 'mercenarize' and 'steal the souls' of Third World countries (Buchanan 1972).

Official aid is more pernicious. Cheryl Payer (1974) has shown, for example, how 'cheap' loans can force developing countries into a 'debt trap'. Similarly, tied aid reduces the burden on the donor by promoting exports and production in the donor economy; and even loans from multilateral institutions such as the IMF mean the abolition of currency controls and trade protection in recipient countries, allowing the multinational corporations of the rich world to syphon off the bulk of the wealth generated in the development process. As Streeten (1968, p. 154) graphically puts it:

The Kings of Siam are said to have ruined obnoxious countries by presenting them with white elephants that had to be maintained at vast expense. In the modern setting this can be achieved best by tying a high-interest loan, called 'aid', to projects and to donors' exports and to confine it to the import content (or better still, some part of it) of the project. But even untied aid on soft terms can be used to promote exports of a white elephantine nature, because capital grants do not cover the subsequent recurrent expenditure which the elephant inflicts on its owners. Receiving aid is not just like receiving an elephant but like making love to an elephant. There is no pleasure in it, you run the risk of being crushed and it takes years before you see the results.

It is also argued that financial aid often intensifies internal political, regional, social, and ethnic inequalities in recipient countries by strengthening the bureaucratic and educated élites who control the distribution of aid. In the same way, urgent social and economic reforms can be more easily postponed whilst it is possible to 'paper the cracks' with foreign aid. In addition, it is pointed out that 'aid' from poor countries to the rich in the form of migrations of skilled man-power has now reached disturbing proportions. A recent study commissioned by the United Nations Conference on Trade and Development (UNCTAD) estimated the equivalent income transferred to the United States in 1970 through the doctors, engineers, and other professionals who left Third World countries for the greener pastures of the United States at $3700 million — more than the total official U.S. aid to the Third World for that year (*New Internationalist* 1975a).

Finally, one of the most powerful arguments against aid relates to its efficiency in promoting economic development, and is shared by critics from both ends of the ideological spectrum (Bauer and Yamey 1972, Griffin 1972). Basically, the argument is that there is no empiri-cal evidence in support of the proposition that aid is at all catalytic in terms of promoting growth in material well-being. There is, of course, still a case for aid on short-term redistributive grounds even if it is assumed that aid does not enhance development prospects at all. Nevertheless, even simple transfers of income from rich *nations* to poor nations are no guarantee of a transfer from rich *people* to poor people. Moreover, redistribution alone, unless implemented with Draconian measures, could never have much impact on global inequali-ties because of the effects of population growth in absorbing the bulk of the transfer payments.

These problems have led to the espousal of more favourable trading arrangements as a less direct but more acceptable form of positive discrimination. Largely the intellectual creation of Prebisch, these ideas have been adopted by UNCTAD, which for several years now has been pressing for lower tariffs on imports from Third World countries and for commodity schemes aimed at stabilizing fluctuations in the prices of the primary commodities on which many Third World countries have to rely for revenue. Unfortunately, this approach suffers from the reluctance of industrial countries to endanger the viability of their own manufacturing industries. The United States, in particular, has objected to unreciprocated preferences on the grounds that they are contrary to the aims of a universal lowering of tariffs through GATT. Furthermore, the findings of economists such as Johnson (1972a) and Little and Clifford (1965) suggest that trading preferences of a substantially resource-transferring kind are unlikely to be either effective or workable.

For various reasons then, the concept of international co-operation for development and equality is wearing rather thin. International conferences on food, population, resources, and trade are becoming less successful in taking the steam out of the Third World's demands for greater justice, and fewer countries are willing to participate in schemes such as the United Nations' 'Strategy for the Second Development Decade'. Bargaining power, rather than positive discrimination, is seen by many as the key to a more equitable relationship between countries, with oil and sugar cartels as opening gambits in the struggle for greater equality. Such an approach may certainly be very effective for those Third World countries fortunate enough to possess scarce and (in the short run) unsubstitutable resources, but there would remain a need for subsequent redistribution of resources from the newly rich to the continuing poor. The experience of the past three decades suggests that levels of beneficence between nation states fall far short of what would be needed to redress the balance through positive discrimination alone. Indeed, it seems that rich nations are only prepared to give aid at present if it promises financial and practical benefits for themselves: a 'new economic order' will need a new philosophy of aid.

Regional Policies as Positive Discrimination. The idea of positive discrimination in favour of disadvantaged regions is familiar to geographers, and a detailed consideration of the theory and practice of regional economics need not detain us here (see Richardson 1969, Boudeville 1966, Isard 1960, McCrone 1969). Regional policies now constitute a familiar part of central government legislation in most countries, although their vigour and the philosophy behind them varies considerably. The importance of a positive approach to regional problems has been confirmed by the relative immobility of both labour and industry in many countries. Other reasons for positive discrimination at the regional level include:
(1) a desire to achieve equality of opportunity and affluence by place of residence;
(2) the need for regulatory mechanisms in order to control national rates of inflation and levels of unemployment;
(3) the desire to make the fullest possible use of regional (and therefore national) resources. As well as fundamental human resources, these include fixed capital investments such as roads, factories, and schools, which might otherwise be under-utilized;
(4) the need to recognize the strength of the political lobby from disadvantaged regions. As McCrone (1969) points out, this factor can become imperative when emotive issues concerning cultural, linguistic, and nationalistic differences are also involved; and
(5) the desire to gain maximum political effect from a minimum of public expenditure.

As with policies of positive discrimination at other scales, simple cash transfers are regarded by politicians, administrators, and economists as 'money down the drain', so that most regional aid takes the form of either investment incentives or selective assistance through rural indus-trialization, new town development, and infra-structure improvements aimed at stimulating growth.

One of the most commonly used forms of positive discrimination is the transfer of financial resources from prosperous to disadvantaged regions in the form of tax concessions, employment premiums, cheap loans, and other regional investment incentives. An important advan-tage of this method is that the consumption of real resources is limited to the administrative costs of taxation and disbursement. On the other hand, unless the tax system is sufficiently progressive, the subsidy of entrepreneurs in disadvantaged regions from national income tax revenues may well end up benefitting the rich in the disadvantaged regions at the expense of the less rich in the prosperous regions (Richardson 1969). In this case, an equitable distribution of prosperity may be achieved at the regional level, but only through an inequitable mechanism which increases intra-regional disparities. Moreover, the designation of areas eligible for aid in the form of 'investment' incen-tives is usually couched in very broad areal terms (see, for example, the Development Areas in Denmark, France, the Netherlands, and the United Kingdom). There are strong grounds for this in terms of ad-ministrative convenience and political expedience, but from the point of view of both regional economic balance and territorial distributive justice, such an approach gives insufficient weighting to sub-regional spatial differentiation. In short, a 'blanket' approach, even at the regional level, will be insensitive to local variations in need and potential for growth.

The main alternative is a strategy based on localized infrastructure investment aimed at improving the physical and economic environment and so promoting economic growth. These investments include road-building, engineering projects, factory construction, urban renewal, and the clearance of derelict land, all of which clearly involve the consumption of real resources. Since governments have only a limited amount of money to spend, the construction of an extra mile of urban motorway in, say, Clydeside means one less in Tyneside, or fewer hospital beds in Yorkshire, or fewer new schools in Ulster. A major problem, therefore, is for governments to decide which types of infra-structure investment are most efficacious, and where. Unfortunately, we are no nearer the resolution of such questions in either theory or practice than we are to knowing which forms of investment incentives are most effective in a given set of circumstances.

In the absence of such knowledge, the best over-all strategy is thought by many to be discrimination in favour of selected *growth points* which can best benefit from the 'natural' advantages of agglomeration: external economies, and economies of scale. The general aim is thus to stimulate (or even create) medium-sized centres in disadvantaged regions in order that they become self-sustaining centres of industrial and service growth. Because of the friction of space, the advantages associated with this growth will decrease with distance from the growth point but, it is argued, through a process analogous to Myrdal's 'spread' effect, surrounding areas would benefit from the prosperity generated in the growth point. The life chances of the rural and small-town poor, for example, would be enhanced by the possibility of commuting to more lucrative employment in the growth point instead of undergoing personal upheaval for the uncertain rewards of long-distance migration. In turn, this brings about the possibility of their use of services (leisure facilities, specialist retail stores, technical colleges, hospitals, etc.) which were previously unavailable or inaccessible. A growth point strategy lends itself both to investment incentive schemes and to direct infrastructure investment, and is thus subject to the advantages and disadvantages of both.

Critics of the growth-pole concept argue that local 'backwash' effects may in fact exacerbate the problems of areas which happen to fall outside the sphere of influence of the growth point. It is also worth noting that a badly chosen growth point may need a permanent subsidy to keep it viable, and that even the advocates of growth-point strategy are uncertain, or at least in disagreement, about their optimal size. In practice, growth-pole strategies have had mixed success, being more effective in the industrial environments of the richer nations than in the primary environments of developing countries, and more successful in circumstances where the strategy is undiluted by administrative and political modifications. In Appalachia, for example, the logic of the growth-point strategy adopted by the Appalachia Regional Commission and the Economic Development Administration was weakened by the proliferation of growth points (around 200) in order to appease local politicians (Alonso 1968). Similarly, southern Italy, which in many ways is ideally suited to a growth-pole strategy, has suffered from fragmented investment because of political pressures and feelings of civic pride (which reached a climax in 1970 with rioting in Reggio di Calabria when it was announced that Catanzaro had been selected as a regional centre in preference to Reggio di Calabria). In contrast, the growth-point strategies adopted in Norway are generally regarded as having been successful in promoting growth, raising levels of living, and reducing regional disparities.

Priority Areas. In contrast to the predominantly growth-oriented approaches to the attenuation of international and regional disparities, metropolitan problems are increasingly being tackled through the designation of priority areas under a 'worst first' philosophy which has emerged with the realization that longer-established strategies such as large-scale urban renewal, slum clearance, zoning, and green belts are unable to cope with the social and environmental problems of contemporary urban areas. Almost all urban planning can be seen as positive discrimination of a sort, but it is the priority area approach — exemplified by 'stress areas', 'action areas', and 'code-enforcement areas' — which is most explicitly directed towards reducing intra-urban disparities in social well-being. In the United Kingdom, the concept was first put forward by the Newsom Report (1963) on education, which strongly recommended special educational help for slum areas. Following the more positive recommendations of the Plowden Report (1967) on primary education, funds were made available for use in Educational Priority Areas, which were to be set up in neighbourhoods where: (1) children were suffering from 'multiple deprivation' through the combination of several disadvantages such as living in overcrowded dwellings and attending schools with high ratios of pupils to teachers and a high turnover of teaching staff; and (2) the physical quality of housing and the environment was also bad.

Similarly, as a result of the Seebohm Report's recommendations (1968), the government set up twelve experimental Community Development Projects in areas of special social need (Carney and Taylor 1974, Lees and Smith 1975). The aim is to help people to 'assume an increasing measure of control over their own lives', to 'use constructively the services which exist', and to 'take some of the load off the statutory services' (Holman 1970b, p.175). Other centrally guided, area-based urban-priority schemes in Britain include the Urban Aid Programme, the General Improvement Area (GIA) scheme, and the Housing Action Area programme (Duncan 1974). The Urban Aid Programme was launched in 1968 to provide funds for educationally oriented projects of all kinds in areas of social need (defined mainly in terms of high rates of overcrowding and a high incidence of immigrant children on school rolls). GIAs were introduced by the Housing Act of 1969, which provides funds for the improvement of environmental quality (through, for example, landscaping and pedestrianization) in physically deteriorated urban areas. Complementary to these are the

Housing Action Areas established under the White Paper of 1973 entitled *Better Homes: The Next Priorities* (Department of the Environment 1973). These are designed to promote internal and external improvements to groups of between 400 and 500 dwellings, not only in inner-city areas where bad housing goes with high levels of demand but also in older industrial areas where poor housing and environment are associated with a declining population and low demand. Similar positive discrimination on an areal basis is to be found in the strategies of some individual cities. The areas of 'Housing Stress' designated by the Greater London Council (1969) in its Development Plan of 1969, for example, were the direct predecessors of the Housing Action Areas. In the United States, where centrally organized schemes are less enthusiastically received, there is a multitude of different priority area projects, of which the Housing Code Enforcement Area Program of the City of St. Louis (St. Louis City Plan Commission 1971) is just one example. Because of the scale of urban problems, however, many urban governments are participating in the federally run Model Cities Program, in which Model Neighbourhood Areas are set up as target areas for various projects aimed at improving the well-being of the most deprived communities.

These programmes, and others like them elsewhere, have achieved some success in a relatively short period of time. They are not, however, without shortcomings. One of the most common failings from an academic point of view is the lack of guidance as to the criteria for the delimitation of priority areas. It is quite common for committee reports and government circulars to lay down general guidelines, only to leave city governments floundering when it comes to the practical methodology of defining areas of need. Social indicators are clearly useful here, but even with the considerable literature on these which now exists, it is most often the biggest and richest local authorities which are first in the queue with the required evidence of need. It is no coincidence, for example, that the first work on delimiting Educational Priority Areas took place in London (Little and Mabey 1972). An attempt to avoid this problem in relation to the British Urban Aid Programme and Housing Action Area scheme is represented by the *national* analysis of small-area census data conducted by the Department of Environment and the Home Office and reported by Sally Holtermann (see p. 73). But in other programmes the problem remains, and is aggravated by the *ad hoc* procedures of some administrators, who see the lack of specific criteria as an opportunity to discriminate between the 'deserving' and the 'undeserving' poor. Thus, for example, GIA designation may avoid 'difficult' neighbourhoods with high proportions of immigrants or the elderly (Duncan 1974).

Apart from criticisms specific to particular projects (Holman 1970b, Duncan 1974), other comments apply equally well to all forms of area-based positive discrimination and lead us to question their utility in achieving the fundamental shifts in the distribution of real income and the means of its production that are clearly necessary. One major objection is that positive discrimination at all levels – international, regional, and intra-urban – is not nearly positive enough. Present levels of munificence are sufficient only to maintain the *status quo* or, at best, to serve as a palliative, although this is not to deny that positive spatial discrimination is extremely beneficial to large numbers of individuals. In addition, it is clear that the adoption of particular forms of aid and priority action is likely to be governed more by speculation than by certainty as to their efficiency in eliminating disparities or creating growth. It is for this reason that writers such as Knox (1974a, 1974c) have urged the institution of a regular series of territorial social indicators which could be used to monitor the need for and effects of positive discrimination and other policies. But our main reservation is that present methods of positive discrimination are insufficiently radical, since they fail to come to grips with the basic processes responsible for the manifestations of inequality that we know exist. Just what these processes are, and how they operate, should be the focus of social geographic research. As Harvey (1974a, p. 23) puts it: 'In order to change the world, we must first understand it'. Some of these processes have been described in this book; others have been all too briefly referred to. Until they are all fully illuminated, and our theoretical knowledge is supplemented by an effective factual monitoring system, positive discrimination must proceed under a cover of confusion and uncertainty, with little effect on the root causes of spatial inequality. And until the public, politicians, and administrators are educated, persuaded, shocked, or forced into adopting more positive attitudes, modest funds will continue to predispose modest results.

SPATIAL REORGANIZATION

In chapter 5 we saw how a partial explanation of aspects of the level of living in a place is its accessibility to others. From such findings, logical deduction is that social well-being could be manipulated by altering the accessibility pattern, which we term 'spatial engineering' here. The accessibility pattern is not constant, however, even without such intervention, so in this section we look first at general trends in the evolution of spatial structures.

The 'Shrinking World'. Improvements in transport technology have much reduced the relative isolation of places, at various spatial scales, through decreases in the time and (relative) cost involved in moving between two points. This 'shrinkage' of time- and cost-distances has been termed 'time-space/cost-space convergence' (Janelle 1968, 1969, Abler 1971). One of its major characteristics is that there have been marked spatial inequalities in its application.

If 'distance shrinkage' occurred at the same rate between every pair of places, following some transport innovation, then the spatial inequality of places relative to each other would not be changing although, because movement may become less of a constraint relative to other costs, the intensity of the inequalities might decline. Unfortunately, this has not been the common trend, for two related reasons. First, not all people are advantaged to the same extent. The bases of greater personal mobility in recent years have been the widespread adoption of the motor car and the fall in relative prices of air travel. Car ownership is still far from universal, however, even in the most affluent countries, and air travel is too expensive for many (Pahl 1970). Thus those who have been unable to buy, operate, and maintain cars — particularly the young and the old, the infirm and the poor — have become relatively under-privileged, as growing car ownership in other sectors of the community has led to a reduction in the provision of public transport facilities: the same is true for long-distance travel, as the plane makes passenger trains and boats obsolescent, with undesirable consequences for those who cannot, or will not fly.

The second reason for growing inequalities consequent on transport improvements is that new facilities are not being universally introduced. Selective location policies occur because motorways, high-speed railway lines, SST aeroplanes, and the like are very expensive items. When introduced by private firms, they will be placed where they are most profitable; when they are government investments (as with most fixed routes) financial return will not necessarily be a major intention, but nevertheless the pressures of cost-benefit analysis in the use of scarce public resources generally require that facilities be placed where they are most demanded, and hence will be most used. There will be exceptions to this, such as roads like the Trans-Amazon Highway which is intended to open up Brazil's interior, and motorway investments in 'problem' regions by British governments as attempts to provide attractive infrastructure in areas where industrial investment is thought desirable.

But the general trend is clear: in Britain the motorway system links the major population centres, as does the inter-city express passenger train service.

Different parts of the world are shrinking at different rates, therefore, mainly to the advantage of the large settlements, which are benefiting from the cumulative advantages of early growth (Forer 1974). As pointed out in Chapter 5, in ocean shipping the innovations — containers, very large tankers etc. — are on the heavily trafficked routes, reducing the per unit costs of transport for the places at either end; elsewhere, older, more expensive technology prevails, which makes imports and exports relatively dearer for the countries concerned, which are usually those already disadvantaged because of their size and location within the world trade system.

In terms of the world's economic geography, the main consequence of these trends is centralization — the growth of the big cities and the super-powers (Janelle 1969, Grötewold 1971). In terms of social geography, the main trend is deconcentration (urban sprawl at the city-scale) as more rapid movement along improved channels knits neighbouring communities more tightly together (Johnston 1975a). The places which lose out are those bypassed by the developments: the small countries off the world's main shipping routes; the towns with no easy connection to a motorway or a railway; the inner suburbs missed by the expressways which carry long-distance commuters to the city centre. Centralization is occurring within the city, too. There have been major changes in the retail grocery trade in recent years (Johnston and Rimmer 1969), with the replacement of a multitude of small shops serving local populations by a few large supermarkets, many of them only accessible to, and useable by, given the amounts purchased, car owners. (This decline of the small shops is often accelerated by their removal in slum-clearance schemes: Berry, Parsons and Platt 1968) school systems are being 'rationalized', with the trend towards fewer larger units, more distant on average from the pupils' homes, with unfortunate consequences in student behaviour resulting from the necessary travel (Lee 1957, 1961); general practitioners are closing their individual surgeries to join neighbourhood health centres, which serve much larger areas; suburban and small-town police stations are being closed and car patrols from large central depots replace the foot and cycle patrols of the British 'local bobby'. In terms of the discussion in Chapter 5, such trends can only lead to greater spatial inequalities.

Centralization is compounded by the nature of the location-decision making process, particularly when this involves decisions made by private, profit-oriented organizations, but also often when they are made by public agencies. However detailed and sophisticated their information gathering and analysis, location-decision-makers must act in states of uncertainty about the consequences of their actions and the decisions of their competitors and others who will influence their well-being. And so they tend to be conservative, favouring proven locations rather than risking capital, and perhaps shareholders' wrath, on a gamble. Someone wishing to live in a prestigious suburb in a town will almost certainly discover which area is considered 'desirable' by other residents: it would be a supremely self-confident optimist who believed he or she alone could alter the social geography of the town by establishing a new prestigious area. (There are some of these people, however, like those who have led the 'gentrification' process of re-establishing high status areas in places like London's Islington and Washington's Georgetown.) And so, as Webber (1971) has made clear, concentration and centralization are the common tendencies, more so than probably would be the case if all decision-makers had perfect information and ability to use it.

All of these trends need not work in the same direction, exacerbating spatial inequalities. Concentration of shops into fewer centres, for example, could reduce the number of spatial monopolists able to charge high prices, by increasing competition. But those living relatively long distances from the centres could be losers, especially if some of them are relatively immobile. This could well result in the continued prosperity of local spatial monopolists: village stores are not disappearing as rapidly from the face of Britain as might have been predicted a few years ago, perhaps because of the rising relative costs of public and private transport. And the industry itself is likely to change: merger activity is very probable —as it is in most sectors of the economy (Galbraith 1975) — which may remove competition and merely rewrite spatial monopoly at a larger scale. Spatial structures are merely the locational manifestations of social and economic structures. While the aim of business remains profit, it is certain that spatial systems will be manipulated to maintain those profits; this is no different from the past and present situations, so the spatial inequalities are unlikely to be different either.

COUNTERING CENTRALIZATION

Centralization of population and economic activity into but a few places is not a new phenomenon and it has worried governments for at least 400 years; Queen Elizabeth I of England took positive, largely unsuccessful steps to curb the growth of London. The health and congestion problems which seem to be so rampant in larger places; the leads which they give to national inflation because of supply: demand imbalances in the labour and housing markets; the relative social, cultural, and economic deprivation of the inhabitants of smaller and less accessible places: all of these have been causes of concern in many places and at many times. A variety of policies has been tried in several countries to redirect jobs towards areas where demand for labour is low relative to supply, in the hope that this will lead to the revitalization of 'depressed areas' and reduce the pressure on the burgeoning metropolises: few analyses suggest that these policies have been particularly successful, although assessment procedures are far from complete or universally accepted (Hall 1975, McCrone 1969, Manners *et al.* 1972).

Why is such redistribution desirable? Arguments for it often are based on notions of 'territorial justice', on a 'fair share for all places', but this may not be the best way of achieving individual justice, which is presumably the major goal of social and economic policy. Might it not be more desirable to allow centralization to continue? Analyses have suggested that, in the long-term, spatial inequalities disappear (Williamson 1965); concentration of economic development into a few parts of a country is necessary for initial 'take-off', but once this occurs, location-decision-makers will see the benefits of alternative locations and development at the latter will remove the supply:demand imbalances between places. Thus some argue that the market forces should be allowed full play, as in time they will produce at least relative spatial equality (Berry 1970). This might be hurried along by some transfer of resources from rich to poor areas, as part of income redistribution procedures, but large-scale interference is unnecessary. Such a view seems to ignore the realities of the political and economic power of vested interest groups in the already prosperous areas, however, and assumes that the factors of production other than labour are relatively mobile, which in the short-term at least is almost certainly not so. Governments are elected for short periods: promises of prosperity in several decades' time will do them little good in a depressed area at the next election.

An alternative pro-centralization argument, forcefully mounted by Richardson (1973b), is that the diseconomies of large cities and conurbations are far from proven. Unfortunately, this case — and that against it — must be based on little hard evidence from which to derive cost-benefit assessments of various settlement patterns. Some detailed work has been done on the costs of traffic congestion in settlements of various sizes (Neutze 1965) and there are the studies already referred to in Chapter 5 on the relationship between city size and crime, health and other indices of social well-being. On the benefit side of the equation, there is a traditional belief in the great advantages to firms of agglomeration economies, of the efficiencies in the flows of goods, ideas, and people resulting from proximity of origin and destination (Pred 1965). Richardson has, from this evidence, suggested a set of cost–benefit curves for settlements of various sizes (Fig. 7.2), which indicate that the financial benefits of growth far outweigh the greater costs until cities are very large.

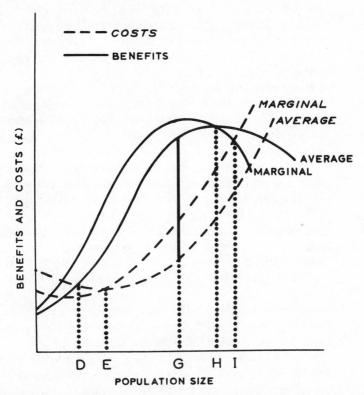

Fig. 7.2. Hypothetical cost and benefit curves by city size. The five population sizes indicated are: D — the minimum viable size for cities; E — the size where average costs are lowest; G — the size where benefits exceed costs by the greatest amount; H — the size where marginal benefits are less than average benefits, and average benefits are maximized; and I — the size where total net benefits are maximised. (Source: Richardson 1973b, p.11.)

Interpretation of diagrams such as Fig. 7.2, assuming them to be reasonable representations of reality, is very much dependent on value judgements. For example, although benefits may be greater than costs for additional growth increments up to size I in the diagram, who obtain the benefits and who pay the costs? In a largely capitalist economy, many of the benefits go to entrepreneurs as profits from business ventures; many of the costs, on the other hand, are carried by the whole population, in pollution and the associated health hazards, traffic congestion, and the expensive technologies needed for its relief (paid for from rates and taxes), climatic modification, high land costs and so on. In other words, the negative externalities of urban growth – the unfortunate by-products of large, densely-occupied agglomerations (Mishan 1967) – are passed on by their developers. And, as Richardson's curves suggest, above a certain population size (on Fig.7.2) the marginal costs of extra growth exceed the marginal benefits, thereby creating relatively greater burdens for the many to bear for the benefit of the few. The new resident – entrepreneur or worker – pays only the average costs, which are less than the marginal costs of his entry: thus beyond a certain population threshold, growth creates greater costs for those already in the city, since the impact of the new development is shared by all.

With regard to population concentration, therefore, it would seem that societies must answer questions such as 'Is a higher crime rate, a greater amount of pollution, and a lower life expectancy an acceptable price to pay for marginal increases in the efficiency of cities as centres of economic production?'. Collecting information which would allow evaluation of such questions – in particular, what city sizes they should be addressed to – is an extremely daunting task, and its analysis even more so (Johnston 1976g). And perhaps other questions would have to be asked too. A number of people now question the 'big is beautiful' syndrome with regard to the economies of large-scale production. It may be that big factories, with automated mass-production processes and menial, repetitive tasks for so many employees, are more productive of worker alienation, strikes, lost time, absenteeism, and so on than are small firms. Certainly it is frequently argued that small firms are more innovative and productive of new industrial ideas (Jacobs 1971) so perhaps the great economic advantages of the big factory and city have begun to outreach themselves.

A number of alternative approaches to the problem of centralization have been suggested. Richardson (1973b), for example, is well aware of many of the unfortunate correlates of city size, such as crime rates, but argues that no causal relationships are involved. The problems arise, he says, because of the internal structure of the city. Most urban areas have congested cores dating from at least the last century – in both

Britain and America, and many other European countries too — and these densely packed areas are totally unsuited to a car-based society. Complete restructuring of the city would remove many of these problems — though the prototype of Los Angeles suggests that the new form will probably create many more of its own.

Rewriting the internal structure of the city is, at best, a very long-term goal, and while it may remove some of the urban ills, it is unlikely to affect other inequalities, such as those of wage differentials and the provision of various public facilities between places. Indeed, if cities are made more attractive places to live in, they could draw even more people to them, leading to greater inflation in wages and prices and greater relative deprivation for the places 'left behind'.

One suggestion for the equalization of place-to-place variations is for government action to depress wages where growth is considered undesirable and to inflate them where it is to be encouraged. Gould, for example, has suggested this as a way of attracting civil servants to the parts of African countries which they would prefer not to live in (Gould and White 1974). But such policies have been tried, with little success. In Britain, there are great spatial variations in the ratio of doctors to patients, and so a policy was introduced which forbade any further doctors practising in areas with fewer than 1800 patients on the average list and encouraged, by financial incentives, more doctors to areas where the average practitioners served 2500 or more patients: in 1972, the incentives were £490 per year for practices with an average of 2500-2999 patients per list, and £750 where the average list was 3000 or more. This policy, in operation in various ways since the creation of the National Health Service in 1948, has not been particularly successful, however (Butler, Bevan and Taylor 1973). Many doctors are not prepared to move to an area they consider unattractive for what is only a marginal increase in income, yet if the incentives were greater, and doctors did respond, then the incentives would be removed, since the average list size would fall, and the move would have been for naught.

An alternative policy, and one we have already mentioned in this chapter, is based on growth poles, which are aimed at inducing growth in relatively deprived areas. Governments often do this through the provision of the necessary infrastructure for economic advancement, such as roads, railways, and factories, perhaps bolstering this by subsidies to developments in the designated poles and by sanctions against developments elsewhere. Thus Friedmann (1966) suggested a hierarchy of growth poles for Venezuela, for example, and recent Labour governments in Australia and New Zealand have announced major new settlements (at Albury/Wodonga in the former and Rolleston in th latter) to counter the hegemony of their major metropolises. (Th Rolleston scheme was abandoned within a week of Labour's elector defeat at the November 1975 General Election in New Zealand.) A the international scale, too, growth poles have been proposed as mear of aiding groups of small, developing countries (Johnston 1975b).

Apart from the economic and social gains from growth poles di cussed above, other benefits may accrue. Studies of the origins c doctors and dentists in Britain, for example, show that many practis either in the area in which they were brought up or in the area of th medical school that they attended (Coates and Rawstron 1971, Butle Bevan, and Taylor 1973). Thus areas without medical schools stand ou as having a deficiency of practitioners, so that use of such a facility a a propulsive element in a growth pole (and universities create conside able volumes of money which are spent locally: Lewes and Kirkne: 1973) could be very beneficial for the social well-being of loca residents.

Growth poles can create backwash as well as trickle-down effect the former involve the 'sucking-in' of society's 'goods' to the designa ted poles, whereas the latter involve spread of the 'goods' to neighbou ing areas. Creation of a growth pole is, of course, creation of a spatia inequality, albeit perhaps to a lesser degree and over a smaller area tha that which it is supposed to remove. But if the backwash effects ar significant relative to the trickle-down effects, such a new spatial ir equality may be magnified. Little is known about the general balanc between the two, and it is probably fear that backwash effects are th greater that makes competition for growth pole status extreme, an makes losers in that process very wary of the whole procedure, a indicated by our earlier reference to riots in Reggio di Calabria. In th international field in particular, governments cannot afford politicall to create economic unions in which, for some time at least, the bene fits are likely to go to growth poles in other countries. Thus severa federations have collapsed (such as Malaysia and the British Wes Indies) through combinations of factors including both the fear o small members that the economic benefits will go to their larger part ners and the fear of the large members that their prosperity will b 'milked' by the smaller partners (Johnston 1975b): even within ar apparently successful union, the Central American Common Market there are fears that spatial inequalities are being created in favou of the initially more developed countries (McConnell and Conklin 1973).

ALTERNATIVE SOCIO–SPATIAL MILIEUX

In Chapter 5, we quoted various studies which suggest that the social composition of an area can have effects on the attitudes and behaviour of its residents. If this is so, then a restructuring of areas, to provide more 'class' mixing instead of the ordered separation of socio-economic groups which is typical of most urban areas, could be very beneficial to society. Neighbourhood effects, as we saw, can both accentuate the 'goods' in society — for example, educational attitudes — and exacerbate the 'bads' — for example, crime rates — but if urban areas could be designed to maximize the former effects and minimize the latter then, in conjunction with the restructuring suggested by Richardson and discussed above (p.242), levels of social well-being could be much improved.

The notion of socially 'mixed' or 'balanced' neighbourhoods is by no means a new one, as Wendy Etherington (1974) shows in her 'critical biography' of the topic. Many of the arguments in support of such mixture have been based on supposed 'improvements' for the 'lower classes'. Thus, from among their middle-class residents, balanced neighbourhoods are supposed to provide community leaders, who can both organize activities in the area and provide effective links with external bodies, such as governments. These middle-class people will also provide models of superior life-styles for the lower-classes to emulate, thus 'educating' them, raising standards, and ensuring co-operation among all strata of society. The distribution of immigrants among their host population, rather than their segregation in separate 'ghettos', should ensure their assimilation into society, as would a similar distribution of 'problem families' on public-housing estates.

Mixing should produce the aesthetic and cultural benefits of diversity according to Jane Jacobs (1961), therefore, although some might argue that, as generally proposed, it involves the imposition of middle-class values on all and the assimilation of all groups into a single life-style rather than the integration of various life-styles into a diverse society. Sennett (1972) has argued that a characteristic of human immaturity is an unwillingness to face the 'unknown', and that by retreating to suburbs peopled only by others like ourselves, we display such immaturity, as well as creating stereotypes of the others and eventual conflict with them over territory. The main examples of such conflict, and the impulse for Sennett's book, were the race riots of the 1960s in American cities. If we were to live among the 'others', rather than to retreat from them, we might come to live in much greater harmony. In a somewhat similar fashion, Downs (1973) argues that,

because suburbs are built around American cities for the white midd
class, low-income blacks are constrained to the relative deprivation
central city environments, and so are unable to participate in tl
mainstream of American urban society. He suggests that the subur
should be 'opened up', that they should retain their white middle-cla
dominance but that small proportions of other groups should I
introduced, to enable the latter to interact with a 'better' soci
economic milieu, producing the sorts of effects observed by Wilson ar
discussed in Chapter 5.

Most of the arguments for balanced neighbourhoods revolve arour
class differences and the need to assimilate ethnic and other mino:
ties, though they could be just as well applied to age groups ar
attempts to bridge the 'generation gaps'. But would the assimilatic
processes operate? Clearly the evidence quoted in chapter 5 indicat
that they do, on a small scale at least, but would they if applied to tl
whole urban society? Gans (1969, 1972) and others have suggest
that we tend not to make lasting contacts with those we have little
common with, and that spatial proximity of homes will generate inte
action only if those homes are under some common threat, like
motorway proposal or some other negative externality. Evidence fro
the British new towns, where there was some initial social mix, sugges
that the middle classes are not prepared to live among their 'inferio:
and help them (Heraud 1966) — or help themselves: Wendy Etheringtc
(1974) suggests that it is, if anything, the middle class which is most
need of education. The establishment of comprehensive schools
Britain has led the middle class to seek even further refuge in exclusi
catchment areas, and despite the sophisticated schemes to ensure int
gration of blacks and whites in American high schools (Hall 1973
there is little evidence that this is producing social integration of tl
two groups. Where it involves only a few 'deviant' individuals in an are
mix may have positive advantages, and indeed most people may acce]
such minimal mix, for Schelling's (1974) simulations suggest that segr
gation is greater than most people want. But minimal mix has minim
effect; it allows some filtering through the system but does not tack
the depth of social inequality.

The case for mixing is far from proven, therefore. Before it is, Wenc
Etherington suggests that we need positive answers to the followir
questions:
(1) Are individuals in mixed areas moved to 'improve' themselv
through 'emulation'?
(2) Do people regard social diversity in their area as a positive conti
bution to their standard of living?

(3) Do people in mixed areas participate in common social and cultural activities, which they consider superior to those in homogeneous areas?
(4) What extra opportunities do mixed areas create for underprivileged people, and are some opportunities in homogeneous areas removed?
(5) Does residential propinquity produce greater tolerance for social and other differences? (or is the black who is our neighbour untypical of blacks who live elsewhere?)
(6) Does middle-class leadership produce benefits for others? and
(7) Do the underprivileged get more, and cheaper, services than they do in homogeneous areas?
Answering these questions will be difficult, for we have few 'mixed' environments to provide valid laboratories, and setting up experiments will be very costly, not only financially but also in social and psychological terms, especially if the answers turn out to be negative.

The seventh of Wendy Etherington's questions suggests that some of the intra-urban inequalities may be removed by a more equitable distribution of public services and facilities. These can involve both positive and negative externalities, the sources of the conflicts which produce and maintain residential patterns. Among the former would be such facilities as doctors' surgeries, fire, police, and ambulance stations, swimming pools, open spaces, shops, and public transport routes: methods are available for testing the locational efficiency of existing patterns (Morrill 1974) and for producing distributions which minimize inequalities (Massam 1975), although Massam (1974) points out that the latter may often be too sophisticated and produce minimal savings. Among the negative externalities are motorways and various noxious facilities, many of which tend to be placed in 'lower-class' areas, both because of weaker political organization there to oppose their installation and because, in accepted cost-benefit terms, they are less affected (Adams 1970: if the average value of land in area A is £1000 per acre, and in area B £10 000, then land values in the latter area are likely to be more affected, in absolute terms, by the noise pollution of a new airport). In many ways, policies of redistributing facilities within the city should be comparable to those of redistributing them among settlements, ensuring reasonable access for all.

ADMINISTRATIVE REORGANIZATION

Chapter 6 was devoted to the theme of variations between administrative units, large and small, in the distribution of society's resources of wealth, status, and power. In it, we showed how the division of the world into independent nations, and the policies of their governments, influences the well-being of inhabitants of different places. Similar patterns were noted within countries, with central governments sometimes being spatially biased in their policies and local governments operating in different ways and at different levels within the constraints imposed by nation-wide regulations. Within cities too, spatial inequalities can arise through local biases — perhaps favouring those areas which voted for the party in power (Glassberg 1973).

One obvious way to circumvent these patterns would appear to be to rewrite the map of administrative districts. This has been done in several parts of the world with the creation of economic unions of various kinds, such as the Comecon, the European Economic Community, the Central American Common Market, and, at a lesser scale, the Australian and New Zealand Free Trade Agreement. The aims of such unions are to benefit all members by creating greater opportunities for economic growth, because of the accessibility to larger markets and the protection of tariffs. As the debate about Britain's membership of the EEC showed, prior to the 1975 referendum, as the 1976 discussion of national devolution in the United Kingdom illustrates, and as the failure of such unions as that of the former East and West Pakistan testifies, the economic benefits may impose considerable costs, notably in the loss of political sovereignty. For many countries — in Africa, America, and Asia — for which economic advantages of unions may appear attractive, political sovereignty has only recently been obtained, often after a long and bitter struggle against imperialist forces, and is not to be signed away lightly. Furthermore, the economic advantages may not be that great, as our earlier discussion of growth poles indicated; a union of equals may be beneficial to all in equal volume, but a union of, for example, the United States and Canada would benefit the former nine times more than it would the latter (Balassa 1967), and small countries fear such economic dominance — which is what most of them suffer now and what they see as the case in unions such as the Comecon.

International unions are feared by many countries, therefore, especially small countries, because they could mean loss of political and economic independence. Very similar arguments are often raised against schemes for reorganization of local government structures within countries. Most urban areas, in Britain, North America, Australasia, and elsewhere, grew with a relatively large central city around which were scattered suburban municipalities with separate administrative powers. The latter are often small and wealthy: they may be parasitic on the central city, whose roads their residents use to get to work and whose public (for example, parks) and private facilities (for example, shops are used more by the suburban inhabitants than central city inhabitants use comparable suburban facilities. Furthermore, the central cities are usually the oldest parts of the built-up area and have the greatest problems of financing urban renewal and providing for many of society's underprivileged who come to live there. Thus city poverty and suburban affluence can be seen side by side, as indicated most forcefully by the problems of New York City in 1975.

Two solutions to such problems suggest themselves. First, the administrative structure could be reorganized to ensure that the whole of a socio-economic complex such as an urban area falls under one jurisdiction, so that resources can then be shared more equitably. This is the course which has been taken in Britain with the extensive reorganization of local government in the 1970s. It encounters much opposition, however, particularly from those residents of the favoured areas, who are probably paying relatively low rates (local taxes) and do not wish to have to pay more to cover the costs of governing the problem areas of the urban complex. In addition, the residents of such small units which disappear into a larger area feel that they are being effectively disenfranchised, in that their voting power in the new authorities is often irrelevant to the over-all balance of power. And so, if the model which suggests that politicians distribute their rewards — public projects and so on — where the votes matter is a correct one (Glassberg 1973), these formerly independent groups may find that their claims are relatively ignored. (This may be considered desirable by many others, of course, if it leads to a redistribution of real income.) Thus small authorities rarely join neighbouring larger ones voluntarily, and reorganization has to be imposed by a strong central government, which does not fear for its own power base by taking such a course. It may, of course, take an intermediate line of action, by creating a hierarchy of authorities, with local control over local issues. But the latter — street-sweeping, fire services and so on — are not usually those over which conflict rages, for they are essential services rather than facilities — such as education and health — which can vary considerably in the amount and cost of provision.

The other solution is for the centralization of power over all services, and the removal of local administration. This might ensure equality of provision by area, though this is unlikely because of the political factor in the distribution of rewards. What it would certainly produce is citizen alienation from decision-making about local issues, an exaggeration of the problems discussed in the previous paragraph. A large, central, remote bureaucracy would be considered by many as the worst way of meeting local needs and problems. It could well set up a separate body within the society with its own identity and loyalties, much like the large industrial corporations (Galbraith 1975), which could become relatively immune from political control and so antithetical to many of the basic notions of democracy.

In very many countries, whether or not their governments are avowedly socialist in orientation, the state has come to play an increasing role in the provision of facilities and services and the general overseeing of levels of social well-being. While wanting local autonomy, they also wish to ensure equality among areas (Judge 1975), so the extent of local control is often considerably constrained especially as, in Britain, the United States, and elsewhere, so much of the income for local government is now provided by the national exchequer.

Local control frequently means control by a certain group of the facilities which they use, which requires definition of administrative areas relevant to such demands. Where there are several groups in an area, each wanting control over its own sector, the problem of defining areas may be immense. This was the case recently in Detroit, where the decision was taken to reduce the number of high-school districts from twenty-one to between seven and eleven, each of which should have 25,000–50,000 students and would be run by a locally elected board, with extensive powers over curricula, appointments, and other major issues. Two major groups were involved — the black and the white communities — and the range of possible alternative strategies aimed at: (1) maximum black control over black children; (2) maximum white control over white children; (3) maximum control over their own children by both groups; and (4) maximum integration. Jenkins and Shepherd (1972) showed that there were 7,300 possible different ways of amalgamating the twenty-one existing districts to form seven, within the size and contiguity constraints set, the majority of which would be most favourable to the white community. The protection of minority interests, and of various levels of equality, could often be a very difficult task, therefore, even when districts are being created explicitly to allow local control.

As we saw in chapter 6, a pervasive inequality which is encouraged if not created, by a spatial system of districts concerns electoral biases. The 'one-man, one-vote, one-value' principle of democracy is frequently violated by the nature of the electoral system. 'Rotten boroughs' - constituencies representing very few voters relative to most other constituencies — and 'gerrymanders' — the drawing of constituency boundaries so as to favour the political fortunes of the cartographers - are widely recognized methods of tampering with the popular expression. In the United States during the 1960s, a series of Supreme Cour rulings outlawed electoral practices which violated the supposed equality of every elector's vote. As Bushman and Stanley (1971) show for the nine south-eastern states, before reapportionment in Florida the smallest state senate district contained only 1/98 of the population of the largest; there were so many small districts in the state that the votes of only 12 per cent of the electorate would have been sufficient to win a majority in the senate. In general, it was the urban areas which were under-represented, because they contained the larger districts and, because reapportionment in the past had been controlled by the party in power — which not surprisingly had a rural base — few steps were taken before the 1960s to correct such a bias.

The same two solutions as are offered to the problem of inequalities between administrative areas are relevant to the removal of electoral biases. First, the constituency system can be redrawn, and much effort has been expended in the United States in recent years in the redistricting procedure (Dixon 1968). One professional geographer was engaged by the State of Washington to produce a redistricting plan; he had to divide the state into forty-nine districts, with an average of 68,495 persons in each and with each district having between 69,180 and 61,180 residents. He had to work with census enumeration districts, and to produce compact constituencies whose boundaries did not cross major natural features, such as the crest-line of the Cascade Mountains (Morrill 1973). Needless to say, this proved to be a very difficult task, with the size constraint being particularly burdensome. In Britain, parliamentary constituency boundaries must coincide with ward boundaries within the borough seats, which is likely to cause quite considerable size differences if the wards themselves vary in size. Taylor and Gudgin (1976) have shown that for Newcastle upon Tyne there are 337 ways of combining groups from the twenty wards to form the four constituencies of the borough. Although over-all Labour gets about just under 60 per cent of the votes there, in 256 (76 per cent) of the districting schemes it would get three of the four seats.

These two examples show some of the many problems of defining electoral districts to avoid the production of biases. In a comprehensive study, Rae (1971) has indicated that constituency systems, with each constituency electing one member, are almost certain to be strongly biased against minority parties (those which get 20 per cent or less of the vote), and usually magnify the majority of the winning party. Many of these biases come about because of the non-uniform distributions of voters from different classes and with different political attitudes (see Johnston 1976b), and it is very unlikely that any electoral system based on constituencies, however the voting in the constituencies is

conducted, can be bias-free (Dixon 1968). This suggests the secon
solution: removal of the constituency system and replacing it by
national election, as in Israel (Lakeman 1974). Such a procedur
would get rid of the biases caused by the interaction between con
stituencies and population distributions, but it would introduce ne
features to the democratic process. In many countries, the constituenc
system is defended because it provides delegates who represent loc:
interests on relevant issues: in others, it reflects the semi-independer
sovereignty of the districts, as with the U.S. Senate. National electior
would probably be fought on national issues alone, thereby perhar
producing voter alienation because the political system is so distar
from the local scene.

CONCLUSIONS

In chapters 4–6 of this book, we showed how where one lives can b
a strong influence on one's standard of living, through the joint effec
of position in the division of labour, relative location to points c
supply and demand for relevant goods, and administrative districtir
procedures. From these findings, it is possible to deduce that spati.
restructuring — the movement of jobs, the relocation of facilities, th
redistricting of administrative units — should produce benefits in soci.
well-being, and in this chapter we have reviewed some of the possib
means of achieving such ends. The relative success of some of them
such as the C.A.C.M., the British regional policies, and the America
reapportionment programmes — is clear, but another major theme i
the present chapter has been the conflict between such policies and th
continuing social processes within a society. We have also shown ho
policies aimed at compensating for the wastage, breakage, and im
balance of contemporary capitalist societies through positive discrim
nation of various sorts, are, at best, inadequate, and at worst, positivel
harmful. Spatial solutions alone seem insufficient, therefore, a findir
to which we ι ay more attention in the final chapter.

Conclusions

Our focus throughout this book has been on spatial patterns and their genesis, with particular attention being paid to the role of locational influences on levels of social well-being. Throughout this presentation, it will have become clear that we are offering only a partial explanation for the inequalities, and so the 'solutions' presented in Chapter 7 must be viewed as, at best, only partial too.

The spatial structure of a place — whether it be continent, country, or city — reflects the interactions between a human society and its physical environment. Thus the patterns which we have studied here — the distributions of settlements and settlement functions; the costs of transport and their influence on the prices of land, labour, and capital; the separation of population groups in the cities and its influence on socialization processes, and so on — can all be appreciated only in the societal context. The spatial structures which men create — their cities and towns, transport routes and terminals — do not have an existence independent of the societies which they reflect. They can, as has been shown here, amplify certain trends in society and reduce others, but only because of the way they are created: thus transport costs can influence the price of goods, and so affect levels of spatial well-being, but only because virtually all human societies have placed monetary values on time, which is a basic component of the 'distance barrier'.

Inequalities are very deeply rooted in the ethic of a capitalist society — and probably are in the so-called 'socialist' societies of the present time, although the route to power may be very different in those than it is under capitalism. To understand the dynamics of spatial patterns in non-socialist countries, therefore, it is necessary to understand the dynamics of capitalism. The driving force is the search for profit, for greater rewards with which to assuage what often seems to be man's inherent and boundless selfishness in pursuing his own interests. Profits are born of shortages, of deficits in supply relative to demand. When such shortages disappear, they must be reinstated, for example by the generation of extra demand through advertizing and related propaganda. Alternatively, capitalists look for new depositing grounds, where the chances of profit are greater, either abandoning their former interests or, as in so many of the great corporate mergers of recent years, extending them. Thus capital moves to profits, just as labour moves to high wages (chapter 5).

If the socio-economic dynamics are based on shortages, then there are bound to be inequalities, since some people must either do without services — those of a doctor perhaps (chapter 2) — or must accept an inferior good, as with housing. Because capital brings power, then it is usually the non-capitalists (the working class in Marxian terms) who are powerless, and must suffer the great brunt of the shortages. Hence position in the division of labour is a major determinant of the distribution of social inequalities. People at various positions in this division tend to live in different parts of the world, because of the way in which the spatial structure of the world economy has been organized by the forces of international capitalism. This we demonstrated in chapter 4, showing the inequalities that result from the concentration of capitalist power in a few cities in a few countries, and also the concentration of the capitalists into a few parts of those cities.

In most societies, time is at a premium despite the frequent claims of the increasing importance of leisure and the decreasing length of the average working day, week, and year for many people during the present century. Thus much energy has been and still is being expended in the search for quicker ways of moving between two places, for the movement of messages and goods, as well as of people. The scale of the investment seems to be increasing, as indicated by the spiralling costs of the Concorde airliner in the early 1970s. Some products, like the bicycle and the motor-car, eventually become widely available, if not ubiquitous throughout a society, but many do not, in part because of their price and in part because of where they are operated. Thus inequalities created by the division of labour are exacerbated, both by financial accessibility to various modes of transport and by spatial accessibility to facilities at different places. As we showed in chapter 5 for most people there is a limited spatial range over which they can travel twice daily to and from work, and this may be very influential on their wage levels. Some circumvent the problem by having two homes; others, if unprepared or unable to migrate permanently, may have to suffer unemployment.

Of the many items which make up the daily life of the resident in a capitalist society, particularly one with what is accepted as a high level of living, only two of the mass media — radio and television services, newspapers and magazines — are virtually ubiquitous with no price differential. Everything else — jobs, consumer goods, leisure facilities etc. — must be obtained by movement, either you to them or them to you, and such movement is costly, perhaps prohibitive. The one exception to this rule is the shelter one lives in, but as we saw in chapter 5, its price, in particular the price of the land it stands on, reflect its accessibility: to be near to things, especially things that most other people want to be near to, you must pay a lot.

Life in a capitalist society is a conflict between individuals and groups for that society's products. Because a capitalist society is almost always a mass society, few, if any, individuals can negotiate on their own behalf, and so they abdicate some of their personal freedom by joining protective associations, such as trade unions, and it is between these that much of society's conflict occurs. One of the bases to many conflicts is territory, for two reasons. First, all people need some territory on which to live, and, some would suggest, in which to invest their personality (Ardrey 1966). Secondly, some places are more desirable than others, because of their accessibility characteristics and their contents. In recognition of these two features, capitalist societies have created the notions of private property and of community property: the former is the territory occupied by an individual, more usually an individual household; the latter is the area organized and operated, in some respects at least, by a collectivity or its representatives, such as a municipal council. Personal property characteristics largely reflect the owners' position in the division of labour: community properties too, may reflect the nature of their owners – in the attitudes and actions of their councils, for example – and can be used to amplify the inequalities between territories, depending on investments which are made. Chapter 6 illustrates many of these differences between community territories.

This brief portrait of capitalist societies indicates how space and the pattern of locations are manipulated for the benefit of capitalism. The consequence is inequality, additional to the inequality which is inherent in capitalism's division of labour, an inequality which most proponents of capitalist society believe is necessary for its survival, and for the 'economic growth' which is one of its major goals. Many individual consciences are upset by these basic inequalities, however, and as a consequence societies have created an institution – the modern welfare state – to protect individuals from extreme inequalities which may ensue from the capitalist system. Part of the function of the state is that which nations have always entrusted to their governments, the provision of goods and services which can only be maintained collectively and not by individuals – notably the 'defence of the realm'. But most of its functions involve the operation of 'liberal humanitarianism', shielding the individual from possible problems of capitalism. Thus there is income redistribution through taxation systems, provision of public goods, such as health, police, and education services, the provision of housing, or of cheap money to finance housing, and protection against unemployment and other social and economic 'ills' (but see Kincaid 1973).

The welfare state, or its equivalent, does not seek to remove the inequalities created by capitalism, therefore, but merely to rectify their extremities. (Many aspects of the welfare state indeed encourage inequalities through their investments in, and encouragement of, capitalist enterprises: Miliband 1969.) Many of these policies, implicitly if not explicitly, have a spatial dimension, and action upon the spatial structure can have significant effects on levels of social well-being (Chisholm and Manners 1971). We discuss some of these policies, potential and actual, in Chapter 7, showing how particular actions — investing in certain places, relocating certain facilities, redrawing certain boundaries — can aid in the removal of inequalities. But it is here that the lack of an independent role for the spatial variables comes clearly into focus: spatial engineering can treat the disease of spatial inequalities but it cannot attack the symptoms, for location is merely a variable used by capitalism to aid in the production of inequalities, not a producer of them *per se*. Thus one can break into the poverty cycle depicted in Fig.5.6 by policies intended to improve the education facilities in certain areas, but unless other variables in the cycle are also altered, notably those relating to income and employment opportunities, it is unlikely that better educational facilities will lead to marked improvements in living standards. (Because, capitalism being what it is, there will still be competition for the 'better' jobs for which education is considered necessary.) Similarly, the creation of mixed neighbourhoods, as discussed in chapter 7, might make 'working-class' people aware of other, 'better' life styles, but unless they are also provided with the extra incomes to support their emulation of these life styles, the consequence is as likely to be feelings of deprivation and alienation as of 'improvement', even if there has been some 'improvement'.

The root causes of spatial inequalities cannot be tackled by spatial policies alone, therefore. Inequalities are products of social and economic structures, of which capitalism in its many guises is the predominant example. Certainly inequalities can be alleviated by spatial policies, as we have shown, but alleviation is not cure: whilst capitalism reigns, however, remedial social action may be the best that is possible. Thus it would seem that we are led to a rather pessimistic conclusion. In part this is so: the spatial, or geographical, approach does not offer the holy grail. Indeed, our conclusion would have to be that this approach, the one taken in this book, is secondary. The real cause of inequalities lies in the structure of societies, and is in part represented by the way in which these organize space; thus the solution of inequalities must be sought in the restructuring of societies. For this, no one academic discipline can claim superior knowledge or ability.

Yet, despite this pessimism, there is much to be learned from the approach which has been followed in this book. In the first place, this relates to time-scales and the approach to social problems. Most capitalist societies are also democracies, ruled by groups elected, frequently and regularly, by the population at large. These ruling groups have self-preservation, the attainment and then retention of power as major political aims. As a consequence, many, if not all of their policies have short-term horizons only, aimed at aiding the electioneering process. Thus little political attention is likely to be given to the long-term restructuring of a social and economic system (and attempts to make rapid changes seem doomed to failure, if the efforts of Britain's Labour governments of the mid–1970s are any guide). Attention will rather be addressed to the amelioration of inequalities, in the search for electoral power, which will mean a patchwork of policies. Our discussion of the spatial element in inequalities shows both what policies may or may not be desirable, and what their by-products may be. In this way, since there are many inequalities needing rapid ameliorative action, spatial policies can be used to treat pressing social problems, whilst permanent solutions are being sought.

Our second argument for the value of the approach presented here is that any alternative social structure to capitalism will need to develop spatial policies. Unless time is given a nil valuation and residents of different places have no need for interaction, distance will still be a barrier and an influence on real incomes. The economics of shortages may not be the dynamic of the new society but, unless communications media develop enormously and the desire for social interaction declines accordingly, people will not be able to have their own doctor and school in their home, their own park alongside, and so on. Accessibility will always be a variable, and location problems for public and private facilities will always exist. If society's resources are to be placed so as to be of the maximum benefit to consumers, rather than to providers, then comprehensive spatial policies will be needed, to ensure both a relative equality in the provision of each element of the level of living and an over-all relative equality in the real incomes which these elements constitute. The topics which we have discussed in this book are very relevant to such a task: just as one cannot investigate and manipulate a spatial structure in ignorance of its encompassing social structure, so one cannot manipulate a social structure in ignorance of the way in which it organizes its territory.

Bibliography

ABLER, R.F. (1971). Distance, intercommunications, and geography. *Proc. Assoc. Am. Geogr.* 3, 1–5.

ADAMS, J.S., and GOULD, P.R. (1971). *Spatial organization: the geographer's view of the world.* Prentice-Hall, Englewood Cliffs, N.J.

JANELLE, D., PHILBRICK, A., and SOMNER, J. (eds.) (1975). *Human geography in a shrinking world.* Duxbury Press, North Scituate, Mass.

ABRAMS, M. (1972). Social indicators and social equity. *New Soc.* 22, 454–5.

ADAMS, J. (1970). Westminster: the fourth London airport? *Area* 2(2), 1–9.

Advisory Commission on Intergovernmental Relations (1964). *The problems of special districts in American government.* U.S.G.P.O., Washington.

AGOC, C. (1970). Social indicators: selected readings. *Ann. Am. Acad. Polit. Soc. Sci.* 388, 127–32.

AHMAD, Z. (1973). Geography of deaths in Orissa: some spatial patterns, trends and correlates of mortality. *Geogr. Observer (India)* 9, 73–86.

ALKER, H.R. (1970). Measuring inequality. In *The quantitative analysis of social problems* (ed. E.R. Tufte), 191–211. Addison-Wesley, Reading, Mass.

ALLARDT, E. (1973). *About dimensions of welfare.* Research Report No. 1, Research Group for Comparative Sociology, University of Helsinki.

ALLEN, K., and McLELLAN, M.C. (1970). *Regional problems and policies in Italy and France.* Allen and Unwin, London.

ALONSO, W. (1964). *Location and land use.* Harvard University Press, Cambridge, Mass.

— (1968). *Aspects of regional planning and theory in the United States.* Working Paper 87, Institute of Urban and Regional Development, University of California.

AMBROSE, P.J., and COLENUTT, R. (1975). *The property machine.* Penguin Books, Harmondsworth, Middx.

ANDREWS, F.M. (1973). Social indicators and socio-economic development. *Jnl. Dev. Areas* 8, 3–12.

ARDILL, J. (1975). Regional policies 'doing more harm than good'. *The Guardian,* 21 July.

ARDREY, R. (1966). *The territorial imperative.* Atheneum Press, New York.

Association of University Teachers (1975). *Regional costs survey.* Association of University Teachers, London.

BALASSA, B. (1967). *Studies in trade diversification.* Johns Hopkins University Press, Baltimore.

— (1969). Country size and trade patterns: a comment. *Am. econ. Rev.* 59, 201–4.

BALDWIN, J. (1975). Urban criminality and the 'problem' estate. *Local Gov. Stud.* N.S. 1(4), 12–20.

— and BOTTOMS, A.E. (1976). *The urban criminal.* Tavistock, London.

BANZHAF, J.F. III (1968). One man, 3·312 votes: a mathematical analysis of the Electoral College. *Villanova Law Rev.* 13, 303–46.

Barlow Report (1940). *Royal Commission on the distribution of the industrial population; report.* Cmd. 6153, H.M.S.O., London.

BARRATT-BROWN, M. (1974). *The economics of imperialism.* Penguin Books, Harmondsworth, Middx.

BAUER, P.T. (1961). *Indian economic policy and development.* Allen and Unwin, London.

and WOOD, J.B. (1961). Foreign aid: the soft option. *Banca Nazionale del Lavoro Quarterly Review* 59, 403–18.

and YAMEY, B.S. (1972). The pearson Report: a review. In BYRES (1972a), 41–76.

BAUER, R.A. (ed.) (1966). *Social indicators.* M.I.T. Press, Cambridge, Mass.

BEDERMAN, S.J. and ADAMS, J.S. (1974). Job, accessibility and underemployment. *Ann. Ass. Am. Geogr.* 64, 378–86.

BELLI, P. (1972). The economic implications of malnutrition: the dismal science revisited. *Econ. Dev. Cult. Change* 20, 1–23.

BENEDICT, B. (ed.) (1967a). *Problems of smaller territories.* Athlone Press, London.

(1967b). Sociological aspects of smallness. In BENEDICT (1976a) 45–55.

BERRY, B.J.L. (1961a). Basic patterns of economic development. In *Atlas of economic development* (ed. N. Ginsburg), 110–19. University of Chicago Press, Chicago.

(1961b). City size distributions and economic development. *Econ. Dev. Cult. Change* 9, 573–87.

(1967). *Geography of market centers and retail distribution.* Prentice-Hall, Englewood Cliffs, N.J.

(1969). Relationships between regional development and the urban system: the case of Chile. *Tijdschr. econ. soc. Geogr.* 60, 283–307.

(1970). City size and economic development. In *Urbanization and national development* (eds. L. Jakobson and V. Prakesh), 111–56. Sage Publications, Beverly Hills.

(1972a). Hierarchical diffusion: the basis of development filtering and spread in a system of growth centres. In *Growth centres in regional economic development* (ed. N.M. HANSEN), 108–38. Free Press, New York.

(1972b). More on relevance and policy analysis. *Area* 7, 77–80.

(1973). *The human consequences of urbanization.* Macmillan, London.

and HORTON, F.E. (1970). *Geographic perspectives on urban systems.* Prentice-Hall, Englewood Cliffs, N.J.

PARSONS, S.J., and PLATT, R.H. (1968). *The impact of urban renewal on small businesses.* Center for Urban Studies, University of Chicago, Chicago.

BERTRAM, I.G. (1970). Television and the decline of the cinema in New Zealand: a study of changing location patterns, 1956–1966. *N. Z. Geogr.* 26, 136–44.

BLOOD, Sir H. (1958). *The smaller territories.* Conservative Central Office, London.

BOADEN, N. (1971). *Urban policy-making: influences on County Boroughs in England and Wales.* Cambridge University Press, London.

BOAL, F.W. (1970). Urban growth and land value patterns: government influences. *Prof. Geogr.* 22, 79–83.

DOHERTY, P., and PRINGLE, D.G. (1974). *The spatial distribution of some social problems in the Belfast urban area.* Northern Ireland Community Relations Commission, Belfast.

BOARD, C., DAVIES, R.J., and FAIR, T.J.D. (1970). The structure of the South African space economy: an integrated approach. *Reg. Stud.* 4, 367–92.

Board of Inland Revenue (1975). *Inland Revenue statistics 1974*, H.M.S.O., London.

BORCHERT, J.R. (1963). *The urbanization of the Upper Midwest, 1930-60*. Urban Report No. 2, Upper Midwest Economic Study, Minneapolis.
    (1967). American metropolitan evolution. *Geogrl Rev.* 57, 301-23.

BOUDEVILLE, J.R. (1966). *Problems of regional economic planning*. Edinburgh University Press, Edinburgh.

BOULDING, K.E., and PFAFF, M. (eds.) (1972). *Redistribution to the rich and poor: the grants economics of income redistribution*. Wadsworth, Belmont, Calif.

BOURNE, L.S. (ed.) (1971). *Internal structure of the city: readings on space and environment*. Oxford University Press, New York.

BRADBURN, N. (1969). *The structure of psychological well-being*. Aldine Press, Chicago.

BRADSHAW, J. (1974). The concept of social need. *Ekistics* 37, 184-7.

BRAMS, S.J. (1975). *Game theory and politics*. Free Press, New York.

BREESE, G. (1966). *Urbanization in newly developing countries*. Prentice-Hall, Englewood Cliffs, N.J.

BROOKFIELD, H.C. (1973). On one geography and a Third World. *Trans. Inst. Br. Geogr.* 58, 1-20.

BROWN, A.J. (1972). *The framework of regional economics in the United Kingdom*. Cambridge University Press, London.

BROWN, L.R. (1973). *World without borders*. Random House, New York.
    (1975). The multinational corporation: economic colossus of modern times. *Horizon USA* 9, 8-12.

BRUNN, S.D., and WHEELER, J.O. (1971). Spatial dimensions of poverty in the United States. *Geogr. Annlr B.* 53, 6-15.

BUCHANAN, J.M. (1974). *The limits of liberty*. University of Chicago Press, Chicago.

BUCHANAN, K. (1964). Profiles of the Third World. *Pacif. Viewpt* 5, 97-126.
    (Reprinted in 1971 in *Developing the underdeveloped countries* (ed. A.B. Mountjoy), 17-44. Macmillan, London.)
    (1972). *The geography of empire*. Spokesman Books, London.

BUCKATZSCH, E.J. (1946). An index of social conditions in the County Boroughs in 1941. *Bull. Oxf. Univ. Inst. Statist.* 8, 365-74.

BUNGE, W. (1975). Detroit humanly viewed: the American urban present. In ABLER *et al.* (1975), 147-82.

BURGHARDT, A.F. (1971). A hypothesis about gateway cities. *Ann. Ass. Am. Geogr.* 61, 269-85.
    (1972). Income density in the United States. *Ann. Ass. Am. Geogr.* 62 455-60.

BURNETT, F.T., and SCOTT, S.F. (1962). A survey of housing conditions in the urban areas of England and Wales, 1960. *Sociol. Rev.* 10, 35-79.

BUSHMAN, D.O., and STANLEY, W.R. (1971). State senate reapportionment in the Southeast. *Ann. Ass. Am. Geogr.* 61, 654-70.

BUTLER, J.R., BEVAN, J.M., and TAYLOR, R.C. (1973). *Family doctors and public policy*. Routledge and Kegan Paul, London.

BYRES, T.J. (ed.) (1972a). *Foreign resources and economic development*. Cass London.

BYRES, T.J. (1972b). The White Man's Burden in a neo-colonial setting. In BYRES (1972a), 77–116.

BYRNE, D.S. (1974). *Problem families: a housing lumpen proletariat.* Working Paper No. 5, Department of Sociology and Social Administration, University of Durham.

CAMPBELL, A., and CONVERSE, P. (1972). *The human meaning of social change.* Russell Sage, New York.

CAMPBELL, M. (1975). A spatial and typological disaggregation of unemployment as a guide to regional policy — a case study of North-West England, 1959–1972. *Reg. Stud.* 9, 157–68.

CANT, R.G. (1975). Territorial socio-economic indicators in development plans in the Asian region. *Int. Soc. Sci. J.* 27, 53–77.

CARLISLE, E. (1972). The conceptual structure of social indicators. In SHONFIELD and SHAW (1972), 23-32.

CARNEY, J.G., and TAYLOR, C. (1974). Community development projects: review and comment. *Area* 6, 226–31.

CASETTI, E., KING, L.J., and WILLIAMS, F. (1972). Concerning the spatial spread of economic development. In *International Geography 1972* (eds. W.P. Adams and F.M. Helleiner), 897–9. University of Toronto Press, Toronto.

CAUDILL, H.M. (1962). *Night comes to the Cumberlands: a biography of a depressed area.* Little Brown, Boston.

Chartered Institute of Public Finance and Accountancy and Society of County Treasurers (1975). *Education Statistics 1973-4.* C.I.P.'F.A., London, and S.C.T., Reading.

CHENERY, H.B. (1971). Targets for development. In WARD *et al.* (1971), 27–47.

CHISHOLM, M. (1962). *Rural settlement and land use.* Hutchinson, London.
    (1964). Must we all live in Southeast England? The location of new employment. *Geography* 49, 1–14.
    and MANNERS, G. (eds.) (1971). *Spatial policy problems of the British economy.* Cambridge University Press, London.

CHORLEY, R.J. and HAGGETT, P. (eds.) (1967). *Socio-economic models in geography.* Methuen, London.

CHURCH, R.J.H. (1969). The Firestone rubber plantations in Liberia. *Geography* 54, 430–7.

CLARK, B.D., and GLEAVE, M.B. (eds.) (1973). *Spatial patterns in cities.* Special Publication No. 5, Institute of British Geographers, London.

CLARKE, J.I. (1966). *Sierra Leone in maps.* University of London Press, London.
    (1972). Urban primacy in tropical Africa. In *La croissance urbaine en Afrique Noire et à Madagascar.* Vol. 1, 447–53. Centre National de la Recherche Scientifique, Paris.

CLIFF, A.D., *et al.* (1975). *Elements of spatial structure: a quantitative approach.* Cambridge University Press, Cambridge.

CLOUT, H. (ed.) (1975). *Regional development in Western Europe.* Wiley, London.

COATES, B.E. (1973). Industrial geography . . . In *Nature in the round: a guide to environmental science* (ed. N. Calder), 79–89. Weidenfeld and Nicolson, London.
    and RAWSTRON, E.M. (1966). Regional variations in incomes. *Westminster Bank Rev.* February, 1–19.
    and RAWSTRON, E.M. (1971). *Regional variations in Britain: selected*

essays in economic and social geography. Batsford, London.

COATES, K., and SILBURN R. (1970). *Poverty: the forgotten Englishmen.* Penguin Books, Harmondsworth, Middx.

COHEN, Y.S. (1972). *The diffusion of planned shopping centers in the United States.* Research Paper 135, Department of Geography, University of Chicago, Chicago.

COUGHLIN, R.E. (1970). *Goal attainment levels in 101 metropolitan areas.* Discussion Paper No. 41, Regional Science Research Institute, Philadelphia.

COUPER, A.D. (1972). *The geography of sea transport.* Hutchinson, London.

COURTENAY, P.P. (1965). *Plantation agriculture.* Bell, London.

COX, K.R. (1972). *Man, location, and behavior: an introduction to human geography,* Wiley, New York.

(1973). *Conflict, power and politics in the city: a geographic view.* McGraw-Hill, New York.

(1974). Territorial organization, optimal scale, and power. In COX *et al.* (1974), 109-39.

and REYNOLDS, D.R. (1974). Locational approaches to power and conflict. In COX, *et al.* (1974), 19-41.

REYNOLDS, D.R., and ROKKAN, S. (eds.) (1974). *Locational approaches to power and conflict.* Halsted Press, New York.

CULLINGWORTH, J.B. (1973). *Problems of an urban society, Vol. 2, The social context of planning.* Allen and Unwin, London.

CYBRIWSKY, R., and LEY, D. (1974). The spatial ecology of stripped cars. *Environ. & Behav.* 6, 53-68.

DAHL, R.A. (1956). *A preface to democratic theory.* University of Chicago Press, Chicago.

DARWENT, D.F. (1969). Growth poles and growth centres in regional planning – a review. *Environ. & Plann.* 1, 5-32.

DAVIDSON, B.R. (1975). The effects of land speculation on the supply of housing in England and Wales. *Urban Stud.* 12, 91-100.

Department of Education and Science (1975). *Statistics of Education.* H.M.S.O. London.

Department of Employment (1973). *British labour statistics year book 1971.* H.M.S.O., London.

Department of the Environment (1973). *Better homes: the next priorities* Cmnd 5339, H.M.S.O., London.

(1974). *Housing and construction statistics.* H.M.S.O., London.

DE VISÉ, P. (1968). *Slum medicine: Chicago style. How the medical needs of the city's Negro poor are met.* Working paper No. 3 IV. 7, Chicago Regional Hospital Study, Chicago.

(1973). *Misused and misplaced hospitals and doctors.* Resource Paper 22 Commission on College Geography, Association of American Geographers Washington.

and DEWEY, D.R. (1972). *More money, more doctors, less care: Chicago' changing distribution of physicians, hospitals, and population, 1950 to 197C* Working Paper No. I.19, Chicago Regional Hospital Study, Chicago.

DEWEY, D.R. (1973). 'Where the doctors have gone: The changing distribution o private practice physicians in the Chicago Metropolitan Area, 1950-1970 Ph.D. thesis, University of Nebraska, Lincoln, Neb.

DICKENSON, J.P. (1974). Imbalances in Brazil's industrialization. In *Spatic aspects of development* (ed. B.S. Hoyle), 291–306. Wiley, London.

DIXON, R.G. (1968). *Democratic representation.* Oxford University Press, New York.

DONALDSON, P. (1973). *Economics of the real world.* British Broadcasting Corporation and Penguin Books, London.

DONNISON, D. (1975). Equality. *New Soc.* 34, 422–4.

DOUGLAS, J.N.H. (1968). Political geography and administrative areas: a method of assessing the effectiveness of local government areas. In *Essays in Political Geography* (ed. C.A. Fisher), 13–26. Methuen, London.

(1973). Politics. In *Evaluating the human environment: essays in applied geography* (eds. J.A. Dawson and J.C. Doornkamp), 159–83, Arnold, London.

DOUGLAS, J.W.B. (1964). *The home and the school.* MacGibbon and Kee, London.

DOWNS, A. (1973). *Opening up the suburbs.* Yale University Press, New Haven.

DREWE, P. (1973). Social costs and benefits of urban development. In STÖBER and SCHUMACHER (1973), 193–209.

DREWNOWSKI, J. (1974). *On measuring and planning the quality of life.* Mouton, The Hague.

and SCOTT, W. (1968). The level of living index. *Ekistics* 25, 226–75.

DUNBAR, A. (1969). *The will to survive: the study of a Mississippi plantation community based on the words of its citizens.* Southern Regional Council, Atlanta.

DUNCAN, O.D. *et al.* (1960). *Metropolis and region.* Johns Hopkins Press, Baltimore.

DUNCAN, S.S. (1974). Cosmetic planning or social engineering? Improvement grants and improvement areas in Huddersfield. *Area* 6, 259–71.

DUNNING, J.H. (ed.) (1972a). *International investment: selected readings.* Penguin Books, Harmondsworth, Middx.

(1972b). Technology, United States investment and European economic growth. In DUNNING (1972a), 377–411.

DWYER, D.J. (1975). *People and housing in Third World cities.* Longmans, London.

DYE, T.R. (1966). *Politics, economics and the public policy outcomes in the American states.* Rand McNally, Chicago.

EAST, W.G. (1960). The geography of land-locked states. *Trans. Inst. Br. Geogr.* 28, 1–22.

EASTON, D. (1965a). *A framework for political analysis.* Prentice-Hall, Englewood Cliffs, N.J.

(1965b). *A systems analysis of political life.* Wiley, New York.

EISENSTADT, S.N., and ROKKAN, S. (eds.) (1973). *Building states and nations.* vol. 1. Sage Publications, Beverly Hills and London.

ESTALL, R.C. (1966). *New England: a study in industrial adjustment.* Bell, London.

ETHERINGTON, W. (1974). *The idea of social mix: a critical biography.* Research Paper 7, Centre for Environmental Studies, London.

FEIS, H. (1930). *Europe: the world's banker, 1870–1914.* Yale University Press, New Haven.

FIRN, J.R. (1975). External control and regional development: the case of Scotland. *Environ. & Plann.* A 7, 393–414.

FORD, J.R. (1975). The role of the building society manager in the urban strat‐
fication system: autonomy versus constraint. *Urban Stud.* 12, 295–302.

FORER, P.C. (1974). Space through time: a case study with New Zealand airline
In *Space-time concepts in urban and regional models* (ed. E.L. Cripps
22–45. London Papers in Regional Science 4, Pion, London.

FORRESTER, J.W. (1971). *World dynamics.* Wright-Allan Press, Cambridge, Mas

FRANKLIN, S.H. (1967). Immaturity and affluence: the social and econom
problems of New Zealand's colonial status. *Geography* 52, 1–11.
  (1975). Regional development — and growth — in New Zealand. *Paci
Viewpt* 16, 143–58.

FRASER, M. (1974). *Children in distress.* Penguin Books, Harmondsworth, Midd

FREEMAN, D.B. (1973). *International trade, migration, and capital flows: a quan‐
titative analysis of spatial economic interaction.* Research Paper 146, Depar
ment of Geography, University of Chicago, Chicago.

FRIEDMAN, M. (1958). Foreign economic aid: means and obligations. *Yale Re
47, 224–38.

FRIEDMANN, J.R.P. (1966). *Regional development policy: a case study (
Venezuela.* M.I.T. Press, Cambridge, Mass.
  (1973). *Urbanization, planning and national development.* Sage, Beverly Hill
and ALONSO, W. (eds.) (1964). *Regional development and planning:
reader.* M.I.T. Press, Cambridge, Mass.
and MILLER, J. (1965). The urban field. *J. Am. Inst. Plann.* 31, 312–19.

FRIEDMANN, W., KALMANOFF, G., and MEAGHER, R.F. (1966). *Internation
financial aid.* Columbia University Press, New York.

FULLER, G. (1974). On the spatial diffusion of fertility decline: the distance-t
clinic variable in a Chilean community. *Econ. Geogr.* 50, 324–32.

GALBRAITH, J.K. (1975). *Economics and the public purpose.* Penguin Book
Harmondsworth, Middx.

GANS, H.J. (1969). Planning for people, not buildings. *Environ. & Plann.* 1, 33–4(
  (1972). *People and plans.* Basic Books, New York.

GARNER, B.J. (1975). The effect of local government reform on access to publ
services: a case study from Denmark. In *Processes in physical and huma
geography: Bristol essays* (eds. R. Peel, M. Chisholm and P. Haggett), 319–3
Heinemann, London.

GILBERT, A. (1974). *Latin American development: a geographical perspectiv
Penguin Books, Harmondsworth, Middx.

GINSBURG, N. (1961). *Atlas of economic development.* University of Chicag
Press, Chicago.

GIRT, J.L. (1973). Distance to general medical practice and its effect on reveale
ill-health in a rural environment. *Can. Geogr.* 17, 154–66.

GLASSBERG, A. (1973). The linkage between urban policy outputs and votin
behavior: New York and London. *Br. J. Polit. Sci.* 3, 341–61.

GLAZER, N. (1975). Ethnicity: a world phenomenon. *Dialogue* 8 (3/4), 34–46.
and MOYNIHAN, D.P. (eds.) (1975). *Ethnicity: theory and experienc
Harvard University Press, Cambridge, Mass.

GODDARD, J.B. (1975). *Office location in urban and regional developmen
Oxford University Press, London.

GODLUND, S. (1961). Population, regional hospitals, transport facilities an
regions: planning the location of regional hospitals in Sweden. *Lund Stud
Geogr.* B 21.

GOLANT, S. (1972). *The residential location and spatial behavior of the elderly.* Research Paper 143, Department of Geography, University of Chicago, Chicago.

GOODALL, B. (1970). Some effects of legislation on land values. *Reg. Stud.* 4, 11–23.

GOSTKOWSKI, Z. (ed.) (1974). *Toward a system of human resources indicators for less developed countries.* Institute of Philosophy and Psychology, Polish Academy of Sciences, Warsaw.

GOTTMANN, J. (1961). *Megalopolis.* Twentieth Century Fund, New York.

(1973). *The significance of territory.* University Press of Virginia, Charlottesville.

GOULD, P., and LEINBACH, T. (1966). An approach to the geographic assignment of hospital services. *Tijdschr. econ. soc. Geogr.* 57, 203–6.

and SPARKS, J. (1969). The geographical context of human diets in southern Guatemala. *Geogrl Rev.* 59, 58–82.

and WHITE, R. (1974). *Mental maps.* Penguin Books, Harmondsworth, Middx.

GRAHAM, R. E. (1964). Factors underlying changes in the geographic distribution of income. *Survey of Current Business* 44 (April), 15–32.

GRAVIER, J. F. (1947). *Paris et le desert Français.* Le Portulan, Paris.

Greater London Council (1966). *The London Traffic Survey, Vol. II.* G.L.C., London.

(1969). *Greater London Development Plan.* G.L.C., London.

GRIFFIN, K. (1970). Foreign capital, domestic savings, and economic development. *Bull. Oxf. Univ. Inst. Econ. & Stat.* 32, 99–112.

(1972). Pearson and the political economy of aid. In BYRES (1972a), 117–34.

and ENOS, J. L. (1970). Foreign assistance: objectives and consequences. *Econ. Dev. Cult. Change* 18, 313–27.

GRIGG, D. B. (1974). Agricultural populations and economic development. *Tijdschr. econ. soc. Geogr.* 65, 414–20.

(1975). The world's agricultural labour force, 1800–1970. *Geography* 60, 194–202.

GROSS, B. (1966). The state of the nation. In BAUER (1966), 198–229.

GRÖTEWOLD, A. (1971). The growth of industrial core areas and patterns of world trade. *Ann. Ass. Am. Geogr.* 61, 361–70.

HAGOOD, M. J. (1943). Development of a 1940 rural farm level of living index for counties. *Rur. Sociol.* 8, 171–80.

HAKAM, A. N. (1966). The motivation to invest and the locational pattern of foreign private industrial investment in Nigeria. *Nigerian J. Econ. & Soc. Stud.* 8, 49–65.

HALL, E. T. (1966). *The hidden dimension.* Doubleday, New York.

HALL, F. (1973). *Location criteria for high schools: student transportation and racial integration.* Research Paper 150, Department of Geography, University of Chicago, Chicago.

HALL, J. (1973). Measuring the quality of life using sample surveys. In STÖBER and SCHUMACHER (1973), 93–102.

and RING, A. J. (1974). 'Indicators of environmental quality and life satisfaction: a subjective approach.' Unpublished paper, Survey Unit, Social Science Research Council, London.

HALL, P.G. (1972). *Forecasting the quality of life in urban Europe.* Geographic Paper 20, Department of Geography, University of Reading.

—— (1975). *Urban and regional planning.* David and Charles, Newton Abbot.

—— et al. (1973). *The containment of urban England.* Allen and Unwin, Londo

HALSEY, A.H. (ed.) (1972). *Educational priority, Vol. 1: Educational Priorii Areas, problems and policies.* H.M.S.O., London.

HAMMOND, E. (1968). *An analysis of regional, economic and social statistic population, employment, housing, education, health, environment, soci characteristics.* Rowntree Research Unit, Durham University.

HAMNETT, C. (1973). Improvement grants as an indicator of gentrification i inner London. *Area* 5, 252–61.

HAMPTON, W. (1966). The county as a political unit. *Parliamentary Aff.* 1 462–74.

HANSEN, J.C. (1972). Regional disparities in Norway with reference t marginality. *Trans. Inst. Br. Geogr.* 57, 15–30.

HANSEN, M.L. (1941). *The Atlantic migration, 1607–1860.* Harvard Universit Press, Cambridge, Mass.

HARRELL, R.F., WOODYARD, E., and GRATES, A.I. (1955). *The effect of die on the intelligence of offspring.* Teachers College, New York.

HARRIES, K.D. (1974). *The geography of crime and justice.* McGraw-Hill, Ne York.

HARRINGTON, M. (1963). *The other America: poverty in the United State* Penguin Books, Harmondsworth, Middx.

HART, R.A., and MACKAY, D.I. (1975). Engineering earnings in Britain: 1914 1968. *Jl R. Statist. Soc.* A 138, 32–50.

HARVEY, D.W. (1971). Social processes, spatial form and the redistribution real income in an urban system. In *Regional forecasting* (eds. M. Chisholm A.E. Frey, and P. Haggett), 270–300. Butterworth, London.

—— (1972). *Society, the city and the space-economy of urbanism.* Resourc Paper No. 18, Commission on College Geography, Association of America Geographers, Washington.

—— (1973). *Social justice and the city.* Arnold, London.

—— (1974a). What kind of geography for what kind of public policy? *Tran. Inst. Br. Geogr.* 63, 18–24.

—— (1974b). Class-monopoly rent, finance capital and the urban revolutio *Reg. Stud.* 8, 239–55.

—— (1975). The political economy of urbanization in advanced capitalist soci ties: the case of the United States. In *The social economy of cities* (ed H.M. Rose and G. Gappert), 119–63. Sage Publications, Beverly Hill California.

HAWLEY, A.H. (1956). *The changing shape of metropolitan America.* Free Pres Glencoe, Ill.

HAY, A.M. (1974). *Economic planning in a developing country: Nigeria.* Region: analysis and development, Unit 14, Open University Press, Milton Keyne:

HAYNES, R.M. (1973). Crime rates and city size in America. *Area* 5, 162–5

HECHTER, M. (1975). *Internal colonialism: the Celtic fringe in British natione development, 1536–1966.* Routledge and Kegan Paul, London.

HELLEINER, G.K. (1972). *International trade and economic developmen* Penguin Books, Harmondsworth, Middx.

HENDERSON, W.L., and LEDEBUR, L.C. (1972). *Urban economics: processes and problems*. Wiley, New York.

HERAUD, B.J. (1966). The new towns and London's housing problem. *Urban Stud.* 2, 8-21.

HERBERT, D.T. (1972). *Urban geography: a social perspective*. David and Charles, Newton Abbott.

and JOHNSTON, R.J. (eds.) (1976). *Social areas in cities*. Vol. 1. Wiley, London.

HICKS, J.R. (1959). *Essays in world economics*. Clarendon Press, Oxford.

HILL, A.G. (1973). Segregation in Kuwait. In CLARK and GLEAVE (1973), 123-42.

HILLYARD, P., ROCHE, D., MURIE, A., and BIRREL, W. (1972). Variations in the standard of housing provision in Northern Ireland. *Reg. Stud.* 6, 393-9.

HIRSCH, W.Z. (1970). The urban challenge to governments. In *American cities* (ed. W.D. Gardner). Michigan Business Papers No. 54, University of Michigan, Ann Arbor.

HIRSCHMAN, A.O. (1958). *The strategy of economic development*. Yale University Press, New Haven.

HOCH, I. (1972a). Income and city size. *Urban Stud.* 9, 299-328.

(1972b). Urban scale and environmental quality. In *Population, resources and the environment* (ed. R.G. Ridker), 231-86. Reseach Report No. 3, U.S. Commission on Population Growth and the American Future, U.S.G.P.O., Washington.

(1974a). Inter-urban differences in the quality of life. In *Transport and the urban environment* (eds. J.G. Rothenberg and I.G. Heggie), 54-90. Macmillan, London.

(1974b). Factors in urban crime. *J. Urban Econ.* 1, 184-229.

HOLLAND, S. (1975). *The socialist challenge*. Quartet Books, London.

HOLMAN, R. (ed.) (1970a). *Socially deprived families in Britain*. Bedford Square Press of National Council of Social Service, London.

(1970b). Combatting social deprivation. In HOLMAN (1970a), 175-221.

HOLMES, J.H. (1971). External commuting as a prelude to suburbanisation. *Ann. Ass. Am. Geogr.* 61, 774-90.

HOLTERMANN, S. (1975). *Census indicators of urban deprivation, Working Note 6, Great Britain*. Department of the Environment, London.

(1975a). Areas of urban deprivation in Great Britain: an analysis of 1971 census data. *Social Trends*, 6, 33-47.

HORTON, F.E., McCONNEL, H., and TIRTHA, R. (1970). Spatial patterns of socio-economic structure in India. *Tijdschr. econ. soc. Geogr.* 61, 101-13.

HOWE, G.M. (1970). *National atlas of disease mortality in the United Kingdom*. Nelson, London.

(1972). *Man, environment and disease in Britain*. David and Charles, Newton Abbott.

HUMPHRYS, G. (1968). A map of housing quality in the U.K. *Trans. Inst. Br. Geogr.* 43, 31-6.

Hunt Report (1969). *The intermediate areas: Report of the Hunt Committee*. Cmnd. 3998, H.M.S.O., London.

ILLICH, I. (1971). *De-schooling society*. Calder and Boyars, London.

(1974). *Energy and equity*. Calder and Boyars, London.

(1975). *Medical nemesis*. Calder and Boyars, London.

Institut National de la Statistique et des Études Économtques (1975). *Données Sociales 1974*. I.N.S.E.E., Paris.

International Labour Organisation (1972). *Yearbook of labour statistics, 1971*. I.L.O., Geneva.

ISARD, W. (1960). *Methods of regional analysis*. M.I.T. Press, Cambridge, Mass.

ITAGAKA, Y. (1973). Economic nationalism and the problem of natural resources. *Develop. Econ.* 11, 219–30.

JACKSON, J.C. (1968). *Planters and speculators. Chinese and European agricultural enterprise in Malaya, 1786–1921*. University of Malaya Press, Kuala Lumpur.

JACOBS, J. (1961). *The death and life of great American cities*. Random House, New York.

— (1971). *The economy of cities*. Random House, New York.

JANELLE, D.G. (1968). Central-place development in a time-space framework. *Prof. Geogr.* 20, 5–10.

— (1969). Spatial reorganization: a model and concept. *Ann. Ass. Am. Geogr.* 59, 348–64.

Japan, Economic Council (1973). *Measuring net national welfare of Japan*, Economic Council of Japan, Tokyo.

JEFFREY, D. (1974). Regional fluctuations in unemployment within the U.S. urban economic system. *Econ. Geogr.* 50, 111–23.

JENKINS, M.A., and SHEPHERD, J.W. (1972). Decentralizing high school administration in Detroit. *Econ. Geogr.* 48, 95–106.

JEWKES, J. (1930). The localization of the cotton industry. *Econ. Hist.* 2, 91–106.

JOHNSON, H.G. (1968). Policy obstacles to trade and development. In THEBERGE (1968), 506–32.

— (1972a). The 'Crisis of Aid' and the Pearson Report. In BYRES (1972a) 135–53.

— (1972b). The efficiency and welfare implications of the international corporation. In DUNNING (1972a), 455–75.

JOHNSON, J.H., SALT, J., and WOOD, P.A. (1974). *Housing and the migration of labour in England and Wales*. Saxon House, Farnborough, Hants.

JOHNSTON, R.J. (1969a). Population change in Australian small towns, 1961–1966. *Rur. Sociol.* 34, 212–18.

— (1969b). Population change in an urban system — the examples of th Republic of Ireland and Scotland. *Scott. Geogr. Mag.* 85, 132–40.

— (1972). Towards a general model of intra-urban residential patterns: som cross-cultural observations. *Prog. Geog.* 4, 83–124.

— (1973). *Spatial structures*. Methuen, London.

— (1975a). New Zealand. In *Essays on world urbanization* (ed. R. Jones) 133–67. Philip, London.

— (1975b). *The world trade system: some enquiries into its spatial structure*. Bell, London.

— (1976a). Parliamentary seat redistribution: more opinions on the theme *Area* 8, 30–4.

— (1976b). Spatial structure, plurality systems, and electoral bias. *Can. Geog* 20.

— (1976c). Territorial justice and political campaigns. *Policy and Politics*,

— (1976d). Spatial and temporal variations in land and property prices in Ne Zealand: 1953–1972. *N.Z. Geogr.* 32, 30–55.

JOHNSTON, R.J. (1976e). Inter-regional and inter-urban income variations in New Zealand: a note. *Pacif. Viewpt* 17, 147–58.

(1976f). Contagion in neighbourhoods: problems of modelling and analysis. *Environ. & Plann.* A., 8, 581–6.

(1976g). Observations on accounting procedures for regional and urban policies. *Environ. & Plann.* A., 8, 327–40.

(1976h). Residential area characteristics. In HERBERT and JOHNSTON (1976), 193–235.

and HERBERT, D.T. (1976). The social area, process and form — an introduction. In HERBERT and JOHNSTON (1976), 5–18.

and RIMMER, P.J. (1969). *Retailing in Melbourne.* Publication HG/3, Department of Human Geography, Australian National University, Canberra.

JONES, M.V., and FLAX, M.J. (1970). *The quality of life in metropolitan Washington D.C. : some statistical benchmarks.* Working Paper 136–1, Urban Institute, Washington, D.C.

JONES, P.N. (1967). *The segregation of the immigrant communities in the city of Birmingham, 1961.* Occasional Papers in Geography 7, University of Hull.

(1970). Some aspects of the changing distribution of coloured immigrants in Birmingham, 1961–66. *Trans. Inst. Br. Geogr.* 50, 199–219.

JONES, S. (1954). A unified field theory of political geography. *Ann. Ass. Am. Geogr.* 44, 111–23.

JUDGE, K. (1975). Territorial justice and local autonomy: loan sanctions in the personal social services. *Policy & Polit.* 3, 43–69.

KAMRANY, N.M., and CHRISTAKIS, A.N. (1970). Social indicators in perspective. *Soc.-Econ. Plann. Sci.* 14, 207–16.

KARAN, P.P., and BLADEN, W.A. (1975). *Inter-regional disparities of income in India.* Mimeographed paper presented at the Annual Conference of the Institute of British Geographers, Oxford.

KASPERSON, R.E. (1969). Environmental stress and the municipal political system. In *The structure of political geography* (eds. R.E. Kasperson and J.V. Minghi), 481–96. Aldine Press, Chicago.

KEEBLE, D.E. (1967). Models of economic development. In CHORLEY and HAGGETT (1967), 243–302.

and HAUSER, D.P. (1971). Spatial analysis of manufacturing growth in outer south-east England, I. *Reg. Stud.* 5, 229–62.

and HAUSER, D.P. (1972). Spatial analysis of manufacturing growth in outer south-east England, II. *Reg. Stud.* 6, 11–36.

KELSALL, R.K., and KELSALL, H.M. (1971). *Social disadvantage and educational opportunity.* Holt, Rinehart and Winston, London.

KEOWN, P.A. (1971). The career cycle and the stepwise migration process. *N.Z. Geogr.* 27, 175–84.

KINCAID, J.C. (1973). *Poverty and inequality in Britain.* Penguin Books, Harmondsworth, Middx.

KINDLEBERGER, C.P. (1958). *Economic development.* McGraw Hill, New York.

KING, L.J., and FOSTER, J.J.H. (1973). Wage-rate change in urban labor markets and intermarket linkages. *Pap. Reg. Sci. Assoc.* 30, 183–96.

KLAASSEN, L.H., KROFT, W.C., and VISKVIL, R. (1973). Regional income differentials in Holland. *Pap. Reg. Sci. Assoc.* 10, 77–81.

KNAPP, J.A. (1973). Economics of political economy. *Lloyds Bank Rev.* 107, 19–43.

KNOX, P.L. (1974a). Level of living: a conceptual framework for monitoring regional variations in well-being. *Reg. Stud.* 8, 11–19.

(1974b). Spatial variations in level of living in England and Wales. *Trans. Inst. Br. Geogr.* 62, 1–24.

(1974c). Social indicators and the concept of level of living. *Sociol. Rev.* 22, 249–57.

(1975). *Social well-being: a spatial perspective.* Clarendon Press, Oxford.

(1976). *Social priorities for social indicators: a survey approach,* Occasional Paper No. 4, Department of Geography, University of Dundee.

KOELLE, H.H. (1974). An experimental study on the determination of a definition for the quality of life. *Reg. Stud.* 8, 1–10.

KONRAD, G., and SZELÉNYI, I. (1969). *Sociological aspects of the allocation of housing: experiences from a socialist non-market economy.* Sociological Research Group, Hungarian Academy of Sciences, Budapest.

KRAENZEL, C.F. (1955). *The Great Plains in transition.* University of Oklahoma Press, Norman.

KRENDEL, E.S. (1971). Social indicators and urban systems dynamics. *Soc. -Econ. Plann. Sci.* 5, 387–94.

KUKLINSKI, A.R. (1971). Regional development, regional policies and regional planning: problems and issues. *Reg. Stud.* 5, 269–78.

KUZNETS, S. (1955). Economic growth and income inequality. *Am. econ. Rev.* 45, 1–28.

(1960). Economic growth of small nations. In *The economic consequences of the size of nations* (ed. E.A.G. Robinson), 14–32. Macmillan, London.

(1963). Quantitative aspects of the economic growth of nations: VIII. Distribution of income by size. *Econ. Dev. Cult. Change* 11 (2ii), 1–80.

(1966). *Modern economic growth.* Yale University Press, New Haven.

KYLLONEN, R.L. (1967). Crime rate vs population density in United States cities: a model. *Gen. Syst.* 12, 137–48.

Labour Party (1957). *The smaller territories.* Labour's colonial policy series, No. 3, London.

LACARTE, J.A. (1973). Aspects of international trade and assistance relating to the expansion of employment in the developing countries. *J. Develop. Plann.* 5, 115–43.

LAKEMAN, E.E. (1974). *How democracies vote.* Faber, London.

LANKFORD, P.W. (1972). *Regional incomes in the United States 1929–1967 level, distribution, stability and growth.* Research Paper 145, Department o Geography, University of Chicago, Chicago.

LASSWELL, H.D. (1958). *Politics: who gets what, when, how.* Meridian Books New York.

LAVE, L.B., and SESKIN, E. (1971). Health and air pollution. In *The economic of environment* (eds. P. Bohn and A.V. Kneese), 119–38. Macmillan, London

LAYTON, C. (1969). *European advanced technology.* Allen and Unwin, London

Le Point (1974). Où vit-on heureux en France. *Le Point* 68 (7 January), 35–50.

LEE, T.R. (1957). On the relation between the school journey and emotiona adjustment in rural infant children. *Br. J. educ. Psychol.* 27, 101–14.

(1961). A test of the hypothesis that school reorganisation is a cause of rura depopulation. *Durham Res. Rev.* 3, 64–73.

LEES, R., and SMITH, G. (1975). *Action research in community developmen.* Routledge and Kegan Paul, London.

LEINBACH, T.R. (1972). The spread of modernisation in Malaya, 1895-1969. *Tijdschr. econ. soc. Geogr.* 63, 262-77.

LEWES, F.M.M., and KIRKNESS, A. (1973). *Exeter, city and university: a study of the economic and social interactions caused by university growth.* University of Exeter, Exeter.

LEWIS, G.M. (1968). Levels of living in the North-eastern United States c. 1960: a new approach to regional geography. *Trans. Inst. Br. Geogr.* 45, 11-37.

LITTLE, A., and MABEY, C. (1972). An index for designation of Educational Priority Areas. In SHONFIELD and SHAW (1972), 67-93.

LITTLE, I.M., and CLIFFORD, J.M. (1965). *International aid.* Allen and Unwin, London.

Liverpool City Council; Planning Department (1970). *Social malaise in Liverpool: interim report on social problems and their distribution.* Liverpool Corporation, Liverpool.

LOGAN, M.I. (1972). The spatial system and planning strategies in developing countries. *Geogrl Rev.* 62, 229-44.

McCONNELL, J.E., and CONKLING, E.C. (1973). A cooperative approach to trade and development. *Tijdschr. econ. soc. Geogr.* 64, 363-77.

McCRONE, G. (1969). *Regional policy in Britain.* Allen and Unwin, London.

McGEE, T.G. (1971). *The urbanization process in the Third World: explorations in search of a theory.* Bell, London.

McKEAN, R. (1947). *Introduction to Aristotle.* Modern Library, London.

MACLARAN, A.C. (1975). *Spatial aspects of relative deprivation.* Mimeographed paper presented to the Urban Geography Study Group of the Institute of British Geographers, Reading.

McVEIGH, T. (1971). *Social indicators: a bibliography.* Exchange Bibliography No. 215, Council of Planning Librarians, Monticello, Ill.

MABOGUNJE, A.L. (1972). Industrialization and metropolitan development in Nigeria. In *La Croissance urbaine en Afrique Noire et à Madagascar.* Vol. 2, 827-40. Centre National de la Recherche Scientifique, Paris.

MAGEE, A. (1971). Emigration and economic growth in southern Europe since 1950, with special reference to Spain. In *Proceedings of the Sixth New Zealand Geography Conference* (eds. R.J. Johnston and J.M. Soons), 179-85. New Zealand Geographical Society, Christchurch.

MAIZELS, A. (1963). *Industrial growth and world trade.* Cambridge University Press, Cambridge.

MANNERS, G., KEEBLE, D.E., RODGERS, H.B., and WARREN, K. (1972). *Regional development in Britain.* Wiley, London.

MARCIS, R.G., and REED, J.D. (1974). Joint estimation of the determinants of wages in subregional labor markets in the United States: 1961-1972. *J. Reg. Sci.* 14, 259-68.

MARRIOTT, O. (1967). *The property boom.* Pan Books, London.

MARTIN, A.E. (1967). Environment, housing and health. *Urban Stud.* 4, 1-21.

MASLOW, A.H. (1954). *Motivation and personality.* Harper, New York.

MASSAM, B.H. (1972). *The spatial structure of administrative systems.* Resource Paper No. 12, Commission on College Geography, Association of American Geographers, Washington.

—— (1974). Political geography and the provision of public services. *Prog. Geog.* 6, 179-210.

—— (1975). *Location and space in social administration.* Arnold, London.

MATHIAS, P. (1969). *The first industrial nation: an economic history of Britain, 1700-1914.* Methuen, London.

MEADOWS, D.L. (1972). *The limits to growth: a report for the Club of Rome.* Universe, New York.

MEIER, G.M. (1970). *Leading issues in economic development: studies in international poverty.* Oxford University Press, London.

MERA, K. (1973). On urban agglomeration and economic efficiency. *Econ. Dev. Cult. Change.* 21, 309–24.

MILIBAND, R. (1969). *The state in capitalist society.* Quartet Books, London.

MILLER, S.M., REIN, M., ROBY, P., and GROSS, B. (1967). Poverty, inequality and conflict. *Ann. Am. Acad. Polit. Soc. Sci.* 2, 16–32.

MISHAN, E.J. (1967). *The costs of economic growth.* Staples Press, London.

MITCHELL, J.B. (1963). *Historical geography.* English Universities Press, London.

MOGRIDGE, M.J.H. (1968). *A discussion of some of the factors influencing the income distribution of households within a city region.* Working Paper 7, Centre for Environmental Studies, London.

MORGAN, W.T.W. (1974). Aid with trade for needy nations. *Geogrl Mag.,* Lond. 66, 281–5.

MORRILL, R.L. (1966). *Historical development of the Chicago hospital system.* Working paper No. 12, Chicago Regional Hospital Study, Chicago.
   (1973). Ideal and reality in reapportionment. *Ann. Ass. Am. Geogr.* 63, 463–77.
   (1974). Efficiency and equity of optimal location models. *Antipode* 6, 41–5.
   and WOHLENBERG, E.H. (1971). *The geography of poverty in the United States.* McGraw-Hill, New York.

MOSER, C.A. (1970). Measuring the quality of life. *New Soc.* 20, 1042–3.
   and SCOTT, W. (1961). *British towns.* Oliver and Boyd, London.

MYINT, H. (1969). International trade and the developing countries. In *International economic relations* (ed. P.A. Samuelson), 15–35. Macmillan and St. Martin's Press, London.

MYRDAL, G.M. (1956). *Development and underdevelopment.* National Bank of Egypt, Cairo.
   (1957a). *Rich lands and poor: the road to world prosperity.* Harper, New York.
   (1957b). *Economic theory and under-developed regions.* Duckworth, London.
   (1971). The economic impact of colonialism. In *Developing the underdeveloped countries* (ed. A.B. Mountjoy), 52–7. Macmillan, London.
   (1974). The transfer of technology to underdeveloped countries. *Scient. Am.* 231 (3), 172–82.

NEUTZE, G.M. (1965). *Economic policy and the size of cities.* Australian National University, Canberra.

New Internationalist (1975a). Aiding the brain drain. *New Int.* May, 5.
   (1975b). New economic order. *New Int.* October, 13–14.

New Zealand Department of Statistics (1974). *New Zealand prices, wages, and labour.* Government Printer, Wellington.

Newcastle upon Tyne City Council (1974). *Social characteristics of Newcastle upon Tyne.*

NEWMAN, O. (1973). *Defensible space.* Architectural Press, London.

Newsom Report (1963). *Half our future: a report of the Central Advisory Council for Education (England).* H.M.S.O., London.

NICHOLSON, R.J., and TOPHAM, N. (1971). The determinants of investment in housing by local authorities: an econometric approach. *Jl. R. Statist. Soc.* A 134, 273–320.

——— (1972). Investment decisions and the size of local authorities. *Policy and Polit.* 1, 23–44.

Northwest Joint Planning Team (1974). *Strategic plan for the North West; report.* H.M.S.O., London.

NOURSE, H.O. (1968). *Regional economics: a study in the economic structure, stability, and growth of regions.* McGraw-Hill, New York.

NURKSE, R. (1953). *Problems of capital formation in underdeveloped countries.* Blackwell, Oxford.

O'CONNELL, J. (1971). Political constraints on planning: Nigeria as a case study in the developing world. *Nigerian J. Econ. & Soc. Stud.* 13, 39–57.

ODELL, P.R. (1971). A European view on regional development and planning in Latin America. *Int. Rev. Community Dev.* 25–6, 3–22.

ODLAND, J., CASETTI, E., and KING, L.J. (1973). Testing hypotheses of polarized growth within a central place hierarchy. *Econ. Geogr.* 49, 74–9.

Organization for Economic Co-operation and Development (1968). *The level and structure of Europe's research and development effort.* Paris.

——— (1971). *Social indicators development programme.* Note by the Secretariat, Paris.

——— (1973). The hungry people of the world wanted bread and they were to be given statistics. *OECD Agric. Rev.* 20, 81–4.

O'FARRELL, P.N., and POOLE, M.A. (1972). Retail grocery price variation in Northern Ireland. *Reg. Stud.* 6, 83–92.

PAHL, R.E. (1965). Class and community in English commuter villages. *Sociol. Rur.* 5, 5–23. (Reprinted in PAHL (1970)).

——— (1970). *Whose city?* Longman, London.

——— (1971). Poverty and the urban system. In CHISHOLM and MANNERS (1971), 126–45.

PALM, R. and PRED, A.R. (1974). *A time-geographic perspective on problems of inequality for women.* Working Paper 236, Institute of Urban and Regional Development, University of California, Berkeley.

PARKER, A.J. (1974a). *Prices survey: Athlone subregion.* Report No. 33, National Prices Commission, Dublin.

——— (1974b). Intra-urban variations in retail grocery prices. *Econ. & Soc. Rev.* 5, 393–403.

PARSONS, G.F. (1972). The giant manufacturing corporations and balanced regional growth in Britain. *Area* 4, 99–103.

PARSONS, T. (1971). *The system of modern societies.* Prentice-Hall, Englewood Cliffs, N.J.

PAYER, C. (1974). *The debt trap.* Penguin Books, Harmondsworth, Middx.

PEARSON, L.B., et al. (1969). *Partners in development: report of the Commission on International Development.* Pall Mall, London.

PEET, J.R. (1969). The spatial expansion of commercial agriculture in the nineteenth century: a von Thünen interpretation. *Econ. Geogr.* 45, 283–301.

PERKINS, H. (1969). *The origins of modern English society, 1780–1880.* Routledge & Kegan Paul, London.

PERLE, E.D. (1970). Local societal indicators: a progress report. *American Statistical Association, Proceedings of the Social Statistics Section*, 114-20.

PERLOFF, H.S., and WINGO, L. (1961). Natural resource endowment and region economic growth. In *Natural resources and economic growth* (ed. J.J. Spenler). (Distributed by) Resources for the Future, Washington. (Reprinted i FRIEDMANN and ALONSO (1964), 215-39.)

DUNN, E.S., LAMPARD, E.E., and MUTH, R.F. (1960). *Regions, resource and economic growth*. University of Nebraska Press, Lincoln, Nebr.

PHILLIPS, A.W. (1958). The relation between unemployment and rate of chang of money wage rate in the U.K., 1861-1957. *Economica* 25, 283-99.

PICKARD, J.P. (1959). *Metropolitanization of the United States*. Research Mon graph 2, Urban Land Institute, Washington.

PLESSAS, D.J., and FEIN, R. (1972). An evaluation of social indicators. *J. An Inst. Plann.* 38, 19-36.

Plowden Report (1967). *Children and their primary schools: a report of the Centr Advisory Council for Education (England)*. H.M.S.O., London.

POOLE, M.A., and BOAL, F.W. (1973). Religious residential segregation in Belfas in mid-1969: a multi-level analysis. In CLARK and GLEAVE (1973), 1-4(

POUNDS, N.J.G. (1963). *Political geography*. McGraw Hill, New York.

PRED, A.R. (1964). The intrametropolitan location of American manufacturing *Ann. Ass. Am. Geogr.* 54, 165-80.

(1965). Industrialization, initial advantage, and American metropolita growth. *Geogrl Rev.* 55, 158-85.

(1974). *Major job-providing organizations and systems of cities*. Resourc Paper No. 27, Commission on College Geography, Association of America Geographers, Washington.

PRYOR, E.G. (1973). *Housing in Hong Kong*. Oxford University Press, Londor

PULLEN, M.J. (1966). Unemployment and regional income per head. *Th Manchester School of Economic and Social Studies* 34, 15-40.

PYLE, G.F. (1968). *The geography of disease in large cities, III. Geosocial patho logy in Chicago*. Working Paper No. IV. 4, Chicago Regional Hospital Study Chicago.

(1974). *The spatial dynamics of crime*. Research Paper 159, Department o Geography, University of Chicago, Chicago.

RAE, D.W. (1971). *The political consequences of electoral laws*. Yale Universit' Press, New Haven.

RAWSTRON, E.M., and COATES, B.E. (1966). Opportunity and affluence *Geography* 51, 1-15.

RAYNOR, J. *et al.* (1974). *The urban context*. Open University, Milton Keynes

Redcliffe Maud Report (1969). *Royal Commission on Local Government i England 1966-69; Report*. Cmnd. 4040, H.M.S.O., London.

REES, P. (1967). *Movement and distribution of physicians in Metropolitar Chicago*. Working Paper No. I.12, Chicago Regional Hospital Study, Chicago

RICHARDSON, H.W. (1969). *Regional economics: location theory, urban an regional change*. Weidenfeld and Nicolson, London.

(1972). British emigration and overseas investment, 1870-1914. *Econ. Hist Rev.* 25, 99-113.

(1973a). *Regional growth theory*. Macmillan, London.

(1973b). *The economics of city size*. Saxon House, London.

RIDDELL, J.B. (1970). *Spatial dynamics of modernisation in Sierra Leone structure, diffusion and response.* Northwestern University Press, Evanston, Ill.

RIVLIN, A.M. (1973). A counter budget for social progress. *N.Y. Times* (8 April), 122 (42078), 91.

ROBINSON, E.A.G. (ed.) (1969). *Backward areas in advanced countries.* Macmillan London.

ROSE, A.J. (1966). Dissent from down under: metropolitan primacy as the normal state. *Pacif. Viewpt* 7, 1–27.

Roskill Commission (1969–72). *Commission on the third London airport: papers and proceedings.* H.M.S.O., London.

ROSSER, C. (1971). Housing for the lowest income group: the Calcutta experience. *Ekistics* 138, 126–31.

ROSTOW, W.W. (1971). *Politics and the stages of growth.* Cambridge University Press, London.

— (1975). *How it all began: origins of a modern economy.* Methuen, London.

Royal Commission on the Distribution of Income and Wealth (1975). *Report No. I.* Cmnd. 6171, H.M.S.O., London.

RUNCIMAN, W.G. (1966). *Relative deprivation and social justice.* Routledge and Kegan Paul, London.

St. Louis City Plan Commission (1971). *A housing program for the city of St. Louis, 1970–1980.* City Plan Commission, St. Louis.

SAMPSON, A. (1975). *The seven sisters: the great oil companies and the world they made.* Hodder and Stoughton, London.

SAMUELSON, P.A. (1973). From GNP to NEW. *Newsweek,* 9 April. Quoted by SMITH (1973b), p. 46.

SANTOS, T. dos (1970). The structure of dependence. *Am. Econ. Rev., Papers and Proceedings* 60, 231–6.

SAUER, C.O. (1948). Geography and the gerrymander. *Am. Polit. Sci. Rev.* 12, 403–26.

SCHELLING, T. (1974). On the ecology of micro-motives. In *The corporate society* (ed. R. Marris), 19–64. Macmillan, London.

SCHNORE, L.F. and PETERSON, G.B. (1958). Urban and metropolitan development in the United States and Canada. *Ann. Am. Acad. Polit. Soc. Sci.* 316, 60–8.

SCHWIND, P.M. (1971). *Migration and regional development in the United States 1950–1960.* Research Paper 133, Department of Geography, University of Chicago, Chicago.

Seebohm Report (1968). *Report of the Committee on Local Authority and allied personal social services.* Cmnd. 3703, H.M.S.O., London.

SEERS, D. (1973). The transmission of inequality. *Ekistics* 214, 163–9.

SELOWSKY, M. and TAYLOR, L. (1974). The economics of mal-nourished children: an example of disinvestment in human capital. *Econ. Dev. Cult. Change* 27, 17–30.

SENNETT, R. (1972). *The uses of disorder.* Penguin Books, Harmondsworth, Middx.

SHANNON, G.W., and DEVER, G.E.A. (1972). *Health care delivery: spatial perspectives.* McGraw-Hill, New York.

SHARKANSKY, I. (1970). Environment, policy, output and impact: problems of theory and method in the analysis of public policy. In *Policy analysis in political science* (ed. I. SHARKANSKY), 61–79, Markham, Chicago.

SHERRARD, I.D. (1968). *Social welfare and urban problems.* Columbia Universit
Press, New York.

SHONFIELD, A. and SHAW, S. (eds.) (1972). *Social indicators and social polic*
Heinemann, London.

SMITH, D.M. (1971). *Industrial location: an economic geographical analysis.* Wile
New York.

(1972). Towards a geography of social well-being: inter-state variations in th
United States. *Antipode Monogr. Soc. Geogr.* 1, 17–46.

(1973a). *The geography of social well-being in the United States.* McGra
Hill, New York.

(1973b). *An introduction to welfare geography.* Occasional Paper No. 1
Department of Geography and Environmental Studies, University
Witwatersrand, Johannesburg.

(1974). Who gets what *where*, and how: a welfare focus for human geograph
Geography 59, 289–97.

(1975a). On the concept of welfare. *Area* 7, 33–6.

(1975b). *Crime rates as territorial social indicators.* Occasional Papers No.
Department of Geography, Queen Mary College, London.

(1976). *Geographical approaches to the allocation of public resources: som
conceptual and practical problems.* Unpublished paper read at the Annu
Conference of the Institute of British Geographers, Coventry.

SMITH, T.E. (1967). Demographic aspects of smallness. In BENEDICT (1967a
11–22.

SMITH, W. (1953). *An economic geography of Great Britain.* Methuen, Londor

SOJA, E.W. (1971). *The political organization of space.* Resource Paper No.
Commission on College Geography, Association of American Geographer
Washington.

(1974). A paradigm for the geographical analysis of political systems.
COX *et al.* (1974), 43–71.

STAGNER, R. (1970). Perception, aspirations, frustrations and satisfactions: a
approach to urban indicators. *Ekistics* 30, 197–9.

STAMP, L.D. (1964). *The geography of life and death.* Collins, London.

STANWORTH, P. and GIDDENS, A. (eds.) (1974). *Élites and power in Britis
society.* Cambridge University Press, London.

STETZER, D.F. (1975). *Special districts in Cook County: toward a geograph
of local government.* Research Paper No. 169, Department of Geography
University of Chicago, Chicago.

STÖBER, G.J., and SCHUMACHER, D. (eds.) (1973). *Technology, assessment an
quality of life.* Elsevier, Amsterdam.

STOHR, W.B. (1974). *Interurban systems and regional economic development
Resource Paper No. 26, Commission on College Geography, Association o
American Geographers, Washington.

STREETEN, P. (1968). A poor nation's guide to getting aid. *New Soc.* 18, 154–6

TACHI, M. (1964). Regional income disparity and internal migration of populatio
in Japan. *Econ. Dev. Cult. Change* 12, 186–204.

TAEUBER, K.E., and TAEUBER, A.F. (1964). White migration and socic
economic differences between cities and suburbs. *Am. Sociol. Rev.* 29
718–29.

TAYLOR, A.H. (1973). Journey time, perceived distance, and electoral turnout -
Victoria Ward, Swansea. *Area* 5, 59–63.

TAYLOR, N. (1973). *The village in the city.* Maurice Temple Smith, London.

TAYLOR, P.J., and GUDGIN, G. (1976). A statistical theory of electoral re-districting. *Environ. & Plann.* A 8, 43–58.

TEITZ, M.B. (1968). Towards a theory of urban public facility location. *Pap. Reg. Sci. Assoc.* 21, 35–51.

TERIBA, O., and PHILIPS, O.A. (1971). Income distribution and national integration. *Nigerian J. Econ. & Soc. Stud.* 13, 77–122.

TERLECKYJ, N.E. (1970). Measuring progress towards social goals: some possibilities at national and local levels. *Manage. Sci.* 16 B, 765–78.

The Times (1972). Bombay shanty dwellers. *The Times* No. 58508 (19 June). Quoted in UN World Report (UN 1975b), Addendum 3, p. 27.

THEBERGE, J.D. (ed.) (1968). *Economics of trade and development.* Wiley, New York.

THIRLWALL, A.P. (1966). Regional unemployment as a cyclical phenomenon. *Scott. J. Polit. Econ.* 13, 205–19.

THOMAN, R.S., and CONKLING, R.C. (1967). *Geography of international trade.* Prentice-Hall, Englewood Cliffs, N.J.

THOMAS, B. (1972). The historical record of international capital movements to 1913. In DUNNING (1972a), 27–58.

THOMPSON, W. (1965). *A preface to urban economics.* Wiley, New York.

THORBECKE, E. (1971). Unemployment and underemployment in the developing world. In WARD *et al.* (1971), 115–22.

TIMMS, D.W.G. (1971). *The urban mosaic.* Cambridge University Press, London.

TOLL, S.I. (1969). *Zoned American.* Grossman, New York.

TOWNSEND, P. (1970). Measures and explanations of poverty in high income and low income countries. In *The concept of poverty* (ed. P. Townsend), 1–45, Heinemann, London.

TREWARTHA, G.T. (1973). Comments on Gilbert White's article 'Geography and public policy'. *Prof. Geogr.* 25, 78–9.

TUFTE, E.R. (1973). The relationship between seats and votes in two-party systems. *Am. Polit. Sci. Rev.* 67, 540–54.

TURNER, F.J. (1920). *The frontier in American history.* Henry Holt, New York.

UDO, R.K. (1965). Sixty years of plantation agriculture in southern Nigeria, 1902–1962. *Econ. Geogr.* 41, 356–68.

United Nations (1954). *Economic survey of Europe 1954.* (Reprinted in FRIEDMANN and ALONSO (1964), 405–39.)

(1971). *Rehabilitation of transitional urban settlements: report of the Secretary General.* E/C. 6/115, U.N. Economic and Social Council, New York.

(1973a). *Statistical Yearbook, Vol. 24, 1972.* U.N. Department of Economic and Social Affairs, New York.

(1973b). *World housing survey: report of the Secretary General.* E/C. 6/129, U.N. Economic and Social Council, New York.

(1974). *Statistical Yearbook Vol. 25, 1973.* U.N. Department of Economic and Social Affairs, New York.

(1975a). *Yearbook of National Accounts Statistics 1973.* U.N. Department of Economic and Social Affairs, New York.

(1975b). *Report on the World Social Situation 1974.* U.N. Economic and Social Council, New York.

United Nations Research Institute for Social Development (1966a). *Social and economic factors in development.* Report No. 3, U.N.R.I.S.D., Geneva.

United Nations Research Institute for Social Development (1966b). *The level of living index.* Report No. 4, U.N.R.I.S.D., Geneva.

(1970). *Studies in the measurement of levels of living and welfare.* Report No. UNRISD/70/C.20. U.N.R.I.S.D., Geneva.

U.S. Department of Health, Education and Welfare (1969). *Toward a social report.* U.S.G.P.O., Washington.

U.S. Management and Budget Office (1974). *Social indicators 1973.* U.S.G.P.O., Washington.

U.S. President's Commission on Income Maintenance Programs (1969). *Poverty amid plenty, the American paradox; report.* U.S.G.P.O., Washington. 13–33. (Reprinted in 1972 in *Poverty: selected readings* (eds. J.L. and J.K. Roach), 109–21. Penguin Books, Harmondsworth, Middx.)

U.S. President's Commission on National Goals (1960). *Goals for Americans.* Prentice-Hall, Englewood Cliffs, N.J.

URRY, J.W. and WAKEFORD, J. (eds.) (1973). *Power in Britain: sociological readings.* Heinemann, London.

VANCE, J.E. (1970). *The merchant's world.* Prentice-Hall, Englewood Cliffs, N.J.

VIPOND, J. (1974). City size and unemployment. *Urban Stud.* 11, 39–46.

WALL, D. (1973). *The charity of nations: the political economy of foreign aid.* Macmillan, London.

WARD, B., RUNNALLS, J.D., and D'AUGOU, L. (eds.) (1971). *The widening gap.* Columbia University Press, New York.

WARNTZ, W. (1959). *Towards a geography of price.* University of Pennsylvania Press, Philadelphia.

(1975). The pattern of patterns: current problems of sources of future solutions. In ABLER *et al.* (1975), 74–86.

WARREN, K. (1966). Steel pricing, regional economic growth and public policy. *Urban Stud.* 3, 185–99.

WEBB, A.E. (1974). *Unemployment, vacancies and the rate of change of earnings: a regional analysis.* Regional Papers, 3, National Institute of Economic and Social Research. Cambridge University Press, London.

WEBB, W.P. (1953). *The great frontier.* Secker and Warburg, London.

WEBBER, M.J. (1971). *The impact of uncertainty on location.* Australian National University Press, Canberra.

WERTHEIM, W.F. (1964). *East–west parallels: sociological approaches to modern Asia.* Van Hoeve, The Hague.

WESTAWAY, J. (1974). The spatial hierarchy of business organizations and its implications for the British urban system. *Reg. Stud.* 8, 145–55.

WHITNEY, J.B.R. (1970). *China: area, administration and nation building.* Research Paper No. 123, Department of Geography, University of Chicago, Chicago.

WILLIAMS, M. (1974). *The making of the South Australian landscape: a study in the historical geography of Australia.* Academic Press, London.

WILLIAMSON, J.G. (1965). Regional income inequality and the process of national development: a description of the patterns. *Econ. Dev. Cult. Change* 13, 3–84.

WILSON, A.B. (1959). Residential segregation of social classes and the aspirations of high school boys. *Am. Sociol. Rev.* 24, 836–45.

WILSON, J.Q. (1969). *Quality of life in the United States: an excursion into the new frontier of socio-economic indicators.* Midwest Research Institute, Kansas City, Mo.

WILSON, R.K. (1973). *Socio-economic indicators applied to sub-districts of Papua and New Guinea.* Discussion Paper No. 1, Economic Geography Department, Melbourne University.

WOLPERT, J. (1972). *Metropolitan neighborhoods: participation and conflict over change.* Resource Paper No. 16, Commission on College Geography, Association of American Geographers, Washington.

WOOD, D.P.J. (1967). The smaller territories: some political considerations. In BENEDICT (1967a), 23-34.

WOOD, R.C. (1961). *1400 governments.* Harvard University Press, Cambridge, Mass.

World Bank (1974). *Nigeria: options for long-term development.* John Hopkins University Press, Baltimore.

WRIGHT, M. (1965). Regional development: problems and lines of advance in Europe. *Tn. Plann. Rev.* 36, 147-64.

YEATES, M.H. and GARNER, B.J. (1971). *The North American City.* Harper and Row, New York.

ZAPF, W. (1975). Systems of social indicators: current approaches and problems. *Int. Soc. Sci. J.* 27, 478-98.

Index

Page numbers in italics refer to maps/diagrams